Bob—

with admiration
and affection for
my friend ^{and} colleague!
Thanks!!!
Lynda

EFFECTIVE
STRATEGIES
FOR DROPOUT
PREVENTION
of At-Risk Youth

Edited by

Lynda L. West, Ph.D.

Associate Professor and Assistant Chair
Department of Teacher Preparation and Special Education
School of Education and Human Development
The George Washington University
Washington, D.C.

AN ASPEN PUBLICATION®
Aspen Publishers, Inc.
Gaithersburg, Maryland
1991

Library of Congress Cataloging-in-Publication Data

Effective strategies for dropout prevention of at-risk youth /
edited by Lynda L. West
p. cm.
Includes bibliographical references and index.
ISBN: 0-8342-0226-3
1. High school dropouts—United States. 2. Dropout behavior, Prediction of.
3. Socially handicapped youth—Education—United States. 4. School
improvement programs—United States. 5. Educational change—United States.
I. West, Lynda L.
LC146.6.E35 1991
373.12'913'0973—dc20
for Library of Congress
91-7691
CIP

Editorial Services: Loma Perkins

Library of Congress Catalog Card Number: 91-7691
ISBN: 0-8342-0226-3

Printed in the United States of America

1 2 3 4 5

Dedicated to

Dean W.R. Miller
College of Education
University of Missouri-Columbia
for his excellence as a
role model, leader, and teacher
with admiration, affection, and gratitude
for all of the lives he touched!

Table of Contents

Preface

This volume was written to address certain issues facing our nation's schools today—namely, those associated with dropouts. After examining the literature and visiting with educators across the country, it became clear that creating new definitions for the terms *dropouts* and *at-risk* was impossible. The authors decided not to add more definitions to the field because they feel there are already too many, which confuses the issues. One universal definition for each term would be helpful and would eliminate the confusion. Further, in reviewing the literature on this subject and related issues, the authors came to question the value of these labels. The Honorable Kenneth G. Nelson from Minnesota, House of Representatives, suggested *at-risk* is useful in the laboratory of higher education, but not when speaking of individual students. If anything, we should refer to individual students as *at-strength*. Clearly, his point is that we have no idea how a student hearing the term *at-risk* applied to him or her may react.

This book is an attempt to fit together the pieces in the giant puzzle of education of at-risk youth, a puzzle that would provide a vision of a positive approach. Together as a team we can use the strength of what we know about learning and the learning environment to prevent students from dropping out or becoming at-risk. As Nash (1990) states, there is no quick fix and certainly no right answer to these issues. Indeed, as this book goes to press, I am still discovering missing pieces of this giant puzzle. The authors hope that individuals who care and share their compassion for special populations of students, and all students, will find in this book renewed support and direction to guide them in their efforts to restructure the educational system at the national, state, and local levels into a more responsive and positive learning environment.

Lynda L. West

REFERENCE

Nash, Margaret A. (1990). *Improving their chances: A handbook for designing and implementing programs for at-risk youth.* Madison, WI: Vocational Studies Center.

Contributors

Arden Boyer-Stephens, PhD
Director, Missouri LINC
University of Missouri-Columbia
Columbia, Missouri

Carl T. Cameron, PhD
Associate Professor
Department of Curriculum and Instruction
George Mason University
Fairfax, Virginia

John Gugerty, PhD
Senior Outreach Specialist
The Vocational Studies Center
University of Wisconsin-Madison
Madison, Wisconsin

Donna Kearns, MEd
Assistant Director, Missouri LINC
University of Missouri-Columbia
Columbia, Missouri

Linda Hudson Parrish, PhD
Professor of Educational Psychology
Texas A&M University
College Station, Texas

James Lewis Ratcliff, PhD
Director and Professor
Center for the Study of Higher Education
The Pennsylvania State University
University Park, Pennsylvania

Michelle D. Sarkees-Wircenski, EdD
Associate Professor
Department of Occupational and Vocational
 Education
University of North Texas
Denton, Texas

Jay Smink, DEd
Executive Director
National Dropout Prevention Center
Professor of Education
College of Education
Clemson University
Clemson, South Carolina

Gregory A. Smith, PhD
Research Associate
Wisconsin Center for Educational Research
University of Wisconsin-Madison
Madison, Wisconsin

Lynda L. West, PhD
Associate Professor and Assistant Chair
Department of Teacher Preparation and
 Special Education
School of Education and Human Development
The George Washington University
Washington, D.C.

Jerry L. Wircenski, PhD
Professor, Trade and Industrial Education
Department of Occupational and Vocational
 Education
University of North Texas
Denton, Texas

Acknowledgments

This book is a collective effort of a dedicated group of colleagues who have endured deadlines and revisions without complaint. Their remarkable ability to bring together diverse strategies and perspectives from all over the country into a central theme creates the vision that we all share—dropout prevention is a reality, not a myth. Efforts made with at-risk youth do make a difference.

I want to thank all of the authors for their expertise, creativity, endurance, and professional follow-through. All of us wish to thank our colleagues in the field who supported us during this endeavor. Many educators contributed through their research, editing, and proofing. A special thanks to Sandy Pritz and Sheila Feichtner for their support, expertise, and friendship!

And a sincere note of gratitude to Loretta Stock and Lorna Perkins at Aspen Publishers for their patience and cooperation. To all my colleagues at the University of Missouri-Columbia and The George Washington University who have shared with me their dedication to "quality education for special populations," I am forever indebted. They motivated me to pursue, examine, reach, persist, and persevere. They taught me the true meaning of the phrase, "when good can be better, then good is not enough!"

Last, but not least, a special expression of gratitude to all the family and friends of the authors, especially to David, Juliana, Carol, and Bob for giving me the time and space that allowed me to complete this professional endeavor. It was at great cost to them that I was allowed to coordinate this project.

chapter 1

Introduction

Lynda L. West

The terms *dropout prevention* and *at-risk* students have been identified, defined, and researched by every education association and organization in the United States during the past decade. Governmental agencies have commissioned research studies and written numerous reports to tell the American public some alarming statistics. Edleman (1988) reports that the first high school graduating class of the 21st century entered first grade in September 1988. They are the future workers, parents, college students, taxpayers, soldiers, leaders, and American hope of the 21st century. Many are off to a healthy start, but millions are not. Today

- one in four of them is poor (this statistic varies by author);
- one in five is at risk of becoming a teen parent;
- one in seven is at risk of dropping out of school;
- one in two has a mother in the labor force, but only a minority have safe, affordable, quality child care. (Edleman, 1988, p. 1)

It is a complex and dismal picture that faces education today, but the future demographic projections only paint a bleaker prospective. The purpose of this book is to shed some light on the issues related to dropout prevention of at-risk youth and to illustrate some strategies that say there is HOPE! There are concrete specific strategies that have already proven to be effective when implemented by a caring, well-trained team that wants to make a difference.

The following chapters have been structured around the major issues that resemble pieces of a giant puzzle; when they are all together, the fit is ideal and the result is impressive. Each of the chapters focuses on a contribution (a piece of the giant puzzle) from a different perspective. Each perspective adds a new dimension and presents educational alternatives. State and local education agencies have taken some dramatic and innovative steps to combat the dropout problem. Some exemplary, successful programs are shared with the reader to illustrate the point that there is hope indeed. The challenges are these: (1) Do educators dare to put tradition aside and try a new philosophical approach? (2) Do educators dare to try a new curriculum? (3) Can educators provide alternative curriculum options rather than impose one academic path on all students in order to meet the increase in graduation requirements? (4) Will educators reach out to parents and the community to cooperate and collaborate, or will they remain suspicious and defensive instead? (5) Can educators respond to a true comprehensive team approach? (6) How can the impact of postsecondary options be used to benefit at-risk students? (7) Will we evaluate dropout prevention programs rigorously for effectiveness and link the findings to actions?

Some say that education needs to be restructured, while others say the existing structure can work if we just open the windows and let in some fresh air. The strategies put forth in this book are a combination of both schools of thought. Some techniques are tried and true; others may sound revolutionary. One fact is clear and certain: no one has all the answers. Dropout prevention is a major challenge for the 1990s. It will take a cooperative and collaborative effort that surpasses any previous effort to date.

Change in the system is clearly paramount at this point. Cuban (1989) believes that unless policymakers and practitioners begin to consider how problems involving schools are framed, they will continue to lunge for quick solutions without considering the fit between the solution and the problem. The description of at-risk students should be familiar by now; it is almost 200 years old. It is as when it first appeared, a formula used by reformers to arouse the public to action.

The problems, Cuban (1989) writes, have been attributed to deficits of families, and the solutions have focused on training adults to do a proper job of rearing their children. Now is the time to consider framing the problem in a less popular way: the inflexible structure of the school itself also contributes to the conditions that breed academic failure and unsatisfactory student performance. The chapters that follow are based on Cuban's premise that schools must be restructured.

In a publication entitled *Making the Grade: A Report Card on American Youth*, Reingold (n.d.) summarizes current reality as follows:

- About 1 million young people drop out of school each year. In June 1986, 2.6 million students graduated from high school, yet there were 3.6 million 17-year-olds in the population.
- In most inner cities, the high school dropout rate is over 50 percent.

- The ratio of dropouts to prospective graduates is notably higher for men than women—30 per 100 versus 24 per 100. (p. 6)

Why are school dropouts a critical problem for our nation? Reingold lists five issues that make school dropouts a major problem for the country: (1) unemployment rates are twice as high for high school dropouts than for high school graduates; (2) it is increasingly difficult for employers to find workers capable of performing the work for which they are hired; (3) each year's class of dropouts will over their lifetimes cost America about $260 billion in lost earnings and foregone taxes, plus the cost to society for welfare dependency; (4) the ratio of dropouts to graduates has remained virtually unchanged for over a decade, in spite of the public attention to education reform and improvement; and (5) as educational requirements in our society rise, a young person without a high school diploma will have a hard time finding any job, let alone one with wages high enough to support a family.

IDENTIFYING AT-RISK STUDENTS

The well-known professional fraternity in education, Phi Delta Kappa, conducted a study to answer the question, what does it mean to say a young person is at risk? Phi Delta Kappa began with the premise that students at risk are likely to fail either in school or in life. For example, if a student fails a course and drops out as a result of failing the course, then he or she is at risk. At the same time, if a student uses drugs, has been physically or sexually abused, or has attempted suicide, he or she also is at risk. Frymier and Gansneder (1989) say that "at-riskness" is a

> function of when bad things happen to a child, how severe they are, how often it happens and what else happens in the child's immediate environment. Moreover, being at risk is not solely a phenomenon of adolescence. Children of all ages are at risk. If we think of human existence as a continuum that ranges from healthy (or good) to unhealthy (or bad), then "at-riskness" shows up on half of the continuum. The good end of the continuum tends in the general direction of health, adjustment, adequacy, happiness, high self-esteem, achievement, and pro-social or life-oriented behavior. The bad end of the continuum tends in the direction of illness, maladjustment, inadequacy, unhappiness, low achievement, low self-esteem, and antisocial or death-oriented behavior. (p. 142)

Tindall (1988) cites the definition the Wisconsin Department of Public Instruction selected to use: "children at risk" means dropouts and other pupils whose school achievement, progress toward graduation, or preparation for employment are in serious jeopardy as a result of one or more of the following:

- one or more years behind grade level group in reading or mathematic basic skills achievement (K–8)
- three or more credits behind age/grade level in credits earned for graduation (9–12)
- chronic truancy
- school-age parent
- parent-adjudicated delinquent
- personal and/or family drug and alcohol abuse
- family trauma, such as death, divorce, violence, separation, or unemployment
- physical, sexual, or emotional abuse
- ethnic, economic, or cultural disadvantage
- disruptive school behavior
- low parental expectations for success
- parents who place little value on education
- cultural diversity (language, customs, or educational expectations)
- family history of dropouts
- school suspensions (p. 3)

Wells, Bechard, and Hamby (1989) note that checklists are most commonly used by schools and agencies to identify potential dropouts. Characteristics are usually gathered from research literature, dropout exit interviews, student records, and other sources. They are concerned, however, that checklists have several weaknesses. Unfortunately, this "gross" approach can lead to students' being mislabeled "at risk" and does not take into account local differences. Yet despite the shortcomings of checklists, they can be useful as initial screening devices. Some of the factors involved in dropping out are listed in Exhibit 1-1.

Wells et al. (1989) write that the development of an identification system is the first step in building a prevention program. They warn that not all variables have the same degree of predictive power but are offered as a guide to help school districts develop screening instruments and prediction formulas. They list the following variables in no particular order of priority:

- attendance
- grade point average

Exhibit 1–1 Factors Involved in Dropping Out

ACADEMIC
Dropouts
- are low achievers
- are 1 or 2 years behind grade level
- are unable to tolerate structured activities
- lack definite educational goals
- are enrolled in a general course of study rather than vocational education or college preparatory programs
- have lower occupational aspirations than their peers
- have difficulty in abstract reasoning, generalizing, and forming relationships
- do not read at grade level
- experience difficulty in mathematics
- have low perceptual performance

BEHAVIORAL
Dropouts
- have a high rate of absenteeism and truancy
- exhibit discipline problems in school
- do not participate in extracurricular activities
- associate with friends who are outside of school, usually older dropouts
- have frequent health problems
- are inclined toward physical rather than mental activities
- are impulsive decision makers
- work more hours per week on a job than do completers
- are over-represented among chemical users and abusers, delinquents, adolescent parents, and persons who attempt suicide or self-mutilation

FAMILY
Dropouts
- come from single-parent homes
- come from low-income homes
- experience little solidarity with their families
- have more older siblings than friends
- are exposed to a dropout at home
- come from families that are more mobile than other students' families
- belong to a minority group
- lack cultural and economic experiences that often relate to success in traditional school programs

PSYCHOLOGICAL
Dropouts
- feel rejected by the school
- have negative attitudes toward school
- do not identify with school life
- feel that courses are not relevant to their individual needs
- lack incentive for achievement in traditional school activities
- are socially isolated or socially and emotionally disturbed
- are loners who are unaccepted by their peers
- have a poor self-concept and lack a clear sense of identity
- have experienced some form of trauma, including abuse
- cannot relate to authority figures
- are attracted to outside jobs, wages, and experiences

Source: From *The School's Choice: Guidelines for Dropout Prevention at the Middle and Junior High School* by R.D. Bhaerman and K.A. Kopp, 1988, Columbus, OH: National Center for Research in Vocational Education, Ohio State University.

- standardized test composite scores
- number of grade retentions
- number of discipline referrals
- education level of parents
- special program placements
- free/reduced lunch program
- number of school moves (transfers)
- reading and math scores
- ethnic/gender distinctions
- language spoken in the home
- number of suspensions
- interests in school
- participation in extracurricular activities
- pregnancy/teen parent
- number of counseling referrals
- family status (broken home, single-parent family, family size) (p. 3)

Wells et al. (1989) adapted a list of suggestions and cautions from Operation Rescue (National Foundation for the Improvement of Education, 1986) and Dropout Prevention (Florida Department of Education, 1986):

1. A team approach involving teachers, parents, administrators, counselors, and students should be used in developing referral systems for at-risk pupils.
2. Total school grade level populations should be surveyed when identifying at-risk students.
3. Objective, accurate data should be used as the basis of subjective judgments that are sometimes necessary.
4. Data should be gathered from student records as well as teacher observations, student attitudinal surveys, school reports, parent questionnaires, or other methods for collecting relevant information.
5. In addition to recent information about dropouts, relevant historical data including elementary and middle school student records should be used when possible, allowing for development of an early identification system in elementary and middle grades. An ongoing monitoring system should include an annual review, possibly each summer, of students who are identified as potential dropouts.
6. Dropout-related variables should be studied in combinations and not as single factors when making decisions about at-risk students. The more

variables available, the better able practitioners will be to develop more targeted interventions.

7. When variables are analyzed in statistical models they should be weighted for their significance to the local student population to obtain the most powerful effect in identification.

8. An identification system, no matter how accurate, is not an end in itself. It should serve the purpose of aiding educators in developing relevant, effective prevention and intervention strategies.

9. Because human behavior is very hard to predict, no statistical formula will identify potential dropouts with 100 percent accuracy. A prediction based on sets of identified characteristics is a probability, not a certainty.

10. Developers of an identification system should reflect on the longitudinal use of instruments in order to confirm their accuracy and usefulness over time.

11. When students are identified at early grade levels as being potentially at risk, labeling should be avoided that might lead to a self-fulfilling prophecy.

12. To be effective, intervention and prevention strategies should always derive from the identified characteristics of the population. (p. 4)

Van Tassel-Baska, Patton, and Prillman (1989) identified yet another population that is frequently overlooked when identifying at-risk students. In addition to students who come from economically and socially disadvantaged backgrounds, educators frequently fail to identify students whose talents may not be actualized because they are culturally different from the mainstream culture; the disadvantaged "gifted" learner is also at risk for educational attention.

THE IMAGE OF YOUTH

The William T. Grant Foundation Commission on Work, Family, and Citizenship (1988) published a report on the school-to-work transition, *The Forgotten Half: Non-College Youth in America*. It states that

a college degree is not the only way to develop the talents of tomorrow's workers. For some it is far from the best. There are many opportunities outside the college classroom to develop skills and talents and many ways to contribute to a stronger America and to successful personal and family life that do not require a college degree. (p. 1)

The report estimates that approximately 20 million 16- to 24-year-old individuals will likely not go on to college but will finish their education at the secondary level, with or without a diploma. A highly competitive and technological economy can offer prosperity to those with advanced skills, while the trend for those with less education is to scramble for unsteady, part-time, low-paying jobs. The study concludes that many are making it by working one or more jobs, living at home with parents, delaying marriage and family, and searching for extra training to advance their careers. The study notes the contrast between this image and the image Americans are most familiar with the picture of a troubled younger generation beset by drugs, crime, and teen pregnancy—a generation on the skids that cannot live up to the standards of the generations that have gone before it. The commission believed that the common portrait of deeply troubled youth is not only misleading but harmful in itself. Complaining about the state of our youth is all too common; a genuine commitment to aiding non–college youth is rare.

Clark (1988) writes that

> traditional sociological and sociopsychological research theories held that a person is disadvantaged to the degree that he or she can be categorized or typed as belonging to a minority group, a low-income group, or a group with low educational and occupational status, or as living in a community that is considered to be unhealthy to well-be-ing—for example, where the crime rate is high, and where the local schools do not provide the mix of resources that are necessary for educational and occupational success. (p. 2)

Clark contrasts this view of a disadvantaged person with individuals who come from an upper-middle class background and have parents with access to wealth and who would appear to have everything "going for them" in an external sense; yet they suffer from low self-esteem, which restricts them from enjoying those advantages. Clark maintains that a person can be both educationally and attitudinally disadvantaged. He suggests that when defining *disadvantaged*, educators must reflect on values and attitudes that appear necessary and sufficient conditions for success.

Ginsburg and Hanson (1990) write that American schools have been mistaken in not understanding the association between student values and success in school and later life. Educators have been reluctant to impose values on children because values are perceived as relative rather than absolute. Values are often related to individual moral or religious beliefs. However, certain values, such as the importance of education, the worth of personal effort, and the importance of acting responsibly, consistently lead to success. Consequently, Ginsburg and Hanson believe that schools should encourage these values on programmatic grounds. For many at-risk children who grow up in an environment that may not reinforce positive values, learning values through school may be particularly important.

Clark (1988) notes that although many studies have shown statistical correlations among background, life chances, and life achievements, few seem to explain adequately the fact that despite disadvantages of social background, many students perform well in school and in later life. He argues that contextual factors probably are more important for identifying populations most likely to be at risk of not succeeding in school. However, educators should not infer that those social background characteristics are the reason why such persons do not succeed. He concludes his report with this statement:

> Research studies have shown that disadvantaged youngsters can have positive attitudes about themselves and about academic achievement. Yet they don't do the work that it takes to ensure the outcome of high achievement. Our challenge as educators is to figure out ways to systematically ensure that these youngsters will have opportunities to do the necessary cognitive work during activities that stimulate and challenge their minds. (p. 19)

DEFINING DROPOUTS

Among the major problems facing educators today is to devise a way to measure and clarify confusion about dropout rates. This confusion exists because the federal government, state educational agencies, and local educational agencies do not use comparable methods to compute them. Hamby (1989) says that there is no single national dropout rate. The United States Department of Education quotes one set of statistics, the Bureau of Census quotes another; both are estimates of dropouts rather than direct measures. There is a need for a single, reliable national dropout rate in order to

- make meaningful comparisons among states;
- make valid judgments about treatment effects;
- target money where needed;
- instill public confidence in educational assessments about at-risk students; and
- support appropriate educational programs. (p. 1)

Hamby (1989) says that there are two primary sources of data found in the literature:

1. the Current Population Survey conducted by the United States Department of Commerce, Bureau of the Census

2. the Common Core of Data Survey conducted by the U.S. Department of Education, Center for Education Statistics (p. 2)

According to Hamby, each month the Bureau of Census conducts a current population survey of approximately 60,000 households throughout the United States. The survey excludes military personnel and their families, and inmates in institutions. The Bureau of Census defines a dropout as one who is not enrolled in school and who is not a high school graduate. The National Center for Education Statistics gathers data from 57 education agencies in 50 states, the District of Columbia, and outlying areas. It provides an adjusted graduation rate, which has been used widely to extrapolate a "dropout rate." Consequently, there are several reasons why no single, accurate national dropout rate currently exists:

- There is no standard, common definition of a school dropout throughout the United States.
- Most states, and even school districts within the same state, use different methods to calculate dropout rates.
- Lack of funding and expertise contributes to the inability to establish an effective tracking system required to obtain accurate data on dropouts. (p. 5)

The Council of Chief State School Officers task force on collecting national dropout statistics in cooperation with the National Center for Educational Statistics is seeking to develop a standardized national dropout rate. Hamby (1989) says that an issue as serious as school dropouts affects every segment of our society and economy. Standardized dropout-related data would permit state policymakers, education leaders, practitioners, and researchers to use standardized information to develop more effective dropout prevention programs. Bhaerman and Kopp (1988) say that individual dropout patterns are well developed before students reach the ninth or tenth grade. There is little consensus, however, among statisticians and educators regarding the dropout rate. Estimates range from 15 to 50 percent. Definitions are not consistent from state to state or from district to district within a state. Gruskin, Campbell, and Paulu (1987) report that most superintendents accept a definition recommended by a task force of the Council of Chief State School Officers. The task force defines a dropout as a pupil who leaves school, for any reason except death, before graduation or completion of a program of studies and without transferring to another school.

However, Gruskin et al. hasten to point out that this definition leaves unanswered questions such as, how long must a student be out of school? Twenty days? Forty days? What about a student who joins the military and pursues an education?

J. M. Weber (1987) states that the term *dropout* has been used to denote a variety of early school leavers:

- *pushouts*—undesirable students (i.e., those removed by suspension from school)
- *disaffiliates*—students who no longer wish to be associated with schools
- *educational mortalities*—students who fail to complete a program-specified course of study
- *capable dropouts*—students whose family socialization does not agree with school demands
- *stopouts*—students who leave, then return to school, usually within the same school year (p. 1)

Lehr and Harris (1988) note that a review of the literature reveals more than one term or label for students who are referred to as at risk. Possible labels include the following:

- disadvantaged
- culturally deprived
- underachiever
- nonachiever
- low ability
- slow learner
- less able
- low socioeconomic status
- language impaired
- dropout prone
- alienated
- marginal
- disenfranchised
- impoverished
- underprivileged
- low-performing
- remedial

Lehr and Harris ask two difficult questions with which educators now struggle: (1) Should students be labeled? (2) If the group is labeled, will the students be treated differently? Research supports the belief that some teachers do communicate inappropriate expectations toward students they believe to be less capable. For example, sometimes these students are

- seated farther away from the teacher
- given less direct instruction
- offered few opportunities to learn new material
- asked to do less work
- called on less often
- given less wait time
- questioned primarily at the knowledge/comprehension levels
- not prompted when they do not know the answer to a question
- given less praise
- rewarded for inappropriate behavior
- criticized more frequently
- given less feedback
- given less eye contact and other nonverbal communication of attention and responsiveness

The National Coalition of Advocates for Students (1988), in a publication entitled *Barriers to Excellence: Our Children at Risk*, suggests that there are a number of barriers in education that put the nation's children at risk. The barriers are

- class discrimination
- racial discrimination
- sex discrimination
- cultural discrimination
- special education
- inflexibility of school structure
- misuses of testing
- narrowness of curriculum and teaching practices
- limits of vocational education
- lack of support services for youth
- lack of democratic governance
- lack of resources for schools (inequitable finance)
- insufficient financing
- limitations of current job market

THE DROPOUT DILEMMA

Frase (1988) identifies three different types of dropout rates:

1. *Event* dropout rates measure the proportion of students who drop out in a single year without completing high school.
2. *Status* dropout rates measure the proportion of the population who have not completed high school and are not enrolled at one point in time, regardless of when they dropped out.
3. *Cohort* dropout rates measure what happens to a single group (or cohort) of students over a period of time.

Frase provides the following examples of each type of dropout rate in an analysis report for The National Center for Education Statistics:

- Between October 1985 and October 1988 an average of 4.4 percent of all students in grades 10 to 12 dropped out of high school. An average of 95.6 percent were retained in grades 10 to 12 each year during that period (event rate).
- In October 1988, nearly 13 percent of all 16- to 24-year-old individuals, (42 million young adults) were out of school and had not completed high school (status rate).
- Among the sophomore class of 1980, 17 percent failed to graduate by June 1982 (cohort rate).
- Dropping out of high school is not an irrevocable action. Many dropouts later complete high school, often within a short period after dropping out. Nearly half (46 percent) of dropouts from the sophomore class of 1980 had completed high school by 1986, that is, within 4 years of the expected date of graduation (cohort rate).

Frase (1988) also reports a number of individual and family demographic and socioeconomic characteristics that are commonly found among dropouts. In general, dropout rates are higher for disadvantaged and/or minority students, while at the same time the majority of dropouts in absolute numbers are white. The study reports the following:

- Whites account for 66 percent of all dropouts.
- Dropout rates are higher for blacks and Hispanics than for whites. Cohort rates were 15 percent white, 22 percent black, and 28 percent Hispanic.

- About one-third of all Hispanics ages 16 to 24 were enrolled in school and were *not* high school graduates in 1988.
- Cohort dropout rates for American Indians/Alaska Natives are quite high (35 percent), while those for Asian students are very low (8 percent) compared with whites (15 percent).
- Dropout rates for male students tend to be higher than those for female students (e.g., status rates of 13.5 percent for male students and 12.2 percent for female students).
- Male students and blacks tend to take longer than female students and whites to complete high school. Higher proportions of male students and blacks are still enrolled in school below the college level at ages 18 and 19.
- Dropout rates are higher for students coming from low socioeconomic backgrounds, from single-parent families, and from non–English language family backgrounds.
- When blacks and whites from similar social backgrounds are compared, dropout rates for blacks are not higher, and in some cases may be lower, than those for whites.

Gastright (1989) writes that since dropouts are a national problem, it has been tempting for some districts to fall back on stereotypical views of the at-risk student, particularly since districts are faced with inadequate data for understanding the local dropout problem. He says that the stereotypical view focuses on lower-achieving, mostly male students with poor attendance, bad discipline problems, and a record of previous school failure. Educators who attempt to reduce dropout rates on the basis of such stereotypes may fail because they neglect local characteristics. One school district in Cincinnati, Ohio, financed by a Ford Foundation Planning Grant, studied the characteristics of its dropouts. Visiting teachers interviewed dropouts for the study. They gave the dropouts two opportunities to state their own reasons for dropping out. The unprompted responses to reasons for dropping out included the following:

- pregnancy/child care/marriage   25%
- failure/overage/low grades   20%
- work   20%
- disliked school   17%
- attendance   11%
- delinquency   6%
- family problems   6%
- suspension/expulsion   4%

- illness/health   4%
- drugs/alcohol   3%
- other students   3%

Gastright (1989) then compared these reasons with a set of variables identified in the study, *High School and Beyond*. The conclusions drawn from this particular local dropout study are that dropout characteristics differ from community to community and that comparisons of local characteristics with national sample studies do not necessarily apply. The study suggests that the dropout problem is not simple and generic, but complex and highly specific. The evidence suggests that we should not make assumptions. Most of all, educators should not base dropout identification and dropout prevention program design on someone else's problem. Each district must do its own homework and design its program on local characteristics. However, one very important concern was raised.

> The fact that a sizable number of graduates were indistinguishable from the average dropout calls into question the wisdom of identifying students at risk. Certainly no combination of risk factors should override the more important evidence that an individual student is attending school consistently, passing most courses, and from all external evidence will graduate. Current performance should be the first and most important factor in deciding whether a student will benefit from being labeled "at risk." (p. 4)

Very few schools maintain records on whether their students are working and for how long, family background, family size, parent education, student arrests, and evidence of incarceration. Yet it is these factors, along with drugs, teen pregnancy, and child care that best discriminate between dropouts and similar at-risk students who are able to graduate.

It is never too early to begin dropout prevention. Prevention begins before formal education starts. The Committee for Economic Development (1987) suggests that it is less costly to society and to individuals to prevent early failure through efforts directed toward parents and children alike. These efforts should include the following:

- prenatal and postnatal care for pregnant teens and other high-risk mothers and follow-up health care and developmental screening for their infants
- parenting education for both mothers and fathers, family health care, and nutritional guidance

- quality child-care arrangements for poor working parents that stress social development and school readiness
- quality preschool programs for all disadvantaged 3- and 4-year-old children

The Committee for Economic Development (1987) states that no two good schools are necessarily alike. The committee believes that the American school system benefits from diversity. However, a successful learning environment for disadvantaged students has a number of key characteristics:

- School must be a place where children want to learn.
- English-language proficiency should be a paramount objective of the school program (a controversial topic in education today).
- Character building through a positive, invisible curriculum should be emphasized.
- Teachers should be given a more important role while being held far more accountable for student progress.
- Principals need to develop better leadership and management skills.
- Schools should encourage greater parental involvement.
- Extracurricular activities should become a more important part of school programs.
- Comprehensive health and social services are needed to address problems that interfere with learning.

In addition to the above characteristics, classroom and school environments are important factors (Exhibit 1-2).

ECONOMIC FACTORS

The Children's Defense Fund and the Center for Labor Market Studies at Northeastern University published a report entitled *Vanishing Dreams: The Growing Economic Plight of America's Young Families*. Johnson, Sum, and Weill (1988) cite 10 key findings:

1. Economic disaster has afflicted America's young families, especially those with children.
2. Poverty among children in young families has skyrocketed.
3. The growing economic plight of young families has been caused by sweeping changes in the American economy that have reduced the earnings of young workers and undermined their ability to marry and form families.

Exhibit 1-2 Optimal Environments

CLASSROOM CLIMATE CHARACTERISTICS THAT BEST HELP DROPOUT-PRONE STUDENTS
- a positive atmosphere and supportive peer culture
- a discipline system that is both fair and effective
- person-oriented rather than rule-oriented classes
- decision-making opportunities for students
- opportunities to develop self-esteem and self-confidence
- instruction and opportunities to help students develop a commitment to social and life values
- opportunities to orient students to the broader world outside school, showing the correlation between education and work
- opportunities for students to become aware of their potential as workers
- parents and community volunteers as mentors
- minimal structure and high flexibility
- individualized and small-group instructional materials and practices
- instructional methods that involve tactile, kinesthetic, and auditory perceptions
- peer teaching and cooperative learning techniques
- instructional activities that build group cohesiveness
- promotion of cooperative behavior among students
- basic skills development, integrating the use of basic and vocational skills
- time on task for repeated practice

SCHOOL ENVIRONMENTAL CHARACTERISTICS THAT BEST HELP DROP-OUT-PRONE STUDENTS
- high but flexible expectations for students
- diverse opportunities for achieving success
- recognition of students' achievements
- opportunities for students to define their goals clearly and realistically
- opportunities to help students monitor their own progress in achieving their goals
- motivational instruction and activities to heighten students' occupational aspirations
- early identification of at-risk students
- more extensive guidance and counseling services for at-risk students
- specific educational plans for dropout-prone at-risk students
- programs that help students address the conditions and stresses that place them at risk
- promotion of students' sense of belonging to the school
- clear, fair, and consistent disciplinary rules
- a high degree of student participation in extracurricular activities
- intimate and caring work environment for staff and students alike
- close adult-student relationships

Source: From *The School's Choice: Guidelines for Dropout Prevention at the Middle and Junior High School*, by R.D. Bhaerman and K.A. Kopp, 1988, Columbus OH: National Center for Research in Vocational Education, Ohio State University.

4. Young black and Hispanic families have suffered particularly severe earning and income losses.
5. Education still pays, but a high school diploma is no longer adequate defense against poverty for young families.
6. While female-headed families are by far at the greatest risk of poverty, young married-couple families have suffered, avoiding large income losses only by having both parents work.
7. Inequality of income has grown substantially among young families.
8. The youngest families find it increasingly difficult to obtain an adequate income.
9. Home ownership is now beyond the reach of most young families.
10. Young adults are least likely to have health insurance or access to the health care they need to start their families.

The economic stability and well-being of young families, defined as two or more related individuals under the age of 30 living in the same household, have a strong impact on the early physical, educational, social and psychological development of America's children. The earnings of heads of young families have fallen sharply since 1973, undermining their capacity to form families and provide care for their children.

Orfield (1988) observes a resurgence of interest in understanding the problems of minority and low-income schools. The term *at risk* has replaced earlier terms such as *poor, culturally deprived, educationally disadvantaged*, and *unconstitutionally segregated*. The new term at risk is a kind of blameless term and suggests that it just happens that some students are in danger of dropping out and that no one is responsible for the problem. The term *at risk* suggests that the problems are individual ones, while the old terms suggest systemic problems affecting entire groups.

Orfield (1988) writes that as the low-income minority proportion of total American students grows, it is urgent to avoid policy actions that may make schools even less successful in dealing with these students. In a situation in which it is far from certain that we know enough or are willing to make sufficient commitments to do what would clearly improve their circumstances, the first clear principle of action should be "Do no additional harm." The general movement to raise academic standards is exactly the sort of action that may make things worse. A serious immediate problem for high school students is too often caused by reforms that have rapidly imposed higher barriers to academic success in elementary and high schools. Higher promotion standards from grade to grade and for high school graduation have been adopted. State governments and local school districts alike have raised graduation requirements, making it much harder for relatively weak students to receive a high school diploma. Supporters argue that the standards will increase the motivation to learn. The costs of the policies, particularly in terms of increasing dropouts among the at-risk students, have usually been ignored. The reality is that high school graduation and the diploma have been the prerequisite for most jobs in our society. Not having a diploma not only punishes the student academically, but may make his or her economic situation virtually hopeless.

Orfield (1988) raises the question with educators of whether standards can be raised without raising barriers in the educational system. He notes that teachers realize that drawing out the full potential of students requires a variety of techniques. Coercion and threats may work for some students, but for many others the key is good teaching, contact with other students excited about learning, or special incentives for successful work. Coercion as a basic approach, however, has not worked well in the past with at-risk children, and it seems unlikely to work well now.

FEMALE DROPOUTS

Fine (1988) notes that Department of Labor data confirm that social class of origin, race, ethnicity, and gender systematically and grossly influence economic outcomes in our society. For example, with a high school diploma, female full-time workers still earn less than males. Even more compelling, these same data indicate that the absence of a high school diploma bears significantly different consequences by race and gender. Although the attainment of a high school diploma does not improve an individual's economic prospects within a demographic group, acquiring a high school diploma does not convert the opportunities of a black woman into those available to a white man.

Earle, Roach, and Fraser (1987) wrote a report on female dropouts for the National Association of State Boards of Education. They say,

> Many problems that we thought had been resolved in the 1960's and the 1970's sex stereotyping in teacher's treatment of boys and girls and in the selection of courses of study, for example, still exist. Many teachers' methods and attitudes favor boys' learning styles and the development of boys' self-confidence, and are correspondingly less attentive to girls' needs in these areas. Because girls tend to be less assertive and less involved in serious disruptive behavior, their academic difficulties are often ignored. Influenced by sex role stereotypes, girls choose not to enroll in certain courses, higher level math and science, for example, in favor of fields for which they are not necessarily best suited, resulting in a lack of prerequisite skills for a wide range of jobs. Further, because girls are more often channeled into

vocational training program for jobs with lower pay, less prestige, and less opportunity for advancement, their chances for achieving economic self-sufficiency are reduced. (p. 3)

When these factors are combined, female students are in a high-risk category for dropping out. The economic consequences for female students who drop out of school are serious. Half of all families headed by a female dropout live in poverty.

What puts female students at risk?

- Socialization—Girls are taught to be unassertive and to expect that a man will take financial care of them in the future.
- Cognitive differences—The teaching structure of most classrooms reflects a bias toward the ways boys learn, placing girls at a disadvantage.
- Teacher interaction—Teachers' responses to students favor male academic development, confidence, and independence.
- Curricular choices—Girls limit their potential by the courses they select. They also choose vocational training. (Earle et al., 1987, p. 5)

Fine (1988) writes that those who are called at-risk are the

students who need the most educationally, suffer disproportionately from practices that may be designed toward better discipline but which empirically facilitate early exit. These practices include, but are not limited to, the following: heavy discipline; higher suspension rates; more notes sent home; increased probability of being retained and tracked down; dull and repetitive pedagogical strategies; remote curricula; low expectations; depressing predictions; and parental exclusion from schools. These institutional experiences predict the tendency to leave high school prior to graduation. (p. 94)

YOUTH UNEMPLOYMENT

The Children's Defense Fund in 1989 published a document entitled Tackling the Youth Employment Problem. Lacy, Johnson, and Heffernan (1989) write that America faces a chronic youth employment problem and, without higher education or specific vocational and technical skills necessary to succeed in today's job market, are finding it increasingly difficult to secure full-time employment with wages adequate to support a family. States' responses to youth unemployment problems are diverse. However, all of them in some way involve remedial education, vocational training, or paid work experience. The strategies fall into four major areas:

1. school-to-work transition programs that provide school-based counseling, peer support, and job placement assistance to high school juniors and seniors about to go directly into the job market
2. out-of-school remedial education for youths who fail to complete high school or who need stronger basic academic skills to compete in the labor market
3. conservation and service corps programs that combine productive work, education activities, and employment preparation for young people
4. policy and program coordination efforts at both state and local levels to ensure that education and training services for young people are administered efficiently and effectively (p. 5)

Lacy et al. (1989) state that the challenge for states is to strengthen vocational training for disadvantaged youths by increasing program quality and accessibility. They strongly encourage all states to do the following:

1. Fund school-to-work transition programs.
2. Establish state and local conservation and service corps.
3. Make creative use of nonprofit corporations to improve remedial education and vocational training.
4. Create a cabinet-level coordinating body focused on at-risk youth.
5. Extend state education financing to alternative programs serving school dropouts.
6. Expand opportunities for out-of-school learning.
7. Link state apprenticeship programs with youth employment initiatives.

These steps are meant to encourage low-cost approaches to job preparation, work experience, discipline, and self-esteem. The emphasis is clearly focused on building partnerships among government, industry, and educational and training institutions to better prepare young people to enter the job market. "Without vocational training and strong basic skills, millions of young Americans leave high school with little hope of finding decent jobs. An array of state-funded initiatives to improve job prospects for youths is encouraging, but much more needs to be done" (Lacy et al., 1989, p. 1).

ROLE OF VOCATIONAL EDUCATION

J. A. Weber (1986) writes that much of the available data suggest that dropping out of high school is related to a variety of individual and social consequences:

- individual consequences
- legal consequences
- health-related consequences
- educational consequences
- economic consequences

J. A. Weber believes that current efforts to address the dropout problem have been affected by two major movements within the educational system: the quest for equity and the quest for excellence.

> The growth of the efforts to achieve "equity" over the past two decades has been paralleled by a growth in the field of vocational education. Proponents of vocational education have argued that it represents one of the few educational alternatives that enable many youth, including those deemed to be disadvantaged, handicapped, and potential dropouts, to become productive members of society. (p. 3)

Jibrell (1987) writes that, even though we are graduating substantially more students than we have at any previous time in our history, the school dropout problem is of major concern today because the consequences of dropping out are more severe than in the past, both for the individual and for society. Dropping out is clearly one of the strongest indicators of future social dependency. The high school diploma has become a required credential for most jobs in America, yet over the next decade it is estimated that dropouts will be 60 percent less likely to be employed than will graduates. When they are employed, dropouts earn about one-third less than graduates. The majority of people in the nation's correctional institutions are school dropouts.

Jibrell (1987) says that there is a decline in young people proportionately at a time when America is moving toward labor shortages and needs workers with basic employability skills; increasing numbers of young people are leaving school with deficiencies in reading, writing, mathematics, science, and reasoning abilities, the very skills that employers say they are looking for in workers.

Johnson and Packer (1987) in their highly publicized report, *Workforce 2000: Work and Workers for the 21st Century*, identify four key trends that they say will shape the last years of the 20th century:

1. The American economy should grow at a relatively healthy pace.
2. United States manufacturing will contribute a much smaller share to the economy in the year 2000.

3. The workforce will grow slowly, becoming older, more female, and more disadvantaged.
4. The new jobs in service industries will demand much higher skill levels than the jobs of today.

Johnson and Packer (1987) contend that if the United States is to continue to prosper, policymakers must find ways to do the following:

- stimulate balanced world growth
- accelerate productivity increases in service
- maintain the dynamism of an aging workforce (ensure that the workforce is adaptable and has a willingness to learn)
- reconcile the conflicting needs of women, work, and families
- integrate black and Hispanic workers fully into the economy
- improve the educational preparation of all workers

Consequently, improving the worker's education and skills is increasingly more critical because

> as a society becomes more complex, the amount of education and knowledge needed to make a productive contribution to the economy becomes greater. A century ago, a high school education was thought to be superfluous for factory workers and a college degree was the mark of an academic or a lawyer. Between now and the year 2000, for the first time in our history, a majority of all new jobs will require post–secondary education. (p. xviii)

The urgency of preventing dropouts has become a national goal not only of educators but of society. Johnson and Packer (1987) believe that "education and training are the primary systems by which the human capital of the nation is preserved and increased" (p. 116). However, they also believe that if a bright future for the United States economy is to be realized, the educational standards that have been established in the nation's schools must be raised dramatically. "Put simply, students must go to school longer, study more, pass more difficult tests covering more advanced subject matter. There is no excuse for vocational programs that warehouse students who perform poorly in academic subjects or for diplomas that register nothing more than years of school attendance" (p. 117).

Frantz, Strickland, and Elson (1988) found that during the past few years graduation requirements have increased in response to school reform initiatives. Vocational educators are worried that increased graduation requirements limit the access to vocational education programs, at a time when technological change and a labor shortage create an even stronger demand for schools to prepare diverse populations. J. M. Weber (1987) identified positive program characteristics commonly noted by proponents of vocational education that justify and strengthen the role of vocational education, particularly in relation to dropout prevention of at-risk students. (See Exhibit 1-3.)

Vocational education, according to J. M. Weber (1987), can enhance student retention and reduce dropout rates. After reviewing nine different programs from seven geographic regions, which represented urban, suburban, rural, and smaller city school districts, J. M. Weber suggested that successful dropout prevention programs possess the following characteristics:

- Programs are holistic and multifaceted in their approach. The most prevalent strategies used were a combination of parental involvement, remedial basic skills instruction, and work experience/job placement, with counseling, supportive services, and in-school vocational instruction all coming in as close seconds and used in the majority of cases.
- Programs are typically operationalized in such manner that about half of the total effort is directed toward addressing and resolving students' education/remediation needs (e.g., basic skills deficiencies); about a quarter of the effort is spent on resolving their personal needs; and the remaining quarter is targeted toward their work-related needs.
- Programs are usually presented in contexts that differ from the "traditional school environment" (even though they may be housed in the same physical plant, for example, a "school-within-a-school" context); involve special motivational strategies such as tying school activities directly to the real world (workplace, daily living, parenting needs, and so forth), building more individualized teacher-student linkages, mentoring, giving special awards, and designing activities to build esprit de corps among affected students; and involve some degree of individualized teaching/learning activities.
- Programs are focused on dropout-prone students who are in the beginning stages of their high school careers (between the ages of 14 and 16), prior to the time when they would "normally" become formally involved in a vocational education program.
- In programs involving a work experience component, that component is intimately tied to the other program components, both logically and operationally, and usually results in the establishment of what are frequently unique and closer relations with business/industry than normally occur in more general, work-study programs.
- Programs require the involvement of special staff/teachers who are committed to the philosophy and goals of the program; are able and willing

Exhibit 1-3 Positive Program Characteristics Noted by Vocational Education Proponents

Vocational Programs	*Other Curricular Offerings*
Active role in learning process	Passive learner role
Concrete, hands-on learning experiences	Abstract, generalized learning experiences
Experiences relevant to learner's life "outside the school"	Experiences not directly relevant to learner's life "outside the school"
Rich, real-life learning environment	Sterile, four-walled classroom
Learning that proceeds from concrete to abstract	Learning that proceeds from abstract to abstract, principle to principle
Learning that occurs within an "application" context	Learning that is context free
Small group, even one-on-one instruction	Classroom and other types of "large group" instruction
Content and delivery variations related to areas of specialization	Standard, "lock-step" curriculum with relatively little variation and minimal review/change
Routinely revised/updated using input from authoritative sources (e.g., business persons)	Relatively little input from outside the "educational establishment"
Preparation for labor market entry; does not necessarily limit learner's post-secondary options	Preparation for additional schooling or a "general" education not directed toward either a job or further education

Source: From *Strengthening Vocational Education's Role in Decreasing the Dropout Rate*, (p. 18) by J.M. Weber, 1987, Columbus, OH: National Center for Research in Vocational Education, Ohio State University.

to establish workable relationships with their students, relationships that are somewhat different and frequently require more commitment than that which is normally required; who are flexible in their approach both to instruction and to dealing with their students; and who maintain a continuing awareness of their students' needs.

The question then remains, Does vocational education lower dropout rates for at-risk youth? Bishop (1988) says, "Yes. Taking one vocational course each year during the four years of high school raises the graduation rate of at-risk youth" (p. 3). Bishop points out that one of the most important ways occupationally specific education can benefit at-risk students is by persuading them to stay in school long enough to graduate, which raises their earning power by nearly 40 percent. Bishop, however, recommends several changes in vocational education:

- counseling before entry into occupationally specific programs
- expanding cooperative education
- developing a strong basic skills foundation
- honoring academic achievement
- helping students obtain good jobs
- restructuring state funding formulas to promote effective service to the disadvantaged

Bishop concludes, however, that strict new mandates regarding procedures for delivering vocational education are not desirable. They would be counterproductive because there is no single best method of serving students.

Senator Edward M. Kennedy (1988) writes,

Vocational education is a good and important education strategy that should be a key part of our national effort. Steps already underway at the local level, coupled with the modest investment the federal government made last year, are a good beginning. We must do more. But above all, we must ensure that vocational education is not seen as the single "solution" to the dropout problem. We need a multifaceted approach that involves all parts of the educational system. There are no magic bullets in this war. (p. 35)

TRANSITION FROM SCHOOL TO WORK

One of the most popular movements in education during the past decade has been transition from the classroom to the workplace. Although educators have been helping individual students with this effort, for the most part it was up to the individual teacher or counselor who took it upon himself or herself to assist a student in finding employment. Vocational instructors specifically have traditionally considered it part of their job, so transition assistance has long been in practice. Federal and state legislation then began to establish and expand initiatives to promote and improve the transition of handicapped and disadvantaged students with transition from school to work.

A position paper by the National Association of Special Needs State Administrators (1989) suggests 11 recommendations:

1. Existing cooperative agreements should be reviewed to ensure responsiveness to recent vocational, special education, and employment and training legislation.

2. Community agencies and employers should be invited to join with parents and schools in planning a comprehensive response to transition.

3. State and local agencies and other community representatives should join together to coordinate programs in order to facilitate transition.

4. State and local systems should seek ways to use human resources more flexibly to better facilitate transition.

5. Special education curricula should be modified for severely handicapped students to focus on post–school needs in order to facilitate transition.

6. School and community counseling services should be made available during and after school hours to help families and individuals involved in the transition process.

7. The Division of Vocational Rehabilitation (DVR) should work closely with local school systems and members of state departments of education to continue to explore ways in which the DVR system may be involved effectively in serving a younger population.

8. Vocational rehabilitation, vocational education, employment and training, and special education staff should work together to develop practical and ongoing vocational assessment for all special needs students.

9. Intensive parent training should be conducted so that parents more ably may assist handicapped and disadvantaged youth in setting realistic goals.

10. State and local staff development efforts should address current issues that affect the transition of handicapped and disadvantaged individuals.

11. State departments of education should provide leadership by initiating a proactive approach, interacting with teachers, employers, and community representatives with the aim of increasing awareness of the many benefits of hiring qualified handicapped disadvantaged individuals.

Feichtner (1989) says that the school-to-work transition process is

> inexorably bound to keeping students in school and helping them de-velop the skills employers need. When the process breaks down the re-sult is unemployment, underemployment, poverty, or public assistance. The unemployment and underemployment problems of at-risk youth are significant enough to the nation's economy (a 1 percent increase in unemployment increases the federal outlay by 64 percent) to merit leg-islative consideration of mandating a systematized school-to-work tran-sition process for all at-risk youth.

RESPONDING TO THE DILEMMA

Gruskin et al. (1987), in a report for the Office of Education Research and Im-provement, state that there are six "best bets" for keeping at-risk students in school and for helping them achieve while they are there:

1. Intervene early. Helping students develop competence and confidence in their ability to learn is a good way to instill a desire to learn and to prepare for a lifetime of learning.
2. Create a positive school climate. Good schools possess strong leaders who stress academic achievement, maintain an orderly and disciplined environment, and work with staff to instill positive values and self-confidence in students.
3. Set high expectations. Research consistently shows that educators who expect students to maintain high standards for attendance, academics, and behavior get more in return. However, expectations must be realistic, and at-risk students must receive the support they need to meet them.
4. Select and develop strong teachers. Teachers exert tremendous influence in students' education and attitudes toward school. It is important to select and train good teachers who are sensitive to the needs of at-risk students.
5. Provide a broad range of instructional programs to accommodate students with diverse needs.
6. Initiate collaborative efforts to develop and administer dropout prevention programs. Schools, communities, churches, and families all influence what and how much students learn as well as their attendance.

Fine (1988) suggests that if schools are to nurture students who grow up to be critical and participatory citizens, we need the following:

- empowerment of teachers and paraprofessionals
- desegregation of teachers by race/ethnicity and students by race/ethnicity, social class, and disability levels
- establishment of curricula and pedagogy that value students and their communities and recognize social inequities as problematic and worthy of academic investigation
- advocacy and community voice
- establishment of school-based health clinics
- reconsideration of retention and promotion policies
- analysis of suspension practices
- establishment of broad-based community support programs
- evaluation of educational policies and practices for discriminatory opportunities and outcomes
- a means of monitoring military and proprietary school programs that recruit students out of high school
- abolishment of educational policies that punish without support
- detiered urban schools
- generation of funding formulas that support at-risk youths
- reduction of school and class size

The Ford Foundation established the Project on Social Welfare and the American Future in 1985. The final report, The Common Good: Social Welfare and the American Future, published in 1989, states that

> reducing the school dropout rate requires a blending of programs that attempt both to improve schools and stimulate individual students who are at risk of failure. Success hinges on making better opportunities available to young adults, increasing their awareness of these opportunities, and providing clear incentives for them to seize the opportunities. In short, there must be a real and personal rather than a bureaucratic and impersonal reason to stay in school. (p. 36)

The Ford Foundation (1989) suggests that local communities must take primary responsibility for designing and coordinating better programs to prepare young people for the job market. The basic elements necessary for success include the following:

- use of schools as centers for delivering integrated services to adolescents

- early detection and early interventions that forestall problems instead of merely reacting to them after the fact
- willingness to recognize the interested nature of such problems as leaving school, teen parenthood, unemployment, and welfare dependency
- positive incentives and life option counseling, so that young people have personal reasons to succeed in school and work
- private-sector involvement in educational and employment programs, together with adequate funding of public-sector programs

Hodgkinson (1989) examined the educational reform movement of the past decade from a demographer's perspective. He concludes that the following are needed:

- "threshold" examinations for students and teachers, establishing minimal competence levels
- more difficult curricula
- choice plans that assume that parents will choose the "good" schools for their children and will shut down the "bad" ones
- restructuring schools to give the individual school more control over its testing

Hodgkinson suggests that these results lead to more urgent educational remedies for the nation:

- Focus attention on the improvement of the "bottom third" of students.
- Reduce youth poverty, currently 40 percent of all poor.
- Prepare at-risk children for school by mandating Head Start-type programs for all eligible children.
- Get more young people to graduate from high school and college.
- Enlarge the talent pool of high-achieving minority and poverty children.
- Develop programs for youth who are at risk from several causes simultaneously (school failure, drugs, pregnancy, and arrests)

He questions how well the reform movement has worked for the demographic agenda:

- There has been no increase in high school or college graduation rates.
- There has been no reduction in youth poverty.
- City schools are today more segregated for Hispanic students than they were for blacks, according to Gary Orfield of the University of Chicago.

- There has been no gain in scores of the "lower third."
- There has been no increase in equity funding to provide the resources to give every child a chance to attain the higher standards that some 40 states have adopted.

Peck, Law, and Mills (1989) state that at one level,

> a new consciousness has emerged that focuses on the ability of schools and communities to identify and assist high-risk students when they need help before the problem becomes so severe that it is more difficult, costly, or impossible to effect meaningful changes. At another level, it is increasingly recognized that the overall climate can be influenced in such a way that school is more attractive and educationally rewarding for all students. (p. 5) The most successful, effective environment and programs involve collaboration among schools, community, business, parents and a wide variety of resources that generate educational experiences that have proved attractive and have holding power for at risk students. They believe that the new agenda for dropout prevention involves substantially rethinking, redesigning and restructuring educational delivery systems, in a way that accommodates the needs for all students, including those for whom the bottom rung of success is just out of reach. (p. 6)

Peck et al. make the following recommendations:

1. Needs assessment and planning efforts should be broadly based.
2. Prevention efforts should include all levels from K through 12, with an emphasis on early intervention.
3. Organizational variables, policies, and procedures affecting the schools' ability to meet the needs of high-risk youth should be revised.
4. Schools should reassess the relevance of all their educational programs.
5. A positive school climate should be a high priority in the school and in the classroom.
6. Programs should continually expand their networking and capacity to create linkages across groups.
7. Staff should be carefully selected.
8. Ongoing staff development should be built into the program.
9. Ongoing program evaluation and feedback should be built in as an integral component of the program.

Carnevale, Gainer, and Meltzer (1989) wrote,

Research shows that in the United States roughly half of the differences in earnings can be attributed to learning in school and on the job. Accidents of geography, career choices, and the selection of an employer account for the other half. Earnings are a function of the skills people have and the choices they make regarding how and where they use those skills. Poor basic skills limit individuals' choice and their potential for earning. (p. 5)

Who, then, has low basic skills? Not surprisingly, the answer to that question is as follows (Carnevale et al., 1989, p. 6):
- 68 percent of those arrested
- 85 percent of unwed mothers
- 79 percent of welfare dependents
- 85 percent of dropouts
- 72 percent of the unemployed

Carnevale et al. (1989) identified the most important skills employers need from any employee. After careful analysis of these skills, they summarized the key skills into seven skill groups:

1. knowing how to learn
2. competence: reading, writing, and computation
3. communication: written and oral
4. adaptability: creative thinking and problem solving
5. personal management: self-esteem, goal setting/motivation, and personal/career development
6. group effectiveness: interpersonal skills, negotiation, and teamwork
7. influence: organizational effectiveness and leadership

Orr (1987) estimates that 25 percent of students who enter high school each year will not graduate:

Instead those young people, who are primarily urban and economically disadvantaged, become school dropouts. Their economic and social opportunities have become increasingly bleak over the past twenty years as business and industry have come to require a more literate and highly trained work force. (p. 1)

Orr believes that the causes of dropping out are numerous and stem not only from economic and social circumstances but from related issues, such as adolescent parenthood, unemployment, drug abuse, and crime. She contends, however, that dropout prevention and service programs are not new. Unfortunately, these programs have simply never been widely available to the extent that they are now needed.

Orr (1987) points out three basic approaches to serving youth dropouts and potential dropouts: (1) compensatory education, (2) alternative education, and (3) employment and training. She contends that *no single system* has the primary responsibility to serve this population; yet it is often presumed that schools have the primary responsibility for dropout prevention and service. She notes, however, that three kinds of service agencies commonly serve dropouts and those at risk of dropping out: schools, employment and training programs, and community agencies. Orr suggests a framework that classifies students into four groups:

1. those still in school, marginally at risk of dropping out, but still motivated to graduate (Their poor grades or postschool plans make them likely candidates to drop out.)
2. those who are interested in staying in school but who cannot because of personal circumstances, such as the need to work
3. those who are at great risk of dropping out, as evidenced by their lack of interest, poor attendance, and poor academic performance
4. those who have already left school but who need services to complete their education in order to be better prepared for employment

Orr (1987) proposes six categories of programs and services:

1. supplemental services—supportive counseling, job readiness preparation support groups, and part-time employment while students are still in school
2. removal of barriers to continued education—includes school-based day care centers, health care, evening instruction, social services, and basic skill remediation
3. comprehensive school-affiliated programs—includes employment preparation, counseling services, and a multiservice approach
4. services for out-of-school youth—offers a menu of services focusing on helping youth to achieve basic skills to obtain a general equivalency diploma and prepare for employment
5. systematic statewide approaches—includes alternative programs and a combination of services that take into consideration ways to restructure the schools to better respond to students' varied educational needs
6. citywide approaches—goes beyond the school systemwide approach to encompass the larger community or city and includes businesses, universities, and social agencies

Lambert, Novak, and Dougherty (1982) wrote a dropout prevention handbook that details a comprehensive K–12 approach to a multidimensional problem. They believe that the comprehensive approach must offer a variety of services that can be tailored to meet the unique characteristics of a school and community, so the approach can be both preventive and therapeutic in nature . They believe that an effective dropout prevention strategy

- centers on the student
- serves all students
- offers a comprehensive scope of services
- coordinates resources and personnel (both in school and out of school)
- transports to various school settings and school populations
- incorporates feedback and evaluation information into the system for improvement

Based on these premises, Lambert et al. identified nine components essential to a comprehensive dropout prevention strategy:

1. assessing the need for dropout prevention
2. focusing on the individual
3. identifying approaches for dropout prevention
4. establishing staff roles and staffing patterns in dropout prevention efforts
5. establishing and maintaining support within the school
6. establishing and maintaining support outside the school
7. involving parents in dropout prevention
8. facilitating an advisory committee for dropout prevention
9. educating the school and community in dropout prevention

Although no one set of strategies will solve the dropout problem completely, successful dropout prevention programs will have components of bonding, basic education, youth advocacy, and planning and evaluation (Exhibit 1-4).

In 1989 Governor Carroll A. Campbell, Jr., of the state of South Carolina established by executive order a Governor's Council on At-Risk Youth. The council held hearings around the state. The hearings included expert testimony from 40 invited witnesses and the participation of hundreds of interested citizens. The consensus was that too many young people were entering adulthood unprepared to meet the challenges of life in an increasingly demanding society. The costs to the state, if the citizens were to support a generation largely incapable of supporting itself, would be high. The council therefore reported the following major findings:

Exhibit 1-4 Components of Dropout Prevention Programs

BONDING
- advisory committees
- attendance improvement projects
- attendance/truancy committees
- business/industry/labor collaboration
- climate supportive for different individual needs and abilities
- community orientation
- community outreach activities
- community resources identified and utilized
- community service projects
- disciplinary alternatives
- home visits by teachers and counselors
- linkages with high school that students are likely to attend
- orientation to school
- parental involvement in child's attendance and homework activities
- partnerships with nonschool agencies
- record keeping accurately verifying student progress

THE BASICS
- academic acceleration
- activities tied to the real world—work, daily living, interpersonal relationships
- alternative curriculum or classes
- balanced curriculum of basic/core subjects and high-interest exploratory courses
- basic skills instruction related to real-world experiences—individualized and intensive
- "block" programs—consecutive instructional periods, followed by work, career education, counseling activities, or community activities
- career education activities
- class size reduction
- community-based evening tutorial and homework assistance programs; community-based learning activities
- community-volunteer involvement in classroom
- competency-based promotion
- computer-assisted instruction
- cooperative learning
- curriculum integration
- encouragement for girls to enroll in math, science, and other nontraditional courses
- expectations—academic and behavioral—clearly communicated
- experimental learning activities
- extracurricular activities
- flexible school schedules and hours
- general education programs integrated with dropout prevention programs
- integration of vocational experiences with core subjects
- individualized and personalized instruction
- clearly defined learning outcomes
- low student-teacher ratios

Exhibit 1-4 continued

- microcomputers for drill and practice in individualized learning
- orientation to the broader world of work outside of school
- peer tutoring
- physical activities in noncompetitive physical education programs
- self-paced progress through the curriculum
- small-group learning activities fostering appropriate group behavior
- specific educational plans—similar to IEPs
- summer learning programs
- teaching methods varied
- team teaching
- time-on-task for repeated practice
- work-related activities
- vocational programs

YOUTH ADVOCACY

- adolescent development principles as foundation
- adopt-a-student activities
- advisement and counseling
- affective domain part of school's concern
- assessment of needs by identifying local reasons students drop out
- coordinated activities of teachers, counselors, principals, and other support staff
- decision-making activities
- drug and alcohol abuse counseling
- early diagnosis and intervention
- environment—personal, informal, nonoppressive
- expectations of success combined with caring for students
- goal attainment activities (short-term attainable goals)
- guidance an integral part of dropout prevention
- health screening
- high standards and expectations in a supportive atmosphere
- identification of developmental needs of at-risk youth
- needs assessment activities
- peer counseling programs
- peer resource centers—classrooms set aside for "dropping in"
- personal relationships and rapport with individual students
- referral systems
- rewards and praise generous but honest
- role models positive
- self-awareness activities
- self-concept and sense of worth; self-esteem enhancement at every opportunity
- sex education—pregnancy prevention, parenting courses
- short-term goals, immediate feedback, and positive reinforcement
- specialized staff with counseling or specialized training background
- training for peer tutors and counselors

Exhibit 1-4 continued

PLANNING AND EVALUATION
- alternative administrative/organizational/instructional arrangements
- articulation: planned linkages with both elementary and high schools
- comprehensive services
- data collection system for dropouts and high-risk students
- evaluation information incorporated into system
- follow-up activities
- participatory decision making by staff in program governance
- program goals carefully monitored
- positive staff/administration relations
- public awareness and information program
- recognition for outstanding instruction
- reduced teacher workloads
- retention—supervisor to review records for early identification
- social worker/counselor on site
- special education programs
- staff committed to philosophy and goals of program
- staff development programs (e.g., classroom management, interpersonal and counseling skills, family intervention skills)
- strong administrative support for program, students, and teachers
- system for identifying and following progress of dropout-prone students

Note: IEP = individualized education program.

Source: From *The School's Choice: Guidelines for Dropout Prevention at the Middle and Junior High School* by R.D. Bhaerman and K.A. Kopp, 1988, Columbus, OH: National Center for Research in Vocational Education, Ohio State University.

1. At-risk youth rarely have a single problem such as deficiencies in basic skills. Rather, problems come in clusters, such as the need for counseling, for a part-time job, and for remediation. But social service delivery in the state is highly fragmented, so that the individual does not receive the full array of services he or she needs. We must find a way to treat individual problems comprehensively, on a broad basis, and not on the present piecemeal one.
2. School reform is highly dependent upon the creation of school/business collaboratives, because the private sector contributes many of the financial and human resource inputs necessary to make the reforms work. These partnerships must be encouraged throughout the state. Public/private ventures are absolutely essential to introducing new, innovative practices into the schools.

3. A youngster does not become "at risk" at some point in school. When children are born, we have a pretty good idea of the future prospects, based on the mother's marital status, the child's birth weight, and the parents' educational background. Therefore, our assistance programs should reach down into the stages of early childhood. Preschool programs for four- and five-year-olds are essential, and these should be coupled with regular visitations in the home. Either we can pay now, and avoid blighted child-hoods—or we can pay much more, later on, for the consequences of these childhoods.

4. Parents are essential actors in the drama of their children's lives. They must be an important part of any program, whether it is counseling, work/study, mentoring, or remediation. Some parents, moreover, need to be taught about parenting, since they themselves often lack parents who could have served as role models for them. Programs must include parents, as well as students.

5. At the state level, there should be some type of permanent state organization to provide policy direction to the efforts of all of the groups and agencies involved in the effort. We need to build an institutional capacity both to identify needs by collecting ongoing research data, and to provide technical assistance to communities as they formulate their own programs.

6. While alternative and enrichment programs are helpful, the best way schools can prevent dropouts is through systemic structural change, including such basic features as redefining the school day and school year; changing the ratio of students to teachers; new curricula that relate school and work experiences; different kinds of pre- and in-service training for teachers; decredentialization so that where there are personnel needs (as in science and math), people without teacher training, but with content know-how, can teach; peer tutoring; intergenerational mentoring; cooperative learning; remediation through computer-assisted instruction; and work/study. Schools are profoundly anachronistic and out-of-step with American business and industry. Single-shot programs will not address a problem of this depth and magnitude.

7. We need accurate dropout data, and a way of tracking students so that we know what happens to them at various points along the trajectory of their education careers. A consistent data collection system could go a long way toward preventing students from dropping through the cracks in the system.

8. Education is a labor-intensive enterprise, and dealing with dropout-prone youngsters requires even more time than is normally

allowed. School counselors have a definite role to play in working with individual at-risk students, scheduling and conducting parent conferences, and coordinating other services. Presently, across the state, many guidance counselors are deflected from providing personal and individual attention to at-risk students because of clerical and administrative duties. We need more guidance counselors and we need them working with students, not filling out forms.

9. The key to excellent schools is local flexibility with responsibility. Since the dropout problem is too diverse for a single solution, no one model or program is "the" answer. Each community must invent its own answer (or answers) based on its particular needs and resources. To exercise this level of creative leadership, schools require broad autonomy and the freedom to experiment. Freedom from unnecessary restrictions and bureaucratic restraints mandated by the Department of Education must be achieved if local school and community groups are to respond to this problem.

10. Solving the dropout problem will require both reallocation of existing resources, and allocation of new resources. Since we estimate that one-third of our school population is at risk, and we have a total of approximately 600,000 youngsters in school, we can conclude that about 200,000 children can be classified as potential dropouts. If we were to spend only $100 per child per year, we would require $20 million. At some point very soon, we are going to have to look at what money will be required to implement which programs and how we are going to raise those funds. This may well mean that while some proposed solutions, such as alternative schools, are very appealing, they may be too costly to mount.

11. In each of the last two years in South Carolina, over 40,000 students in grades 1–8 were retained. This is roughly 10 percent of all students in those grades. Last year alone, it cost South Carolina $130 million for students retained in elementary or middle/junior high schools. This policy has continued in spite of its costs, and in spite of the fact that the educational research in this area suggests that promotion to the next grade with intensive remediation is more effective than retention alone. A hard look needs to be taken at how we group students (age/grade level), our promotion policies, and alternatives beyond social promotion.

12. To elicit community support, there needs to be a generalized awareness that we do, in fact, have a problem that we must do something about. In South Carolina, while there are segments of the population that are aware of this, there are many people who

are either unaware of these issues or who are apathetic about them. Through a major public relations and advertising effort, we need to raise the present level of consciousness in this state about the dropout problem and what it means to us as a people in terms of its negative effects. Unaware people will be unwilling to contribute their time and resources toward solutions.

13. Unless everyone has high expectations of everyone else, we will not be able to implement successful programs. This means that schools must have high expectations of their students and must communicate those expectations to them in a variety of ways. It also means that the general public must have high expectations for school administrators and teachers. Finally, it requires that the general public of South Carolina have high expectations of policy-makers and public officials.

14. Without executive leadership at the highest levels of the state, nothing will happen. This means that everyone from the Governor on down must demonstrate commitment to solving the dropout problem. This commitment can be made apparent in a variety of ways: by publicly speaking out on the issues; by pressing ahead with new policies; by urging the creation of new entities designed to deal with the problem; by allocating funds; and by reaching out to the community to participate and help.

Only through concerted action can we fulfill the promise we have made to our children and to ourselves: not to let another decade dawn without real hope of change for the better. It is probably high time we all began making it our business to effect that change. (pp. iii–v)

SUMMARY

Nash (1990) says that there are a number of issues with which we must concern ourselves if we want to help our children. The problems are so complex and interrelated that the individual differences within communities and young people make a quick fix impossible. However, she is hopeful, as are the authors of this book, that there are some underlying ideas and principles that are basic to a positive learning environment. The following chapters identify policies, practices, and standards that need to be implemented if progress is to be made and hope exist. Nash (1990) says it best when she writes:

The point of all these discussions of school reform, restructing, and changing of policies is that our current system is not reaching all of our children. In addition to many personal and social problems that put children and youth at risk, the schools themselves also may contribute to pushing our young people out of the school doors before they are adequately trained for the working world. (p. 26)

It is the intent of this book to examine a variety of carefully selected issues that educators can use to make a difference in the restructuring process, whether it be a change in philosophy or policy at the district level, choice of curricula or the selection of the instructional activities in the classroom.

REFERENCES

Bhaerman, R.D., & Kopp, K.A. (1988). *The school's choice: Guidelines for dropout prevention at the middle and junior high school.* Columbus, OH: National Center for Research in Vocational Education.

Bishop, J. (1988). *Making vocational education more effective for at-risk youth.* Ithaca, NY: New York State School of Industrial and Labor Relations, Cornell University.

Carnevale, A.P., Gainer, L.J., & Meltzer, A.S. (1989). *Workplace basics: The skills employers want.* Alexandria,VA: American Society for Training and Development.

Clark, R. (1988). *Critical factors in why disadvantaged students succeed or fail in school.* Washington, DC: Academy for Educational Development.

Committee for Economic Development. (1987). *Children in need: Investment strategies for the educationally disadvantaged.* A Statement by the Research and Policy Committee of the Committee for Economic Development. Washington, DC: Author.

Cuban, L. (1989). The "at-risk" label and the problem of urban school reform. *Phi Delta Kappan, 70,* 780–782.

Earle, J., Roach, V., & Fraser, K. (1987). *Female dropouts: A new perspective.* Alexandria, VA: Youth Services Program, National Association of State Boards of Education.

Edleman, M.W. (1988). *Who's watching the children?* Washington, DC: Children's Defense Fund.

Feichtner, Sheila H. (1989). *School-to-work-transition for at-risk youth.* Columbus, OH: ERIC Clearinghouse on Adult, Career, and Vocational Education.

Fine, M. (1988). De-institutionalizing educational inequality. In *School success for students at-risk.* Orlando FL: Harcourt Brace Jovanovich. (Council for Chief State School Officers)

Ford Foundation (1989). Project on Social Welfare and the American Future. *The common good: Social welfare and the American future.* New York: Author.

Frantz, N.R., Jr., Strickland, D.C., & Elson, D.E. (1988). Is secondary vocational education at risk? *Vocational Education Journal, 63* (7), 34–37.

Frase, (1988). *Dropout rates in the United States.* Washington,DC: National Center for Education Statistics.

Frymier, & Gansneder (1989). *Phi Delta Kappan, 70,* 142.

Gastright, J.F. (1989). Don't base your dropout program on somebody else's problem. *Phi Delta Kappan, 70,* 3–4. (Research Bulletin, Center on Evaluation, Development and Research)

Ginsburg & Hanson. (1990). *Values and success: Strategies for at-risk children and youth.* Paper presented at The U.S. Department of Education Conference, Washington, DC.

Gruskin, S.J., Campbell, M.A., & Paulu, N. (1987). *Dealing with dropouts: The urban superintendents' call to action.* Washington, DC: Office of Educational Research and Improvement.

Hamby, J.V. (1989). National dropout rates: *Sources, problems, and efforts toward solutions: A series of solutions and strategies.* Clemson, SC: National Dropout Prevention Center, Clemson University.

Hodgkinson, H. (1989). *The same client: The demographics of education and service delivery systems.* Washington, DC: Center for Demographic Policy, Institute for Educational Leadership.

Jibrell, S. (1987). *School dropouts: A national dilemma.* Washington, DC: National Governor's Association. (Labor Notes)

Johnson, C.M., Sum, A.M., & Weill, J.D. (1988). *Vanishing dreams: The growing economic plight of America's young families.* Washington, DC: Children's Defense Fund.

Johnson, W.B., & Packer, A.H. (1987). *Workforce 2000: Work and workers for the 21st century.* Indianapolis, IN: Hudson Institute.

Kennedy, E.M. (1988). When students drop out, we all lose. *Vocational Education Journal, 63,* 35.

Lacy, G., Johnson, C., & Heffernan, D. (1989). *Tackling the youth employment problem.* Adolescent Pregnancy Prevention Clearinghouse. Washington, DC: Children's Defense Fund.

Lambert, R., Novak, J., & Dougherty, B. (1982). *Staying in: A dropout prevention handbook K–12.* Madison, WI: Vocational Studies Center.

Lehr, J.B., & Harris, H.W. (1988). *At-risk, low-achieving students in the classroom.* Washington, DC: National Education Association.

Meeting the needs of at-risk youth in South Carolina: Executive Summary. (1989). Testimony presented during public hearings of the Governor's Council on at-risk youth, ii-v.

National Association of Special Needs State Administrators. (1989). *Transition for at-risk students in vocational education.*

Nash, Margaret A. (1990). *Improving their chances: A handbook for designing and implementing programs for at-risk youth.* Madison, WI: Vocational Studies Center.

National Coalition of Advocates for Students. (1988). *Barriers to excellence: Our children at risk.* Boston: Author.

Orfield, G. (1988). Race, income and educational inequity. In *School success for students at-risk.* Orlando, FL: Harcourt Brace Jovanovich. (Council for Chief State School Officers)

Orr, M.T. (1987). *Keeping students in school.* San Francisco: Josey-Bass.

Peck, N., Law, A., & Mills, R.C. (1989). *Dropout prevention: What we have learned.* Ann Arbor, MI: ERIC Counseling and Personnel Services Clearinghouse.

Reingold, J.R. (n.d.) *Making the grade: A report card on American youth.* Washington, DC: National Collaboration for Youth.

Tindall, L.W. (1988). *Retraining at-risk students: The role of career and vocational education.* Columbus, OH: ERIC Clearinghouse on Adult, Career, and Vocational Education, Center on Education and Training for Employment.

Weber, J.A. (1986). *The role of vocational education in decreasing the dropout rate.* Columbus, OH: National Center for Research in Vocational Education, Ohio State University.

Weber, J.M. (1987). *Strengthening vocational education's role in decreasing the dropout rate.* Columbus, OH: National Center for Research in Vocational Education, Ohio State University.

Wells, S., Bechard, S., & Hamby, J.V. (1989). *How to identify at-risk students: A series of solutions and strategies.* Clemson, SC: National Dropout Prevention Center, Clemson University.

William T. Grant Foundation (1988). Commission on Work, Family, and Citizenship. *The forgotten half: Non-college youth in America: An interim report on the school-to-work transition.* Washington, DC: Author.

Van Tassel-Baska, J., Patton, J., & Prillman, D. (1989). *Disadvantaged gifted learners at-risk for educational attention. Focus on Exceptional Children, 22,* 1.

chapter **2**

Program Planning for At-Risk Students

Gregory A. Smith

Much of the debate about how to deal with the problem of school dropout has tended to remain in the realm of abstractions. Scholars and policymakers discuss the need for developing a common definition of *dropout*, compare the dropout rates of different populations of students, and suggest on one hand that dropout is not significant since a majority of school leavers eventually earn a diploma or a general equivalency diploma (GED), or on the other hand that dropout is an increasingly serious problem because of the absence of economic opportunities for those unprepared to enter the labor market of the late 20th century. While this discussion is necessary as a means for alerting the general public to a complex and thorny issue, it is not at this level that the problems of school failure and disengagement will be solved. Those problems will be solved as educators in specific schools come to accept their own accountability for the failure of a proportion of their students to acquire the skills required to make their way in the rapidly changing world adults have bequeathed to them.

Such accountability has been slow in coming. Throughout most of the 20th century educators have tended to blame students themselves for their inability to master the requirements and expectations of the school. Lack of parental support, low intelligence, poor motivation, cultural deprivation, attention deficits, and emotional or behavioral disabilities, among others, have been held up as reasons underlying the inability of teachers to teach all students. The blame for student failure has almost invariably been directed away from the

---

Note: This chapter was prepared at the National Center on Effective Secondary Schools, supported by the U.S. Department of Education, Office of Educational Research and Improvement (Grant No. G-008690007-9) and by the Wisconsin Center for Education Research, School of Education, University of Wisconsin-Madison. The opinions expressed in this chapter are those of the author and do not necessarily reflect the views of the supporting agencies.

behavioral and programmatic regularities of the school. This is not to say that students' background characteristics and personal problems have no impact on their ability or willingness to undergo the rigors of formal education; they do. This kind of analysis, however, has disregarded the fact that measures related to school performance such as failure and grade retention rates as well as suspension and expulsion rates are among the most powerful predictors of drop-out (Ekstrom, Goertz, Pollack, & Rock, 1986; Wehlage & Rutter, 1986). In other words, in schools where many students fail, are retained, or are suspended or expelled, dropout rates are higher. Students therefore do not drop out in isolation from the school; they drop out as a result of their interaction with the teachers, administrators, peers, and activities they encounter there. The nature of that interaction is at least partly the responsibility of educators.

It is in recognizing this shared responsibility that educators in an increasing number of communities throughout the United States have begun to develop educational alternatives that respond to students at risk of school failure in new ways. Instead of accepting that failure as a natural consequence that must follow the inability or unwillingness of certain students to align their lives with the expectations and requirements of the school, they have begun to shape programs more successful in meeting at-risk youth halfway, programs able to draw them into the life of the school and to engage them in productive learning activities.

In a study conducted under the auspices of the National Center on Effective Secondary Schools at the University of Wisconsin-Madison, 14 of these schools were the subject a major research effort. These schools were located in urban, suburban, and rural communities around the United States and served a wide range of students: white, black, Hispanic, Native American, economically disadvantaged, middle class, emotionally troubled, pregnant, academically able, and academically slow. The aim of this research was to explore the diversity of responses that have arisen in regard to the problem of school dropout and to discover commonalities that might link them together. More extensive information about this study and the theoretical conclusions drawn from it can be found in *Reducing the Risk: Schools as Communities of Support* (Wehlage, Rutter, Smith, Lesko, & Fernandez, 1989). The comments about program planning that follow are grounded in information drawn from this research project.

This chapter begins with a review of steps educators commonly take as they attempt to create innovative programs for at-risk youth. In that section, reference is made to two contrasting programs in an effort to describe how these steps are likely to take different configurations from place to place. The ability to respond appropriately to local conditions is a central characteristic of most effective dropout prevention programs. Regardless of their particularity, however, effective programs for students at risk tend to demonstrate common characteristics related to school climate, curriculum and instruction, and patterns of governance. The second section focuses on more general principles abstracted from these characteristics. A number of changes in practice and organizational structure can contribute to a realization of these principles. In the final section, specific strategies that have been adopted elsewhere to accomplish this purpose are described. These strategies demonstrate the kind of creative and nontraditional thinking that may be necessary to invent schools where all children are likely to succeed.

STEPS IN PROGRAM PLANNING

Programs designed specifically for potential dropouts are developed for a variety of reasons. The schools described below tended to be the result of actions taken by concerned educators who recognized a need and then addressed it. As the problem of school dropout has received increasing attention from state and national policymakers, the motivation for the creation of such programs has to some extent shifted away from local districts to state houses and state departments of education through the mandating of specific measures aimed at reducing dropout rates or providing funding for the creation of different categorical programs. Regardless of the source of motivation behind the creation of such programs, however, the response of educators at the local level to the characteristics of their own students and to the social, economic, and political dynamics of the immediate community is of primary importance. Programs that fail to respond to particular local conditions will be less likely to address the needs of those students who require additional support to become academically successful. In some districts, students who constitute this group may in fact be a majority. In this situation, more than the creation of special programs may be necessary; policymakers will need to consider a more thoroughgoing restructuring of schools throughout the district. The focus here, however, is on the creation of more self-contained programs.

Six initial steps should guide the planning process. They include the following:

1. identification of student population to be served
2. formation of a collaborative team
3. identification of program vision and goals
4. research into programs that have demonstrated success in working with the target population
5. development of proposal and implementation strategies, including the identification of potential supporters and sources of funding
6. evaluation of program outcomes: creation of an evaluation process aimed at measuring changes in selected student outcome measures to demonstrate the program's effectiveness in working with its target population

Although these steps might be followed in a different order, each appears to play an important role in assuring the success of innovative educational ventures.

Identification of Student Population To Be Served

The identification of a target student population can be the result of a more formal needs assessment on the part of the district or can arise from the perceptions of individual educators who see a need for alternative educational practices among their students. It is often helpful to be somewhat specific in choosing which group of students will be addressed. The nature of the program itself ideally will be predicated on the population chosen.

The School-within-a-School at Memorial High School in Madison, Wisconsin, for example, was created in 1984 as part of a districtwide effort to reduce the dropout rate. The superintendent of schools at that time had been pleased with the success and popularity of a vocationally oriented alternative called the Work and Learn Center, a program that served high school students who were seriously credit deficient. He was interested in creating comparable programs that could be housed in two of the district's four high schools. These programs would work with juniors and seniors whose chances of graduation could be improved by taking modified course offerings and participating in vocational learning experiences that would allow them to accumulate credits more rapidly than would be possible by following a regular schedule. In addition to a modified schedule, the program would also offer smaller classes taught by teachers willing to assume direct responsibility for the academic success of their students.

Although students at the School-within-a-School share the common experience of credit deficiency, the reasons for their course failure are varied. Some students in the program are intellectually able but are alienated from the school; others have serious emotional problems; and still others have difficulty in dealing with the school's academic demands. Not all students experiencing credit deficiency, however, are admitted to this program. Students with fewer than seven credits at the beginning of their junior year are referred to the Work and Learn Center, which continues to exist. Only students who can be reasonably expected to graduate within 2 years, given the program's provisions for accelerated credit accumulation, are admitted.

In contrast, the choice of the student population to be served at the Sierra Mountain High School in Grass Valley, California, arose in a less systematic way. When interviewing for a job as truant officer for the high school, the school's future principal told district administrators that he would accept the position only if allowed to create a special program that would attract ninth and tenth graders to school. The district already had a continuation school for students over 15 years of age. No alternatives were available for younger secondary school students. The future principal believed that if students who were regularly truant were provided with a school that offered a more accepting, supportive, and academically appealing environment, they could be reconnected to the educational process. Most students who attend Sierra Mountain are characterized not so much by credit deficiency–although many have histories of course failure–but by a shared dislike of the district's two comprehensive high schools. Furthermore, most students at Sierra Mountain tend to be viewed by educators and students at these schools as misfits and behavior problems. Not surprisingly, the nature of the educational program offered at Sierra Mountain focuses on strategies likely to draw these students into an experience of social bonding with their teachers and peers. The provision of an embracing educational community is the central aim of this school.

Educators at other programs involved in our study similarly identified specific populations of students to serve. The New Futures School in Albuquerque, New Mexico, for example, works only with pregnant or parenting teens ranging in age from approximately 12 to 21. The Croom Vocational High School in Prince George's County, Maryland, has chosen to direct its energies to 16- through 18-year-old students whose academic difficulties are likely to prevent them from graduating or seeking postsecondary training. The Media Academy, a school-within-a-school at Fremont High School in Oakland, California, works primarily with able but unmotivated black and Hispanic students who have not become engaged in more conventional classes. What is important to note in each of these instances is the fact that educators have chosen not to work with all at-risk students but with a selected proportion of that population. A single program may not be able to assist all students at risk of school failure; multiple approaches to the problems of such students may be necessary.

Formation of a Collaborative Team

The formation of a core group of colleagues who share a common vision about the program they wish to establish is perhaps one of the most important elements of the entire planning and implementation process. Often, the motivation to develop a new program is the result of the action of individual teachers who are willing to act as educational entrepreneurs. Individuals on their own, however, rarely are able to create schools. They need the support and participation of others. It is critical that these educational entrepreneurs develop a group of allies who are willing to contribute their energy to what must eventually become a collective project. The choice of team members will continue to be a critical matter throughout the life of the program.

Prior to the establishment of the School-within-a-School, the program's two core teachers as well as their future district-level supervisor had been participants in a university course in which the specific design of the program was developed. All shared a common desire to work with at-risk students, and after this shared venture all possessed a clear vision of what they wanted to accomplish. During the first 2 years of the program, the third teacher hired to work in the School-within-a-School shared their values and orientation. Hiring practices in the district rendered this teacher surplus during the third and subsequent years, however, and led to the transfer of a series of teachers into the School-within-a-School who did not wish to work with the program's student population. These teachers generally regarded their stay at the School-within-a-School as temporary and undesirable. The sense of common purpose and direction that existed in the initial years of the program was lost. This has been highly problematic in that the staff at the program no longer approach their work or their students from the same perspective, a factor that has impeded the creation of a supportive school environment in which expectations for students from one class to another are clear. These difficulties underline the importance of recognizing that effective programs for at-risk students must involve more than the introduction of new educational structures. The teachers responsible for working within these structures appear to be considerably more important than the structures themselves.

The formation of the team of teachers at Sierra Mountain occurred somewhat serendipitously. At the outset, the principal was given one other teacher to establish the program. After a report from the California State Department of Education made accreditation of the program contingent upon more funding, the district hired two more teachers, both of whom had had extensive experience in working in innovative private schools. All four educators shared a desire to create a school they could consider their own. To one extent or another, all four were also mavericks, people who questioned many of the assumptions that tend to govern the practices encountered in most conventional schools. They were willing to experiment, to take risks, and to invest their lives in the evolution of a new institution. In the next years of Sierra Mountain's development, four more teachers, a counselor, and support staff were hired. These people, as well, have shared a common desire to work with students often poorly served in regular classrooms; they also have shared a common interest in the creation of a new kind of school. Their commitment and their willingness to act collectively have been central to the school's success. Sierra Mountain has not had to deal with conflicts set in motion by districtwide hiring and transfer practices, conflicts that have hampered the work of teachers at the School-within-a-School.

The collection of teachers and administrators who can act as a supportive community for one another is often essential to the long-term success of programs for at-risk youth. Such students can be highly demanding in their need for attention, care, and patience. By working as a team, however, teachers become more able to tolerate these demands. Rather than having to face students alone, teachers know that their colleagues are there to back them up, help them through difficult periods, and act together to change policies or improve conditions that may be counterproductive to their educational efforts as a whole. Collegial relations such as those that characterized the School-within-a-School during its first 2 years and continue to characterize staff relations at Sierra Mountain were observed in the most successful of the 14 schools. Assembling the "right" people must be a central aim of the planning process. Without them, it may not be possible to build and sustain the momentum needed to create a new kind of school.

Identification of Program Vision and Goals

The identification of a program's vision and goals is necessarily related to its choice of target population and the formation of a core team of teachers. The evolution of this vision is likely to depend on a variety of factors related to the unique mix of people who choose to participate in the project itself; such a vision may not become clear and defined early in the development of the program. Eventually, however, it will be important for those who are interested in creating an innovative program to articulate some agreed on direction; it will be this shared intention that will become the bedrock upon which their new school community will be constructed.

The program vision at the School-within-a-School is closely tied to a belief that if students are to become self-supporting adults they must learn how to adjust to the requirements of life in the organizational settings that characterize contemporary society. This means that they must learn how to get along with others and be willing to comply with institutional regulations. The primary goal of the School-within-a-School is to help students complete requirements for a high school diploma and enter the workplace, institutions of higher education, or the military. As the lead teacher at the School-within-a-School noted,

> I guess we are a behavior modification program. Because if these kids can't get their acts together, no matter how much factual material we teach them, they're still not going to be successful in life.... They have to learn how to get along with other people, which a lot of them haven't been able to do. They have to learn some respect for law and the society; whether they agree with it or not, they have to learn how to function in that society. (Smith, 1987a, p. 21)

At the School-within-a-School, teachers strive to help students learn lessons about institutional conformity, lessons that in many respects are essential if they hope to have any success in most conventional work environments once they graduate.

On the other hand, the program vision at Sierra Mountain is predicated on an orientation to social relations with students that emphasizes tolerance, affection, and respect. The school's primary goal is to enhance student self-esteem on the assumption that people who believe in their own ability to deal with problems will be more able to adjust to the requirements of adult society than those who feel that they are failures. In their comments about the school, student informants mentioned the four A's, describing them as the Sierra Mountain motto. The four *A*'s include acceptance, appreciation, affection, and attention. One girl, a student leader, observed, "People are taught that. People here live by that" (Smith, 1987b, p. 5). On their first day at the school, new students may find themselves hugged by the principal or one of their teachers. Although such gestures of friendliness may seem contrived or out of place, many students come to feel accepted for who they are; they do not feel that they are being asked to fit into a particular mold. A former student who was working full-time in a local grocery store said that teachers at Sierra Mountain ". . . helped me to become more of who I am. . . . I wasn't suppressed or held down. They let me try to find out . . . what I could be" (Smith, 1987b, p. 6).

Although the specific educational visions that underlie the School-within-a-School and Sierra Mountain are distinctive and in some respects opposed to one another, teachers in both programs share a fundamental sense of responsibility for at-risk students that could also be considered as part of their visions. The teachers who have chosen to work in these programs believe that they can have an impact on the lives of students who more often than not had become marginal to the experience of schooling. Central to this deeper vision is a faith in the ability of most if not all students to learn. In the most successful of the 14 schools, staff shared a commitment to at-risk youth similar to that encountered in the original teachers at the School-within-a-School and their colleagues at Sierra Mountain. Most were motivated by a deep sense of mission toward students too often disregarded in conventional classrooms. As one of the teachers at the Media Academy said, "This is God's work we are engaged in. . . . Unlike some teachers, we care about our students' success, we have a stake in it. These kids will shine when they leave here" (Wehlage, 1987, p. 24). Such determination often fuels the efforts of teachers in these schools and informs their vision of what they wish to accomplish with their students.

Research into Programs that Have Demonstrated Success in Working with the Target Population

Taking advantage of the experience of others is an important step in the creation of new educational ventures. How this is done may vary from school to school. In some cases, educators who are creating the program may carry out research in a systematic and scholarly fashion. In others, knowledge of comparable programs may be based on personal experience. In yet others, outside consultants may assist in the process of developing alternative schools appropriate for a given population of at-risk students.

As indicated earlier, the design of the School-within-a-School grew out of a university course aimed at exploring characteristics of successful schools for at-risk youth. This course was cotaught by a professor at the University of Wisconsin knowledgeable about alternative programs aimed at enhancing academic achievement and retention and a Madison Metropolitan School District administrator responsible for the development of special programs for potential dropouts. Teachers, counselors, and administrators interested in partici-pating in the School-within-a-School project were invited to attend this class. During this short course, participants identified important characteristics of successful programs for potential dropouts, including a strong vocational component aimed more at the transmission of behaviors appropriate for the worksite than at specific skills, exposure to a variety of occupations, the opportunity to learn within a small and moderately stable educational communi-ty, and the chance to work with a team of committed teachers for a 2-year period. They designed their own program with these characteristics in mind.

At the Sierra Mountain High School, the principal relied more on his experience as a teacher and administrator in a successful continuation school in Southern California than on a systematic investigation of literature about programs for at-risk youth. Sierra Mountain's supportive and accepting teacher-student relations, its provision of independent learning opportunities, its consensual governance patterns, and many of its slogans were borrowed outright from this other school. In addition, teachers at Sierra Mountain brought with them their own experiences in alternative institutions. One teacher had taught for several years in an innovative Quaker high school in which teachers assumed a multiplicity of roles vis-à-vis their students and had full responsibility for the development of their own curriculum. At this institution, as well, schoolwide decisions were made by the staff as a whole rather than by the principal. These accumulated experiences all contributed to shaping the unique environment of Sierra Mountain High School. Staff at Sierra Mountain have continued their education through their involvement with both state and national organizations for alternative educators. They regularly share their experiences at these meetings and learn firsthand from the experience of others.

This willingness to reach out to the broader educational community is characteristic of teachers and administrators in many of the programs we studied. The principal as well as other staff from the New Futures School in Albuquerque, for example, regularly participate in national conventions and forums in which issues related to the education of pregnant and mothering teens as well as at-risk youth in general are raised. The same is true of teachers at the Wayne Enrichment Center in Indianapolis, Indiana, a school that works on both a short- and long-term basis with high school students who are experiencing academic and behavioral problems, and educators involved with the Federation of Alternative Schools, a consortium of six different alternative programs in Minneapolis, Minnesota. Planning for program innovation is an ongoing process for these teachers. They are continually seeking new ways to meet the needs of the students they encounter in their schools. That learning is predicated on a desire to improve their programs through more research, visitation to other schools, and participation in associations composed of similarly committed educators. Innovation in these schools, while local, thus does not occur in a vacuum but is informed with the experience of other practitioners from around the nation.

Development of a Proposal and Implementation Strategy

The School-within-a-School and Sierra Mountain exemplify two different approaches to the development of a proposal and implementation strategy. As indicated above, the proposal that led to the creation of the School-within-a-School was largely the product of a group of concerned university and public school educators who had been given at least a partial mandate from the local district to develop a program for students nearing the end of their high school careers without enough credits to graduate. The district administrator who cotaught this course was at the time completing a doctoral program at the University of Wisconsin-Madison. His studies focused on the educational needs of at-risk youth. This man has continued to be intimately involved with both the Work and Learn Center and the two schools-within-a-school that grew out of this effort. He initially assisted in the construction of a proposal that met district requirements and then helped to locate the additional local, state, and federal funding needed to bring these programs into existence. He brought with him a working knowledge of the local district, expertise in the characteristics of innovative programs for students with histories of school failure, and familiarity with different funding options. His long-term commitment to these programs as a supervisor and fund-raiser has undoubtedly contributed to their continued operation. Finding someone within the organizational structure of the local school district with the kind of knowledge and connections possessed by this individual could well be an important step in developing a proposal likely to meet with district approval and in negotiating the multiplicity of barriers that almost inevitably stand between program conception and implementation.

The situation faced by the future principal of Sierra Mountain High School was very different. Instead of being an insider, he was an outsider with an untried plan. Fortuitously, two lower-level district administrators (who subsequently became the superintendent and assistant superintendent in charge of business) became interested in his ideas. They urged him to complete a needs assessment that led to the development of a proposal suggesting the establishment of a dual-focus alternative. One component would serve freshmen and sophomores who were still in school but in danger of dropping out. They would meet in regular classes but work with an individualized curriculum, a process not dissimilar to that used in many continuation high schools. The second component would be aimed at older students who had already dropped out. They would be given the opportunity to earn credits toward graduation through independent study. Because the state of California funds students in independent study programs at the same rate as students in full-day schools, state monies for the latter could be used to pay for a lower student-teacher ratio in the former. The superintendent and the school board liked his idea, but instead of providing the six teachers, several thousand dollars, and the site requested in his proposal, they offered the future principal an additional teacher and $2,000, and told him to find his own building. Undeterred by such details, the now-principal of this new program located another teacher interested in the plan, found a run-down building on the county bus lot, and went about the job of collecting students. Despite limited staff and facilities, at the end of 2 months, 30 to 40 students were enrolled; another 100 were engaged in independent study.

The development of the proposal that led to the creation of Sierra Mountain High School as well as the strategies that furthered its implementation were dependent to some extent on lucky breaks. If two district personnel had not been interested in the ideas of Sierra Mountain's future principal and if the California Department of Education had not recommended that the program be adequately funded, it is doubtful that this educational experiment would have succeeded. This points out the degree to which serendipity can shape the evolution of alternative educational settings. Not everything can be well planned or anticipated. It is important that those responsible for developing proposals and implementation strategies be prepared to adapt to the conditions they encounter while at the same time remaining loyal to their underlying vision. It is also important to cultivate ties to individuals so placed that they can influence decisions about the acceptance or funding of these new ideas. In the case of Sierra Mountain, the support of the future superintendent and assistant superintendent has been a critical factor in the continued funding of the program; the superintendent has also played a very helpful role in protecting a group of educational mavericks from intradistrict critics.

In other programs, teachers cultivated similar forms of support by going beyond district personnel to other groups within the community. At the Media Academy, for example, an advisory board composed of executives from a number of Oakland media establishments as well as professors of journalism from local colleges and universities has provided guidance and protection for the program in times of fiscal constraint. In Minneapolis, the Federation of Alternative Schools has made it possible for a number of smaller programs to negotiate a contract with the Minneapolis public schools to offer educational services to at-risk youth. An important part of planning, therefore, is the cultivation of constituencies of interested and potentially supportive individuals from throughout the community. By broadening their base of support, innovative programs become more able to withstand the opposition and budgetary trials that almost inevitably accompany institutional experimentation. The cultivation of such support needs to be seen as one of the primary tasks of the implementation process.

Evaluation of Program Outcomes

The development of systematic measures of the impact of programs for at-risk youth is often neglected by educators. This is not surprising given the variety of other legitimate and generally more pressing demands that accompany the creation of any new institution. The political environment in which these programs are established is rarely a favorable one, and the problems of the students themselves can be so compelling that teachers and administrators are often forced to spend the majority of their time dealing with immediate problems rather than evaluating the overall effect of their efforts. This is unfortunate, because in the long run the ability to demonstrate outcomes such as reduced suspension and expulsion rates, increased attendance, higher retention, improved graduation rates, growth in academic skills, and positive postgraduation experiences can provide important forms of validation for teaching strategies that often appear iconoclastic and questionable to decision makers and members of the public unfamiliar with schools that work with potential dropouts.

The district-level administrator who has played such a central role in the evolution of the School-within-a-School has been very sensitive to this issue. Perhaps because he has been in a supervisory position rather than involved in the day-to-day operation of the program, he has been able to oversee the continued monitoring of program outcomes. Data on social adjustment, academic achievement, attendance, and grade point average are regularly gathered and incorporated into reports to the district as well as to funders. These data provide an important vehicle for chronicling the degree to which innovative practices are efficacious both for people outside the program and for those within.

Similar data were not collected systematically at Sierra Mountain prior to the school's involvement in our study. In part, this was the result of the fact that students at Sierra Mountain could transfer to a variety of programs in the district after they had reached the age of 16. While it is possible to track students by using the district's management information system, this process is cumbersome, and no one at the school had compiled records about academic achievement or retention rates for the school's former students. Other information about credit accumulation, grade point average, and disciplinary referrals, while easier to gather, had also not been tabulated. For Sierra Mountain, such information could have been very helpful in demonstrating to critics that the efforts of teachers in the program were having a positive impact on students who had been known for their truancy, misbehavior, and academic failure in the district's comprehensive high schools.

When educators in programs for at-risk students are asked to evaluate their work, they often turn to anecdotal information. Although such information is valuable, it tends not to possess the same authority or generalizability as figures that demonstrate explicit changes in the school-related behavior of potential dropouts. The continued existence of programs marginal to mainstream classrooms is often dependent on their ability to show that they are achieving outcomes with at-risk students that conventional schools are unable to demonstrate. The collection of such information, although time-consuming, should be a priority. Not only can these data play an important role in convincing skeptics of the value of alternative educational settings, they can potentially help teachers and administrators involved in dropout prevention and recovery programs to evaluate their own work as it is affecting groups of students rather than the isolated individuals who are so often mentioned in their conversations when they are asked about the worth of their schools.

Conclusion

The importance of the planning process leading to the creation of programs for at-risk students cannot be underestimated. Without the identification of a specific student population to be served, the clarification of program goals, and the collection of a group of colleagues committed to the development of a new educational venture, there is little likelihood that a program will move beyond the conceptual stage. Research into comparable programs, an assessment of their appropriateness for local conditions, and the development of implementation and evaluation strategies will contribute to the program's credibility and efficacy once established. As Sarason (1972) notes, one of the most important periods in the development of any new social institution occurs before it has been created. Those involved in the design and implementation of new institutions must anticipate as systematically as they can the kinds of issues they will be likely to confront once their program is established. Often, decisions made at the outset can have long-term consequences. Sarason points to the process by which the United States Constitution was conceived and written and suggests that if similar care were directed to the planning of all social institutions, more would be able to achieve their ends and persist over time. His advice is particularly relevant for those who attempt to construct new models of schooling. Such schools, like the fledgling democracy constructed over two centuries ago in the United States, must challenge many of the habits, practices, and dispositions associated with more traditional institutions.

PRINCIPLES UNDERLYING SUCCESSFUL DROPOUT PREVENTION PROGRAMS

Although exemplary programs for at-risk students tend to be those that address the needs of a specific, rather than a general, student population, it is still possible to articulate a set of characteristics that appear to cut across the diversity of responses that have accompanied this approach. In the next section, the outlines of a theory of dropout prevention that arose to make sense of these common characteristics is presented. Programs able to reconnect at-risk youth to the demands and opportunities of education achieve their success by acting on three important principles. First, they are able to help students who have become increasingly marginalized in their relations with teachers and peers to feel as though they are once again members of a school community. Second, they have developed instructional practices that are more likely to encourage academic engagement. In short, these successful schools provide a sense of family and a set of activities that tend to be more interesting than those encountered in conventional classrooms. Finally, these programs create not only places where students want to be; they also create good places for teachers. They frequently offer their teaching staff the opportunity to be involved in the life of the institution in ways generally absent in most public schools. These broader principles should inform the efforts of both planners and building-level staff as they attempt to design and implement dropout prevention programs that are responsive to local needs.

School Membership

Instead of assuming that the experience of belonging to the school community occurs naturally and is to some degree inevitable, teachers in effective programs for at-risk youth take an active role in reaching out to children who have often experienced various forms of rejection in their previous schools. Teachers do this through developing programs that cultivate social relations premised on care and mutual respect. In doing so, they demonstrate the importance of drawing students into an experience of school membership as the basis for behavioral change. Their programs actively attempt to help students encounter the attachment, involvement, commitment, and belief identified by Hirschi (1969) as instrumental to the experience of social bonding. Students at risk of school failure are frequently those who have lost the sense of personal interconnectedness with people in the school within which care and motivation are sustained. They furthermore often demonstrate minimal levels of involvement in both the curricular and extracurricular activities of the school. Few feel commitment to the norms and values of the school environment, and while most acknowledge the importance of schooling for their own economic well-being, potential dropouts rarely believe that teachers are deeply concerned about their personal welfare. Their likelihood of dropping out is reduced if they are drawn into supportive school communities in which teachers demonstrate commitment to their success both as learners and as people.

In successful dropout prevention programs, teachers not only demonstrate commitment to their students; they also take steps to overcome what can be identified as four impediments to the experience of school membership. These impediments–which include poor adjustment, difficulty, incongruence, and isolation–were first described by Tinto (1987) in his study of college retention; they describe factors that can contribute to the withdrawal of students from secondary school as well. By adjustment, Tinto refers to the problems many students encounter as they attempt to learn and internalize the norms and expectations associated with a specific college environment. Prior to college, adjustment can become a serious problem when secondary students make a transition from one school to another. These transitions—from elementary school to intermediate school or from intermediate school to high school—are often difficult for all students. Students who already are experiencing problems negotiating the demands of schooling become even more in jeopardy of academic failure when they are required to enter a new environment without adequate explanation or support. For Tinto, difficulty refers to the way problems related to success in academics can preclude the experience of membership. Academic failure can cause a student to question his or her own ability to live up to institutional standards presented as a condition for acceptance. The experience of incongruence is related to the degree to which a student's cultural or class background parallels the behaviors, practices, and beliefs encountered within the school. For students from non-middle class and nonwhite backgrounds, the discontinuity between home and school can be so great as to preclude social bonding. Finally, some students experience personal isolation for a variety of reasons. In some cases, isolation may be tied to personality or appearance; in others, to an inability to break into already established social groups. Discrimination against students who are members of economic or cultural groups scorned by more dominant groups can also contribute to isolation.

By providing support and care as well as overcoming a number of impediments to membership, educators in effective dropout prevention programs are able to help at-risk youth become reattached to the school and the people there. The formation of interpersonal ties can contribute to students' willingness to commit themselves to school values and goals and to believe that those who represent the institution—their teachers—have their best interests at heart. For many students, the experience of social bondedness can help them overcome patterns of truancy and misbehavior, a crucial step if they are to graduate from high school.

Educational Engagement

Besides drawing students into an experience of school membership, the most successful programs for at-risk youth also strive to generate genuine academic engagement. As teachers in these schools do not assume that membership occurs naturally for all students, they similarly do not assume that all students wish to be willing participants in their classrooms. In response, they take it upon themselves to make their course offerings appealing and meaningful. It must be noted, however, that it is in this area that programs for youth at risk have demonstrated the least innovation and creativity. There is a tendency among teachers drawn to such schools to believe that a supportive social environment and training in a variety of vocational areas are all that educationally disadvantaged children need. While such programs are accomplishing an important task in helping at-risk students graduate from high school, many frequently fail to help students become committed learners. Their failure to do so is becomingly increasingly problematic in an economic environment in which adequate employment is available only to those who possess some form of post-secondary training (William T. Grant Foundation, 1988). Particularly effective programs for these students are those that combine a supportive social environment with a demanding academic program or vocational program, or both.

Newmann (1989) suggests that engaging students in the act of learning involves addressing five factors. In addition to social support, these factors include students' need for competence and their desire for extrinsic rewards, intrinsic interest, and a sense of ownership over their own activities. The experience of competence, for example, can act as a powerful motivator for continued learning. When students master skills that allow them to affect the world, their own sense of power and efficacy are enhanced. Students also need to know that their efforts will have some future payoff or extrinsic reward. Learning is not easy. It requires effort and perseverance. Unless students under-stand how the labor and denial that are part of any discipline can lead to some future good, teachers will find it difficult to sustain their attention and involvement. The act of learning, itself, must also be intrinsically interesting, at least on occasion. Some activities necessarily require drill and repetition, but in the end practice must lead to performance. In sports, games follow the hours of training; in school, students rarely experience the satisfaction that can come from such culminating activities. Finally, students, like workers in any setting, need to believe that they have some ownership of their activities–some involvement, in other words, in decisions about the nature of the learning environment in which they must live.

Few contemporary educational settings, however, address these factors with any consistency. Teachers' concerns about covering course material in a limited amount of time often preclude the mastery of intellectual skills or disciplines. Most children are graded on what they do not know rather than on what they do know. Often, only a minority of students are able to develop and demonstrate competence in ways that are personally satisfying and validating. For many students, particularly those who do not intend to seek a college education, there is little relationship between what occurs in their classrooms and what they intend to do after graduation. Education for them provides few extrinsic rewards. Because of a narrowly conceived curriculum that focuses primarily on the acquisition of teacher-determined information, students also have little intrinsic interest in formal learning. Their concerns and involvement are seen as less important than their ability to answer questions correctly. Partly as a result of this, students rarely experience a sense of ownership of what they learn. Education is something that is imposed on them, not something they have sought themselves. Finally, most classrooms are structured as competitive environments in which children are fearful of making mistakes. As was suggested in the preceding section, they experience little social support from peers or teachers, and often only the able are willing to take the risks associated with extending their own competence and knowledge. Youth at risk are particularly vulnerable in a school that disregards these fundamental needs and fails to accommodate their special requirements.

The most effective dropout prevention and recovery programs are those that have taken these factors into account. In doing so they come to resemble the learning environments encountered in desirable workplaces. Resnick (1987) argues that in such settings, learning occurs in a social context in which skills and information are acquired in order to complete specific tasks. She contrasts this kind of learning with the individualized acquisition of symbolic and generalized knowledge that takes place in most classrooms. By constructing educational settings in which students are able to work with one another toward the accomplishment of meaningful and socially valued tasks, teachers in dropout prevention programs can help students fulfill the five needs seen by Newmann (1989) as central to the experience of academic engagement.

Teacher Ownership and Collegiality

Working with initially resistant learners, many of whom may have serious personal problems, is not easy. If teachers are expected to support such students over time without "burning out," they need to be sustained by other elements of their worklife. In effective dropout prevention programs this sustenance comes from opportunities to act as educational entrepreneurs, to become involved in the school's governance, and to participate in a staff culture characterized by collegiality rather than isolation.

As should be clear from the earlier discussion of steps in program planning, educators who work in programs for at-risk youth tend to be activists and risk takers. In this sense, they resemble entrepreneurs in the business world. Their continued enthusiasm depends to some extent on their ability to develop and act on their ideas. Few traditional schools, however, are prepared to deal with such people. Teachers typically are expected to fulfill specific tasks within large and complex organizations. Those who propose innovations that challenge the regularities of that organization are generally inhibited by accepted conventions and bureaucratic regulations. Districts interested in genuinely serving at-risk youth need to be willing to give such educators the support and resources they require to experiment. This will almost certainly entail the granting of waivers and the willingness of central office administrators to buffer innovators from people both within and outside of the school who oppose their efforts.

Associated with teachers' freedom to innovate is their ability to govern themselves. In the United States, schools historically have been managed as hierarchical institutions with little room for the participation of teachers in the development of either policies or practices. This situation is not encountered in effective dropout prevention programs. In these schools teachers and administrators collaborate closely in the shaping of the educational experiences they offer to students. This opportunity to create and act on deeply held beliefs and dreams can be a powerful incentive for teacher involvement and commitment. Teachers in these schools rarely exhibit the sense of powerlessness too often encountered in most public school systems. As a new teacher at Sierra Mountain who had previously taught at a large comprehensive high school noted,

> I feel I've had more impact on decision-making in the last 3 weeks than I ever had at [my former school. There] I did what I was told, with a certain amount of my own interpretation, but here I have input. The staff meeting process is remarkable to me. I guess I always figured that's the way it should be, but I . . . never had the kind of freedom to express my opinion, be it good or bad, or the unstated support. I mean, it doesn't matter when we're brainstorming whether your idea is good

or bad. If it's an idea, it can come out and be tossed around and there's no personal loss or gain. . . . It's all goal-oriented to the collective good of the school. (Smith, 1987b, p. 19)

Not only do teachers have the opportunity to govern the school, they also are encouraged to shape their own courses with a degree of flexibility uncommon in most school settings.

A final characteristic of many dropout prevention and recovery programs can also be found in the working relations that exist among staff. Teaching in most schools is a moderately lonely occupation. Adults rarely have time to interact in anything more than a fleeting way with their colleagues. In contrast, teachers in many of the programs involved in our study met regularly with one another about student needs and the direction and development of their schools. They acted as the guardians of educational communities that required their involvement and good will. The collegial interaction and support offered by teachers to one another can act as important sources of validation and encouragement for adults who might not always be certain of their positive impact on difficult students.

Conclusion

Programs effective in reconnecting at-risk students to schooling achieve their success largely by translating three principles into educational practice.

1. They help students feel as though they are valued and cared for members of an educational community.
2. They elicit from students a willingness to participate in the tasks of learning by presenting curriculum and instruction in ways that are extrinsically rewarding and intrinsically valuable.
3. They provide teachers with a work environment in which they are encouraged to innovate, participate in the governance of their school, and interact with one another as supportive colleagues.

Those who wish to create programs for at-risk youth should keep these factors clearly in mind as they establish priorities and attempt to evaluate their own efforts. In the section that follows a number of changes in educational practice and organizational structures that encourage the realization of these principles are discussed.

STRATEGIES FOR ENCOURAGING MEMBERSHIP, ENGAGEMENT, AND TEACHER OWNERSHIP

A number of structural features as well as educational and administrative practices contribute to the experience of membership, engagement, and teacher collegiality. Some of these concrete strategies are described below in an effort to give the reader a clearer sense about how educators in the 14 schools went about translating theoretical principles into concrete innovations. These features and practices challenge many of our common assumptions about the nature of contemporary schooling. They are offered as a stimulus to experimentation and innovation.

Small Size

The majority of the schools involved in our study had student populations ranging from 60 to 150. In this, they resembled smaller educational institutions of the past before the drive in the 1950s to consolidate schools and districts to increase efficiency and offerings. The primary advantage of small size is that it allows for more personal student-teacher and student-student relations than can be achieved normally in most conventional secondary schools. As Barker and Gump (1964) noted more than two decades ago, small schools tend to be more effective in drawing students into the experience of membership. Gregory and Smith (1987) have recently argued that small high schools are more able to engender the experience of community and mutual support they believe to be necessary if students are to become personally committed to their own education. Small size is important not only to students; it can also be a critical factor for teachers, as well. In a small school, teachers are more likely to assume responsibility for the entire institution rather than just their own department or classroom. This kind of accountability, born of an identification with the school as a whole, can be a critical factor in the development of the collegiality that plays such an important role in sustaining teacher commitment and energy.

Given the current nature of secondary education in the United States, the replacement of large high schools by smaller institutions seems improbable. There is no reason, however, that smaller educational units or communities cannot be constructed even within facilities that exist presently. The movement toward the creation of subunits within large schools–such as the School-within-a-School and the Media Academy–is one that promises to reduce some of the anonymity associated with secondary education and yet work within the budgetary constraints faced by most school districts.

Extended Role

Although a smaller student population may provide the necessary precondi-tion for the development of a supportive educational community, small size in itself does not guarantee the experience of school membership. In the most effective of the 14 schools, teachers played an active role in seeing that this occurred by adopting an extended role vis-à-vis their students. Instead of presenting themselves as subject-matter specialists and instructors, they took on the roles of counselor, friend, and confidant. In so doing, they helped to create a qualitatively different school environment, one in which social interaction mirrored the commitment and accountability encountered in healthy families. Many students who are at risk of school failure are in need of the stability that arises from such commitment; access to an environment that provides it can often make the difference between success and failure.

Teachers and administrators at Sierra Mountain High School, for example, go out of their way to help students become members of their school community. The principal or counselor meets personally with each incoming student. As if to emphasize the informality and familylike atmosphere of the school, classrooms are marked by teachers' first rather than last names. More important than these gestures of friendliness, however, is the teachers' attitudes to students. As one experienced teacher said,

> I tend to treat the kids with respect and come straight across with them. I have expectations of what their behavior should be and what their achievement should be in my classes, and I put that out without any conditions to my respect other than respect returned. I think that I put out affection for these kids. I feel real protective of them. They're my kids. I think that helps. Treating the kids with a feeling that they are your kids, the kids sense that. They sense that I care about them and what happens to them. (Smith, 1987b, p. 6)

Students at Sierra Mountain responded positively to the personal attention they were given by school adults. One girl noted in regard to her teachers that ". . . they'll take you aside and they'll help you, whatever it is, whether it's school problems, problems in that class, or family problems. And I've known several teachers that I can go to and talk to them about personal things that I never would have dreamed about talking [over] with any other teachers" (Smith, 1986). Another student said, "Even if I didn't have any friends out of the people that go to school here, I'd still be friends with the teachers" (Smith, 1986). By expanding their own sense of responsibility and enlarging the scope of their interaction with students, teachers at Sierra Mountain and other schools we studied are able to create an environment in which school membership is both desirable and possible for students.

Scheduled Time for Advising and Decision Making

Changes in daily and weekly schedules can also enhance students' experience of school membership as well as contribute to higher levels of teacher collegiality. If teachers hope to assume a more extended role with students, for example, they must be given the time to interact in a more informal and personal manner with the young people in their classes. One way to facilitate this is to include a regular advising period in the daily or weekly schedule. The Wayne Enrichment Center had taken this step by scheduling "family meetings" during which student accomplishments and issues related to school rules, social relations, and credit accumulation are discussed. Similarly, if teachers are expected to work more collaboratively with one another, opportunities for regular staff meetings must also be built into the daily routine. Teachers cannot be expected to add these new responsibilities to already overburdened schedules. Too often, educational reforms are presented to teachers without a realistic appraisal of their consequences in regard to teacher workloads. Programs for students who are educationally at risk must be especially sensitive to what they require of teachers, avoiding unnecessary demands and making choices about which kinds of activities are most critical to the task of improving their pupils' school experience. In many of the 14 programs, frequent staff meetings were included in the regular schedule in an effort to give teachers an opportunity to keep one another informed about students' progress and to allow them the time needed to make fundamental program decisions.

Long-Term Rather than Short-Term Student-Teacher Relations

Higher levels of student membership and engagement also can be fostered by allowing for the development of long-term rather than brief relations between students and teachers. Frequently, students who are at risk of school failure resent the limited personal interaction they have with teachers. Feeling uncared for themselves, they respond in kind. To get back at teachers, they refuse to do their work. In contrast, when such students believe that teachers are genuinely interested in their welfare, they begin to complete their assignments as a sign of respect and concern. This kind of reciprocity is more likely to evolve in a setting in which students and teachers have the opportunity to know one another for extended rather than brief periods of time.

At the School-within-a-School, a 2-year enrollment period provides teachers with the opportunity to develop closer interpersonal relationships with their students. At the Media Academy, students and teachers remain together for up to 3 years as students "major" in courses related to print and electronic media and also assume increasingly greater responsibility for the production of school publications. During this period of time, people have the opportunity to develop the kind of respect and bondedness that can lead to the experience of obligation and care. Teachers in these programs become something more than the dispensers of knowledge and grades. They become people with feelings, people who both need and give support. In this situation, students who have withdrawn from the competitive ethos that exists in most classrooms encounter another reason to commit themselves to the demands of learning.

Clear Demonstration of Link between School Activities and Extrinsic Rewards

Bishop (1987) argues that one of the primary reasons behind the lack of academic engagement on the part of youth who do not anticipate going on to college is the limited relationship between school performance and employment. What is learned in school seems divorced from the requirements of the workplace, and as a result students invest little of themselves in learning activities presented to them by their teachers. In a number of the 14 schools, that relationship was made abundantly clear to students in ways that were both immediate and visceral.

The Media Academy was perhaps most successful in demonstrating the link between academic work and future occupations. One of its central strengths lay in its ability to translate abstract learning into socially valued products. Students enrolled in the Media Academy are helped to develop their writing and thinking skills over a sustained period of time, knowing that their efforts will be turned into publications distributed among their peers, families, and community. In addition to publishing a school newspaper and yearbook, students in the program also publish a Spanish-language community paper and a teen magazine, and produce essays and public service announcements aired by local radio stations. Their schoolwork mirrors the work of media professionals.

In addition, teachers strive to acquaint students with staff in local media establishments who have come from low-income, minority backgrounds similar to their own. These professionals demonstrate to youth who have stopped believing in their ability to construct meaningful careers for themselves that there are ways to realize personal dreams despite economic disadvantage and apparently limited opportunities. The Media Academy also offers students summer internships in Bay Area newspapers and radio and television stations to help them gain firsthand experience of what it is like to be a reporter, a camera operator, or a radio announcer. For students in the Media Academy, learning is intimately linked to the world of work. Even though not all graduates of this program in fact pursue media careers, their exposure to the activities of adults confirms the way formal learning can be translated into desirable jobs.

Development of Intrinsically Rewarding Learning Activities

Programs like the Media Academy also allow students to experience the pleasure that comes from participating in activities that are intrinsically interesting and personally valuable. Students are frequently encouraged to write about issues that concern them and are allowed great flexibility in what is published in both the school and community newspapers. The variety of tasks that accompany any publishing venture also gives students the chance to share and develop more personal interests as well. Students thus not only have a chance to become stronger writers, they can also develop their competence in areas such as photography, layout, advertising, and management.

The New Futures School in Albuquerque has also been especially successful in developing academic coursework immediately relevant to the needs of the pregnant and mothering teens who enroll in this program. Three special parenting classes, for example, deal specifically with diet, exercise, anatomy, growth of the fetus, labor and delivery, child development, and the care of toddlers. These topics are covered in depth with the aim of preparing girls for the demands of labor and parenthood. As one girl noted, "When I went into labor, I knew *everything* that was going to happen to me." A companion agreed, "You learn the name of every part of you and what's happening. You know *so much*" (Lekso, 1987, p. 2).

Issues related to parenthood are drawn into other courses as well. A math teacher, for example, developed a text on math applications in the home that was written to be adaptable to regular math classes and to GED classes and to be used by students alone. In addition, employment-seeking and -training classes are provided at the school in an effort to help prepare young mothers for the financial obligations of parenthood. In these ways, teachers develop learning activities that touch students in personal and meaningful ways, activities that are much more likely to be intrinsically valuable to them than those often encountered in conventional classrooms.

Innovative Grading Practices/Shortened Grading Periods

When the success of all rather than only a proportion of students becomes a fundamental goal, educators begin to question commonly accepted evaluation practices as well as the configuration of the academic year. In some programs for at-risk youth, for example, students are graded on work completed rather than on work assigned. At the Wayne Enrichment Center, credits are awarded on the basis of whether or not students have mastered all of the assignments in an individualized learning packet. Students know that they must complete a minimal number of credits in a given grading period to remain in the program, but they have the opportunity to establish their own pace. Individualized learning materials are also available at Sierra Mountain for students who wish to do extra work. In addition, students are awarded variable credit during each grading period. If they have completed three-fifths of the assigned work and been awarded a *C* for these assignments, they will be given a *C* and three-fifths of the possible credits for this class. This contrasts with the situation they would face in a more conventional classroom, where uncompleted work would be averaged into their final grade–in this case resulting in an *F*, or no credit for the work that they had done. This strategy rewards students for beginning to make a turnaround in their efforts to meet class requirements.

At Sierra Mountain as well as at a number of other schools, teachers have also acknowledged the difficulty many at-risk students have in sustaining interest in a course for a 9- or 18-week grading period. In response, teachers at Sierra Mountain have shortened academic units to 5 weeks; furthermore, they have modified the academic calendar, scheduling a weeklong vacation at the end of each of these units. This has meant that they must begin school in early August and end the third week in June. Although inconvenient in some ways, this schedule has proved to be very helpful in terms of both student motivation and curricular flexibility. With the additional planning time provided by these breaks, teachers are able to adjust courses to the actual rather than anticipated students who populate their classrooms.

Close Monitoring of Student Performance

In part because of their small size and teachers' adoption of an extended role, student performance is much more closely monitored in effective dropout prevention and recovery programs than in conventional schools. Too often, teachers in regular classrooms fail to respond quickly enough to warning signals exhibited by students who may be on the verge of withdrawing their commitment and effort from the tasks of learning. In programs that consciously cultivate student success, teachers attempt to catch small problems before they result in major difficulties. In some programs, this monitoring may be undertaken in an informal manner. At the Wayne Enrichment Center, for example, teachers demonstrate an extraordinary degree of sensitivity to the way in which their students present themselves when they enter their classrooms each morning. If someone appears to be having a difficult time emotionally or academically, teachers attempt to draw students into conversations during which the difficulty might be aired and possibly resolved.

At the School-within-a-School, teachers have developed a much more structured strategy for making sure that students are adopting behavioral patterns associated with school success. After recognizing that many of their students had fallen into habitual patterns of truancy, inattention, or misbehavior, the teachers developed a point system aimed at making students more immediately accountable for their behavior. If students accumulate more than five points in a quarter, they are dropped from the program. If they go through an entire week without receiving any points, they are awarded a positive point. Teachers review on a daily basis any student who has received a point, and they arrange for a conference or a letter home to parents when students accumulate two or four points. Students who fail to turn in all of their assignments during a given week are also required to stay after school for a Friday study hall. In this way, students are given ongoing feedback about their performance and are helped to correct problems before they lead to expulsion from the program. Although on one level this system appears Draconian, students are remarkably appreciative of this form of support. They believe that it indicates that their teachers are genuinely concerned about helping them to graduate, something they had not felt in their interaction with teachers in previous classrooms, who appeared not to care about whether or not they were in school.

Rewards for Improvement

In most classrooms, students are rewarded primarily for achievement rather than for improvement. For at-risk students, such rewards may appear to be beyond their grasp. It is critical, therefore, to acknowledge smaller steps along the way. Schools successful in working with this population often demonstrate a variety of techniques to acknowledge these more incremental stages of growth. The Sierra Mountain High School staff, for example, have been especially creative in rewarding student improvement. During monthly awards assemblies, certificates are given by teachers to the most outstanding and most improved students in each of their classes. Furthermore, the most outstanding and most improved students from the school as a whole are invited to make presentations to the monthly school board meeting and have their pictures featured in the local paper.

In addition to this more formal recognition, the staff also offer field trips, which are made available to students who are participating with responsibility in selected classes or activities. Biology classes, for example, make regular camping trips to the Sierra Nevada Mountains or the Pacific Coast to engage in studies of natural history. Similar opportunities are made available to students who take a leadership role in extracurricular activities. Members of the drama club, for example, are given the chance to travel to the Oregon Shakespearean Festival to observe plays. Participation is predicated on the students' involvement in fund-raising activities and drama productions.

Opportunities To Be Needed

Perhaps one of the most effective strategies for offering at-risk students the experience of success is the creation of opportunities for them to be of service to others. Langberg (1986), a nationally recognized administrator of alternative schools in Colorado, has said that demonstrating to needy students that they themselves are needed can provide just the leverage required to reconnect them to the school and the broader community surrounding it. The experience of marginality is often linked to a belief that one's community values nothing that one might offer to it. If at-risk students are shown that they possess the ability to have a beneficial impact on the lives of those around them, their sense of personal efficacy and self-esteem are likely to be enhanced.

Community service opportunities provide an important vehicle for giving students the chance to experience the responsibilities and rewards that accompany the process of caring for others. Students in a leadership club at the Wayne Enrichment Center, for example, organized a food bank and Christmas party for elementary school children from economically disadvantaged families. Many of the children in fact may have been from circumstances very similar to those of the students who were sponsoring the event; but for the older students, the opportunity to give rather than receive contributed to their view of themselves as competent, able, and responsible people. Peer tutoring programs have been shown to have a similar effect (Cohen, Kulick, & Kulick, 1982).

Program Autonomy

The adoption of these innovative strategies generally involves giving teachers and administrators at the building level the authority to make fundamental decisions about budgetary matters, curriculum, and scheduling. This authority allows practitioners the flexibility they need to respond to the educational needs of specific students. It furthermore allows them the freedom to fine-tune their courses and their program as a whole in ways rarely possible in most comprehensive high schools. Such flexibility can be critical to the development of educational experiences capable of generating student interest and involvement. As indicated earlier, authority over hiring can also be a particularly crucial factor in the long-range viability of a given program. Without the ability to select staff members who must fulfill not only their own classroom responsibilities but broader responsibilities to their colleagues as well, programs for potential dropouts run the risk of jeopardizing the sense of communal vision and interdependence that undergirds the efforts of their teachers. Educators who work in such programs must be given permission to create unique school environments, environments that depend as much on the people who work in them as on the way in which instruction is presented.

Collaborative Rather than Directive Administrative Style

Administrators who assume the role of coordinators and encouragers rather than managers can also facilitate the experience of staff ownership and commitment. Teachers must feel that their observations and experience are taken into account when decisions affecting their worklives are made. Too frequently in many conventional secondary schools, the opportunity to participate in school governance is denied teachers by principals who are unwilling or unable to share their administrative authority more broadly. Such participation, however, can be a critical factor in sustaining the high levels of teacher involvement and enthusiasm needed as antidotes against the difficulties of working with at-risk students.

This does not mean that more hierarchical administrative structures are not workable. The administrative style encountered at the New Futures School, for example, remains more traditional. What does seem to characterize faculty-administrator relations in many programs for at-risk students is the treatment of teachers as full participants in the life of the school, people whose insights and skills are comparable to the insights and skills of program administrators. The flatter organizational structures that have arisen from this recognition are becoming increasingly favored in business and industry because of their positive impact on worker motivation and productivity (Dertouzos, Lester, & Solow, 1989). The more participatory governance structures encountered in many effective programs for at-risk youth demonstrate their suitability for school environments as well.

Summary

Planners concerned about creating programs that are likely to lead to higher levels of student membership, engagement, and teacher collegiality therefore have a number of strategies from which to draw. As they consider the design of a school aimed at improving the educational performance of at-risk youth, serious consideration should be given to the implementation of such innovations. To summarize, positive features encountered in effective dropout prevention programs include the following:

- a small-enough student population to allow individuals to feel that they are members of a supportive and personally meaningful school community
- a teacher culture that emphasizes the adoption of an extended role with students that includes counseling and mentoring as well as classroom instruction
- a daily or weekly schedule that permits teachers and students as well as teachers and teachers to support one another and participate in the governance of the school
- grouping and scheduling practices that allow students to experience long-term rather than short-term relations with teachers
- learning activities that demonstrate to students a clear link between what is taught in school and the skills needed in desirable workplaces
- curriculum and instructional practices that are responsive to student concerns and interests
- grading practices, including the scheduling of academic units, that are more sensitive to the characteristics of students who have not responded well to traditional classrooms
- close monitoring of student behavior and academic performance in an effort to provide assistance rather than administer punishment
- recognition and rewards for incremental signs of improvement
- activities, including community service and peer tutoring, that allow students to know that they are needed
- enough program autonomy from central office directives and policies to permit needed forms of experimentation
- administrative practices that encourage teacher collaboration and account-ability

CONCLUSION

This chapter has focused on the characteristics of effective dropout prevention programs and a set of strategies for planning and implementing them, but it is important to note that the cultivation of school membership, engagement, and teacher collegiality encountered in these programs may be educationally sound not only for at-risk students but for all students. In a fundamental sense, add-on dropout prevention programs stand as an indictment of conventional educational practice, pointing to the way in which regular classrooms have failed to draw all students into the forms of emotional support and intellectual commitment that must undergird successful learning.

Although one might argue that 75 to 85 percent of American students are able to earn a high school diploma despite these inadequacies, it remains the case that a significant proportion of these graduates have not achieved the levels of numeracy and literacy now demanded by many contemporary worksites. While they may have met the minimal standards of attendance and credit accumulation required to graduate, it is likely that these students have not encountered enough of the experience of membership or engagement to lead them to become involved and committed learners. In this sense, they are similar to their peers who are at risk of dropping out.

Instead of thinking of potential dropouts as qualitatively different from other students, it is perhaps more accurate to think of all students on a continuum running between the poles of marginal-disengaged to member-engaged. In most classrooms, particularly at the secondary level, neither the structure of the institution nor the instructional practices of most teachers serve to encourage the experience of membership or engagement. If this experience is achieved at all, it is generally the result of student characteristics and motivation. Those students who for a variety of reasons are motivated to perform well in school receive the school's blessing and to varying degrees are shown that they have been accepted as members of the institution. They find themselves, for example, on the honor roll and in advanced classes. Those who do not demonstrate such motivation are allowed to settle into less institutionally desirable courses and categories; some drop out altogether. Whether or not students buy into the process of learning is seen as the result of student choice rather than teacher effort.

If American schools are to become more successful in enhancing the educational achievement of all students, it is exactly this orientation that must be changed. Educators can no longer leave the experience of membership and engagement up to student choice. They must strive, as do educators in effective dropout prevention programs, to draw their students into this experience. With a shrinking labor supply and more intellectually demanding worksites, we cannot afford to waste any of our human resources. Effective programs for at-risk youth demonstrate ways in which this might be accomplished. Such programs should be seen not as alternatives but as harbingers of the educational practices that should come to characterize all schools.

REFERENCES

Barker, R.G., & Gump, P.A. (1964). *Big school, small school: High school size and student behavior.* Stanford, CA: Stanford University Press.

Bishop, J.H. (1987, October 1). *Why high school students learn so little and what can be done about it.* Paper presented at the hearings conducted by the Subcommittee on Education and Health of the Joint Economic Committee on "Competitiveness and the Quality of the American Workforce," Washington, DC.

Cohen, P., Kulick, P., & Kulick, C. (1982). Educational outcomes of tutoring: A meta-analysis of findings. *American Educational Research Journal, 19,* 237–248.

Dertouzos, M.L., Lester, R.K., & Solow, R.M. (1989). *Made in America: Regaining the productive edge.* Cambridge, MA: MIT Press.

Ekstrom, R., Goertz, M. E., Pollack, J. M., & Rock, D.A. (1986). Who drops out of high school and why? *Teachers College Record, 87,* 356-373.

Gregory, T., & Smith, G. (1987). *High schools as communities: The small school reconsidered.* Bloomington, IN: Phi Delta Kappa.

Hirschi, T. (1969). *Causes of delinquency.* Berkeley, CA: University of California Press.

Langberg, A. (1986, May 30). Address at the National Foundation for the Improvement of Education, Washington, DC.

Lesko, N. (1987). New futures school. In *Dropout prevention and recovery: Fourteen case studies.* Madison, WI: National Center on Effective Secondary Schools.

Newmann, F.M. (1989, February). Student engagement and high school reform, *Educational Leadership, 46,* 34–36.

Resnick, L.B. (1987, December). Learning in school and out, *Educational Researcher,* 13–20.

Sarason, S.B. (1972). *The creation of settings and the future societies.* San Francisco: Jossey-Bass.

Smith, G.A. (1986). Student interviews, field notes. Sierra Mountain High School, Grass Valley, CA.

Smith, G.A. (1987a). School-within-a-school at Madison Memorial High School. In *Dropout prevention and recovery: Fourteen case studies.* Madison, WI: National Center on Effective Secondary Schools.

Smith, G.A. (1987b). Sierra Mountain High School. In *Dropout prevention and recovery: Fourteen case studies.* Madison, WI: National Center on Effective Secondary Schools.

Tinto, V. (1987). *Leaving college: Rethinking the causes and cures of student attrition.* Chicago: University of Chicago Press.

Wehlage, G. (1987). Media academy. In *Dropout prevention and recovery: Fourteen case studies.* Madison, WI: National Center on Effective Secondary Schools.

Wehlage, G., & Rutter, R. (1986). Dropping out: How much do schools contribute to the problem? *Teachers College Record, 87,* 374–392.

Wehlage, G., Rutter, R., Smith, G.A., Lesko, N., & Fernandez, R.R. (1989). *Reducing the risk: Schools as communities of support.* Philadelphia: Falmer Press.

William T. Grant Foundation. (1988). Commission on Work, Family, and Citizenship. *The forgotten half: Non-college youth in America: An interim report on the school-to-work transition.* Washington, DC: Author.

chapter 3

Curriculum Design and Implementation: A Futures Perspective

Donna Kearns

INTRODUCTION TO CURRICULUM DESIGN

Finch and Crunkilton (1989) state, "Any curriculum that hopes to be relevant tomorrow must be responsive to tomorrow's as well as today's needs" (p. 20). The educational needs of today's students at risk must be assessed and modifications must be made in order to reduce the number of dropouts and other casualties of education. The curriculum for at-risk students may require modifications to reflect the needs students will face tomorrow. Some of the modifications that must take place in order to reduce the number of at-risk students include changing the curriculum. Before examining the changes needed, it is important to reflect on curriculum designs of the past.

Curriculum design has changed greatly over the years. The changes reflect the beliefs of various time periods, and for more than 4,000 years included "apprenticeships" and other hands-on experiences for students. However, in the 1800s and early 1900s many school curricula changed and were made up solely of reading, writing, and arithmetic. In 1893, the first Committee of Ten reported on courses, electives, college preparatory subjects, and practical subjects—all issues concerning curriculum. About this same time, John Dewey began his studies of curriculum in his laboratory school. A number of these laboratory schools appeared during the early 1900s, enticing city schools to launch systemwide curriculum improvement projects. Laboratory schools began to spring up in university settings, and "curriculum" became a field of study in many colleges during the 1930s. The curriculum of these laboratory schools included not only courses, but general goals that were to be met in those courses. The curriculum was designed to meet the needs of all students and prepare them for today and tomorrow. However, laboratory schools are scarce today. They have not proven effective for all students.

The currently popular developmental curriculum began in the late 1940s and early 1950s. It was based on the belief that children generally develop at about the same rate. Therefore, they will learn the same subject areas at about the same time. For many students this may be true; but for some, this simply does not occur. Problems associated with the use of a developmental curriculum to educate students include the following: (1) not all students develop at the same rate; (2) developmental stages represent averages, which lead teachers to focus instruction on what a student cannot do; (3) teachers are often frustrated because of lack of student progress; (4) when few, if any, gains are made, students are simply seen as "not ready" to engage in age-appropriate activities and are required to repeat grades or subjects; and (5) deficits widen with age.

Another method that has been used in educational settings is the functional life skills approach, which helps both the student and the environment adapt. This method of education builds on skills students possess, focuses on real-life skills, uses natural environments, is age-appropriate, and helps students train for present and future needs. Both the curriculum and the instruction are based on the student as opposed to an idealistic content.

Preparation for tomorrow is what education is all about; yet some educators continue to examine ways to include more courses in the curriculum, more days in the school year, and more time spent per day in each class. People using these methods of improving education may be ignoring the fact that some students do not learn by adding on more information or lengthening the time spent in the classroom. Curriculum is not simply the course offerings; it must prepare at-risk students for the future. This preparation is likely to be hindered by lengthening the time required to complete the coursework necessary to receive a diploma and to result only in an increased dropout rate, as has been recorded over the past several years. It is important to remember that "the central focus of the curriculum is the student" (Finch & Crunkilton, 1989, p. 9).

Kauffman and Pullen (1989) report that "we can provide appropriate education for mildly handicapped and at-risk students only if we recognize that their needs are different from most students and that they therefore require special programs" (p. 13). Today a great deal of change in the needs of students is apparent. The world has changed drastically and so too have the needs of students in that world. Curriculum has continued to increase, but only in relation to the areas that have been taught for decades, as opposed to the areas needed for functioning in today's adult roles. The developmental approach in education may not allow for the diversity required to educate students in today's world. Methods used to instruct today's students must activate and support learning of the individual student (Gagne, Briggs, & Wager, 1988). A more functional/relevant curriculum needs to be designed to allow students to achieve as individuals.

TRADITIONAL APPROACHES TO CURRICULUM DESIGN FOR AT-RISK YOUTH

Programs targeted toward assisting the student at risk traditionally include goals such as (1) improving daily school attendance, (2) parental participation, (3) tutorial assistance, (4) babysitting services for student parents, (5) remedial academic curriculum, and (6) vocational options. Programs targeted at reducing the dropout rate traditionally have been flavored with one or more of these goals. Although some of the above goals have contributed to the success rate of students involved in programs for at-risk youth, the number of students dropping out of school (or at risk of dropping out) has continued to increase. It is important to examine some of the programs that have attempted to meet the above-mentioned goals.

In an effort to increase daily attendance, the School-within-a-School in Madison, Wisconsin, awards students for daily attendance. Students receive positive points for attending daily. Points are lost for each absence. Teachers provide ongoing feedback to both students and parents regarding their attendance and work completed. These efforts have proved effective in keeping some students in school. However, experience tells us there will always be the student who is required by his or her parents to stay home and take care of the younger children, drive a parent to the doctor, or care for other family matters. These students need more than just points and parent contact to keep them in school and learning.

Parental participation is one goal found in a number of effective programs across the country. For example, the Comprehensive Dropout Prevention Plan in Jacksonville, Florida, includes a program to involve parents and interested citizens. Parents receive frequent reports regarding student attendance. Parent participation is extremely important if we accept the idea that education means teaching students to learn how to learn. When children learn how to learn, they should be able to apply skills in a number of situations—including the home. Parental involvement does not mean that the parents have to come to the school or that the school calls the parents to give reports. It means that parents are involved in educating the child whenever and wherever possible.

Tutorial assistance has aided a number of students in the educational process and has likely provided a major reason for their completion of high school. In some dropout prevention programs, teachers are made available to tutor students. In other programs, students are providing peer tutoring. A high school in Oregon has had positive results from providing an opportunity for students to meet together daily, develop goals, and earn credits for successful efforts (Conrath, 1984). This type of tutorial assistance can help students succeed in the goal of completing high school.

In-school babysitting services for students identified as being at risk and who are also teenage parents have been utilized in an attempt to remediate the problem a teenager faces when she desires to return to school after the birth of a child. Programs that include child care have likely contributed to the return and possible completion of high school for some of these young parents. However, simply providing child care is not enough. Educational offerings for these students must meet their needs if they are to become successful members of society tomorrow as well as successful parents today.

Academic deficits have been addressed by offering remedial programs for students at risk. Remedial reading and remedial mathematics at the secondary level tend to focus on teaching basic academics that were taught in previous years. Often these programs enroll small groups of students who have failed the coursework in the past. Often the methods of teaching vary only slightly from those used in previous years. Although the books may be different, the students might not differ! These students need more than remedial academics. They need relevant academics.

Vocational education (practical education for many students) has provided an opportunity for learning to occur along with the chance to perform as an adult in a job situation. This option has contributed greatly to allowing many students to continue their education while learning a skill for the future. The future for students at risk is often very uncertain. Providing a method of examining the future and preparing for it allows each student to see clearly his or her importance in that planning process. Vocational education programs currently are hosting large numbers of handicapped or disadvantaged students, or both. Many of these students are considered at risk and benefit greatly from the vocational (practical) option.

All of the above program goals for youth at risk have provided attempts to educate students in new ways. However, all of the programs based on these goals have not resulted in a substantial reduction in the dropout rate. This reduction will be more likely to take place if the curriculum is changed to meet students' needs. It is especially important for districts to consider the relevance of their programs. Although programs for at-risk youth are springing up in most school districts across the country, few of those programs are actually assessing the relevance of all their educational programs. Offering tutoring, attendance incentives, vocational options, babysitting services, and so forth will do little to really educate today's students for tomorrow. Those students must not only stay in school through these incentives; they must learn through a curriculum that includes relevant material that will prepare them for the future.

BALANCING INSTRUCTIONAL CONTENT WITH SERVICES

It is important to integrate appropriate curriculum approaches with necessary educational services in order for learning to take place. To do this successfully, educators need to determine (1) what service options exist within the community and (2) how those options might be used in the instructional content.

Service delivery options existing for students include the regular classroom setting, a special classroom, an after-school program, an evening program, a special school setting, and a weekend program or a vocational program that includes academic content for credit. Use of this range of service delivery options is but one example of the flexibility necessary in providing services for students who are at risk now as well as in the future.

When considering these options, it is important to determine what the content might be in each of the settings. It is equally important to determine how the content can be made relevant in order to increase the generalization of skills taught and those required by society. Today's concerns in education relate to students' grades on tests, amount of homework completed, and participation in class discussions. For today's student who is at risk, this approach is unmotivating and often appears to be controlling. Being controlled by teachers is often one of the factors that lead to resentment toward education by students at risk. Educators must attempt to determine the appropriate service delivery options within the community as well as the content required by students in that setting. Traditional educational approaches often limit the options as well as the content, which may create student resentment.

LIMITATIONS OF TRADITIONAL APPROACHES TO GOAL SELECTION

If we recognize that students who are at risk require a different approach to education, then we must begin to explore the limitations that exist in the current developmental curriculum and make necessary modifications. Often students at risk are not making developmental progress and may be unable to reach a functional level given the skills being taught. Remedial programs accommodating students who are reading or performing math at a lower grade level often do little to prepare students for the future. These programs too often are still accused by dropouts of being boring and not challenging. Even students who are not reading at their developmental level need challenges.

Developmental objectives and activities may not be readily adaptable to the interests and needs of a young adult. Students leaving school before graduating often state they want to "get on with their life." The interests of some students today are quite different from those John Dewey studied nearly 70 years ago in his laboratory school. These students come from a variety of home environments and have experienced much more than the youths of the 1920s and 1930s. Simply telling the student that a certain subject must be taken and passed in order to graduate is not as acceptable as it might have been years ago. Their exposure to life's joys and tragedies on a daily basis reinforces the need to "get on with life." In those cases, an algebra requirement for graduation is not going to stand in their way unless a logical explanation of its use in life is also provided.

Often the activities utilized in a developmental curriculum are not functional or age-appropriate. When students cannot see the relationship between the "real world" and the "school world," the real world wins their attention. Curriculum offered in schools must relate to the needs of the students in their world and must be appropriate for their age or peer group. It is inappropriate to insist that a student continue to spell third-grade spelling words because that is the student's spelling level. If spelling is to be improved, it must be done by providing strategies to learn spelling words needed by students of the same age, not the same spelling level.

When the objectives being taught throughout the curriculum are not practiced in daily life with sufficient frequency to result in maintenance, they may no longer be appropriate for the curriculum. Schools continue to insist on the attainment of skills that are no longer required except in the educational setting. Education must make the connection with the community to better enable students to maintain skills.

Finally, developmentally based objectives often require excessive drill and practice in order for a student to learn the skills required. Drill and practice are two of the reasons students often complain of school as "boring." If drill and practice are required, educators must be creative in their attempts, allowing for individual differences as well as guiding the learning by matching individual learning styles and interests.

AN ALTERNATIVE APPROACH THAT FOCUSES ON THE
FUTURE

Preparing people for the future is the purpose of education. Curriculum that prepares students for the future must be based on knowledge of how individual learners learn. It is important for education to assist in the development of abilities and not simply the skills an instructor or author may care to dispense. Curriculum, then, must be developed with the idea of helping the student acquire skills, thus allowing the student to learn how to learn. This type of alternative curriculum will allow students who are at risk to prepare for the future.

Curriculum that prepares students for the future is student-centered. This student-centered curriculum is established after determining the needs of students. Not all students are the same–in development, economics or interests. A preestablished curriculum may impose inappropriate instructional content on some students. We must keep in mind that some dropouts and other at-risk students are functioning very highly, but they have reported that they are bored or understimulated. Determining students' needs will better serve the student at both ends of the spectrum. Any curriculum developed must allow for the acquisition of skills that will enable a student to learn on his or her own—a necessity for the future.

Curriculum that allows students to learn how to learn considers a number of components. Those components include assessing the learner and the instructional context, using the community as a curriculum resource, integrating community demands with the traditional curriculum, pretesting the at-risk youth, providing appropriate instruction, teaching strategies for learning, post-testing the at-risk youth, and setting new goals.

Assessing the Learner and the Instructional Context

The first component, assessing the learner and the instructional context, is extremely important. It is essential to assess the learner developmentally as well as to determine areas of interest. It is also necessary to assess speed, accuracy, and strategies used for learning. Standardized achievement tests may not reflect the true abilities of a student who has few, if any, strategies for learning. A more appropriate assessment includes observations of student experiences in a number of settings. A portion of this assessment may be conducted by the parent to determine whether the child is using (generalizing) specified skills in the home. Parental involvement in the assessment as well as the instructional process might also increase the role that parents play in the child's future plans. Assessing a child's interest to plan educational experiences may increase the amount of motivation the student demonstrates in that experience. Often educators feel that they have taught a concept in every way possible, but forgot to utilize the student's interest and abilities within that instructional context to teach a concept.

When assessing students, it is important to determine speed and accuracy in acquiring new skills. Many students who are at risk have few, if any, strategies for acquiring new information, thus reducing the speed and accuracy with which skills might be learned. To determine a student's speed and accuracy, a sample task might be assigned to the student to complete in a given period of time. It is important first to determine the average rate of speed it takes students of the same age to complete the task. It is then possible to determine the speed in acquiring new skills of the student being assessed, as compared with his or her peers. At the same time, the student can verbalize the steps used to plan for completing the task. These steps can be recorded by the instructor and checked to determine whether the student followed the plan. This information may assist in determining accuracy and efficiency in tackling new skills. Effective teaching strategies are reported to be especially relevant for at-risk children who are often at a disadvantage in developing basic skills as well as self-esteem (Askamit, 1990). An alternative curriculum would include the assessment and teaching of strategies to improve speed and accuracy for acquiring new skills.

If students are not using strategies to acquire new skills or are using the same strategies for all skills attempted, new strategies need to be taught. Along with strategy training, students need to acquire the ability to select the appropriate strategy for completing a task. For some students, this may mean conceptualizing the parts to make the whole. For others, it may mean identifying the project and determining how to find the parts based on knowledge of the whole. Students must be taught to attack a problem from a number of angles and must have this demonstrated to them. Mere exposure to information may create the boredom and lack of motivation students often report. Boredom and a lack of motivation may, in turn, result in lowered scores and increased dropout rates.

The personal interests and expectations of a student must be taken into account in order to plan instruction. These interests and expectations must therefore be assessed. It is well known that students learn to read by using a variety of methods, including whole language, phonics, language experience, and so on. Not only reading is learned through a variety of methods, but so are other subjects. The first (and often the best) way to determine a student's interest is to ask the student. It is also helpful to ask parents, examine school records, and administer an interest inventory. Frequently students are caught reading auto mechanics or fashion magazines in classrooms instead of their assigned reading. This should be a clue that assigned reading needs to be of interest to the student, keeping in mind that reading is the purpose. When a student is allowed to read something of interest often enough, some reading skills may be acquired. These reading skills may later enable the student to read less interesting yet more complex material or to find other reading more interesting.

Educators planning the instruction of students at risk must use student ideas in order to develop effective instructional units. Student input into the sequence and content of instruction should be considered in order to motivate students who are lost in the educational maze. Student ideas may be used to generate a wider variety of activities per class period. This variety may help stimulate student involvement, hopefully to result in not only increased attention but also retention. Use of familiar, concrete objectives as teaching tools and hands-on learning techniques must be employed with students who may have lost interest in education years ago. Educators must also learn how the topics being taught relate to everyday environments and occupational opportunities.

In order for students to determine the quality of their work, it is important for the teacher to establish levels of expectations as well as demonstrate quality work. The teacher must clearly define the competency level at which the student is expected to perform; this should help the student determine when the objectives for a particular lesson have been met. Simply stating the objective of the lesson is not enough. If a student is to write a report, a sample completed report may need to be made available to each student along with labels detailing the components that make this a complete report. The students will then have his or her own method of checking the work for quality. Students must be taught to reward themselves intrinsically in order to prepare for the future. These rewards come naturally only after repeated direction and successful experiences.

The instructional resources on hand must be scrutinized closely. Today's classrooms are often limited in space, books, and supplies. When this occurs, the teacher is expected to be creative. A careful examination of the activities in the community can help the teacher choose functional context and materials to add relevance to the curriculum content. A great deal of education takes place outside the four walls of the school room, and making use of other settings and resources enables students to see how the information being taught applies to the real world. Educators must assess students' knowledge of these resources as well as their need to use the resources in the future.

Another component to be assessed is the student's future opportunities to practice and benefit from the skills acquired. If a student will use the skills being taught in the school only minimally as an adult, those skills may need to be deleted in the secondary education of students at risk. For example, as an adult the need to know how to spell *spleen* may not exist. The more important concept is to know what the spleen does. In fact, very few adults know the function of the spleen, but students in high schools are required to acquire that skill for a test in most biology classrooms. As adults, if we do not know what the spleen does, we can look it up in a book or we can ask someone. As educators we do not know all the skills that might be required in the future, but we must assess as best we can the obvious skills needed for the future. We often hear of the need for today's youth to become computer literate. Many students who are at risk have little if any difficulty using today's computers. Technology has not passed them by; education has.

The final components to be assessed are the social and interpersonal competencies of students at risk. In the rapidly changing world in which we live, the need to interact socially with others and to care for others in our world becomes more and more important. Deci (1989) states, "Educators need to become concerned with individuals' adjustment and personal growth—i.e., with affective outcomes—as well as with academic achievement." Educators need to assess the level of social and interpersonal competence of students in order to determine what affective skills need to be taught. Assessment may involve a child's ability to solve problems (personal as well as social), to display respect for various cultures and populations, and to understand and demonstrate community concern. Educators must take responsibility to relate education to today's world with the hope of preparing students to be well-equipped adults in the future.

Using the Community as a Curriculum Resource

In order to prepare for the future, education must take place within the community. One of the greatest resources for educating students is the community. Within our communities lies a world that is ever-changing, one that addresses the needs and concerns of some of its individuals on a daily basis. Students participate in that world and need to learn better methods of interaction in order to succeed there. As educators it is important that we identify the skills necessary for success in a community and the methods of integrating those skills into the curriculum.

The first step in using the community as a curriculum resource is to identify future settings in which the student is expected to participate. Educators must examine the events of today's world and determine how they might affect a student's future. When the curriculum is student-centered, it focuses on the needs of the students both today and in the future. It would be ludicrous to assume that educators could predict the future of each student. It also would be ludicrous to assume that each would have the same future. We can, however, survey the community and determine some of the growth that is occurring and how it is affecting today's society to gauge how it might affect us in the future. This type of survey activity might be conducted with students. Students' written reports of the research conducted would prove much more beneficial than writing a research paper on an assigned topic or historical event. Curriculum should be developed based in part on these types of data.

If students are expected to pay bills, live alone, acquire employment, negotiate traffic, and so forth, we need to utilize these community skills in our curriculum. It is important to interview, observe, and collect reference materials from individuals in these settings to determine what will be necessary in the future. Students may be given an assignment to find a place to live and budget for that experience given a predetermined income. Difficulty in living within that planned budget would allow the student to ascertain (through problem solving and other strategies) what would need to be adjusted. Students might also be expected to discuss and demonstrate their responsibility on community streets. Placing students in a decision-making role allows them to see the outcome of their efforts. It may be beneficial to place students on community committees that make decisions regarding the placement of traffic lights, licensing of bicycles, or various other community problems. Students would not only learn to make decisions on a team with adults, but gain self-confidence and a greater understanding of the necessity for these community rules. Why can't we have a class in our schools called Utilizing Community Agencies in which students are involved in community agencies for a semester or a year? This type of interaction may be more beneficial to some students at risk than English composition and grammar. Such community interaction might even complement a composition and grammar course. It might also result in a student who reads more about various aspects of the community and has the ability to write reports read by community leaders.

Conducting an assessment of the student's ability to perform in community settings may prove very beneficial in planning a curriculum. Conducting a job analysis as a portion of that assessment may benefit the student as well as community personnel. Often those in the community do not know what goes on at the local school, other than an upcoming sports event or musical. Frequently the school is not involved in community activities. To prepare students for jobs in the future, it is important to conduct job analyses of jobs in that community. Jobs are analyzed according to turnover rate, skills required, salary and benefits, and the like. This type of information enables the teacher to prepare tasks that will allow the student to acquire skills needed for a chosen occupation. As teachers, we often tell students that they must constantly work hard on the job, and that they only get two 15-minute breaks per day. Yet, students sometimes see construction workers standing around on the job site, secretaries filing their nails, and nurses smoking cigarettes! They hear their parents talking about what they "got away with," and the students themselves often hold jobs in which they "get away with" much more than we admit. The skills that are required on the job, however, vary from situation to situation. As teachers we must know those skills and relate them to the educational setting so that our students can be better prepared to compete in the work world. A job analysis can provide important information for teachers who need to relate what they are teaching to job opportunities. Too often we forget the truth in Kathleen Turner's lines in the movie *Peggy Sue Got Married*: "I happen to know I will never need algebra!" If the skills are truly needed for the future, educators should be equipped with answers as to how and when those skills will be used.

The job analysis shown in Exhibit 3-1 is an example of the type of information gathered by teachers who observe and interview employers in order to apply the curriculum to real job situations. By examining the job skills needed for a specific job, the curriculum can be adapted to be more functional in the areas of language arts, reading, writing, social studies, science, math, vocational education, and physical requirements.

Teaching students strategies as well as the content necessary for various job situations is extremely important. The teaching of strategies may be a major element missing in the educational link. Arizona State University's program for learning-disabled college students stresses the development of independence and responsibility, self-advocacy, and realistic self-knowledge. These skills have been associated with college success for learning-disabled students (Barbaro, 1982; Cordoni, 1982). These skills also are necessary for success for many students identified as being at risk and need to be taught in public schools.

Exhibit 3-1 Job Analysis Form

Business Name: _____

Address: _____

Phone: _____ Number Employed: _____

Positions: _____   _____

_____   _____

_____   _____

1. **QUALIFICATIONS**

   Age: Minimum _____   Maximum _____

   General Education: Elementary _____   High School _____
   Courses

   College _____   Courses _____

   Specific Education Skills

   Language: _____
   _____

   Reading: _____
   _____

   Writing: _____
   _____

   Social Studies: _____
   _____

   Science: _____
   _____

   Math: _____
   _____

   Vocational Education: _____
   _____

   Offers

   _____ Apprenticeship _____ Inplant Training _____ On-the-Job Training
   Experience Required? ___ Yes ___ No
   Licenses, certificates required, etc. _____

Exhibit 3-1 continued

Physical Requirements

Hearing (perceiving nature of sounds by ear)

Exceptional ____   Average ____   Not important to the job ____

Comment _____

Talking (expressing or exchanging ideas by means of spoken word)

Exceptional ____   Average ____   Not important to the job ____

Comment _____

Seeing (perceiving nature of objects by the eye: acuity far; acuity near; depth perception)

Exceptional ____   Average ____   Not important to the job ____

Strength

____ *Sedentary work* (lifting 10 lb maximum)

____ *Medium work* (lifting 50 lb maximum with frequent lifting and/or carrying objects up to 50 lb)

____ *Heavy work* (lifting 100 lb maximum with frequent lifting and/or carrying objects up to 50 lb)

____ *Very heavy work* (lifting objects in excess of 100 lb with frequent lifting and/or carrying of objects weighing up to 50 lb)

____ Climbing and/or balancing   ____ Stooping, kneeling, crouching, and/or crawling

____ Reaching, handling

Manual Skills Required

____ Manual dexterity   ____ Finger dexterity

Specific abilities/skills required (e.g., paying attention to detail, reading blueprints, size and/or color discrimination, eye-hand coordination, etc.): _____

2. **WORKING CONDITIONS**

Wages: Beginning pay _____   Pay period _____   Overtime _____

Raise potential _____

Hours: Amount: _____   Work schedule: _____

Job stability: Temporary ____   Permanent ____   Seasonal ____

Benefits: Vacation _____

Illness ____   Medical Ins. ____   Pension ____   Workers' Comp. ____

Other _____

Working environment:

Inside/out ____   Noise level ____   Wet and/or humid ____   Temperature ____

Fumes/odors ____

Amount of supervision: _____

Position of supervisor: _____

Type of supervision: _____

Employee interaction: Works alone ____   With a group ____

Promotion possibilities:

From_____   to   _____

3. **JOB TASKS:** _____

_____

Source: Adapted from *A Guide to Job Analysis* (pp. 381–387) by the U.S. Department of Labor, 1982, Stout, WI: Materials Development Center.

In order to assess skills for living independently in a community, it may be necessary to construct a hierarchy of enabling skills in a task sequence. These skills are identified by walking through community job sites, businesses, utility and governmental offices, real estate agencies, and so forth. The skills are identified and sequenced according to the steps needed to function successfully in each. For example, the tasks are sequenced for paying the telephone bill (both in person and by mail). It is necessary to gather the required materials such as the bill itself, the checkbook or cash, pencil or pen, and sometimes a budget book. The simple organizational skills that are required for paying a bill may not have been acquired by some students who are in the at-risk population. They must first be taught organizational skills through demonstration and practice. Learning the task of paying the telephone bill may prove easier when the bill actually belongs to the student. It is reported that when the material is directly relevant to a student's real-life experience, motivation is enhanced, and there is greater potential for success (Posthill & Roffman, 1990).

As educators, we need to assess a student's ability to function in a number of community settings such as those listed in Exhibit 3-2.

A skills checklist can be constructed for each skill to be taught. By listing the skills as well as the tasks included in each, the instructor can better determine areas needing remediation in order to assess levels of accomplishment. Later, the student also can use the checklist for self-monitoring, thus learning how to learn. A skills checklist can be designed for use by individual learners, groups, or instructors. It may be a simple checklist of skills such as paying utilities, paying taxes, maintaining a checkbook, using public transportation, applying for a job, seeking medical care, and so forth; or it may be a checklist of larger clusters. These clusters might include such categories as language skills, interpersonal/social skills, independent living skills, organizational skills, math skills, and so forth. The checklist should include columns to indicate the level of performance such as (1) performs independently, (2) performs with assistance, or (3) does not perform (Schloss & Sedlak, 1986).

A skills checklist might also allow space for strategies used when the student attempts specific skills. If a student has no idea how to tackle a problem (thus no strategies), it will be necessary to examine some strategies that might work in that particular situation. We can determine not only whether the student does or does not have the skill, but what strategies are necessary to enable the student to acquire and maintain the skill. Exhibit 3-3 offers an example of a skills checklist.

Integrating Community Demands with Traditional Curriculum

Existing in today's community is no easy task, but cooperating in today's community requires even greater skills. Those skills must be taught by educators in the public school system to students who may not have witnessed the skills in their own homes or neighborhoods. Schoolteachers must consider the skills

Exhibit 3-2 Sample Community Settings and Skills

Setting	*Skills*
Hospital:	Following directions
	Remembering information given
	Identifying emergency room, cafeteria, laboratory, X-ray, etc.
	Checking bills for accuracy
	Contacting the appropriate person regarding changes in bill
	Using appropriate communication techniques to discuss problems
	Paying bills
	Calling for information about parents, appropriate clients, etc.
	Parking in appropriate lots
	Identifying listed visiting hours
Bus Station:	Identifying information desk
	Reading bus schedule
	Determining bus to take in a given location
	Transferring busses
	Paying fares
	Using appropriate social skill on the bus
	Storing packages
	Determining when to leave home to catch a bus for a given schedule
Courthouse:	Paying taxes
	Paying child support
	Visiting with juvenile officer
	Arriving on time
	Checking court docket
	Using appropriate social skills
	Determining appropriate dress for task
Mall:	Using any type of banking facility
	Demonstrating appropriate behavior
	Ordering food
	Cleaning up after eating
	Demonstrating wise shopping
	Identifying job possibilities and duties
	Using coupons
	Planning and designing display
	Comparing and contrasting salespersons' tactics at various stores

Source: © Donna Kearns, 1989.

Exhibit 3-3 Sample Skills Checklist

	Performs Independently	Performs with Assistance	Does Not Perform
Language Skills			
1. Asks for help	___	___	___
2. Describes problem	___	___	___
3. Communicates with strangers appropriately	___	___	___
4. Questions information	___	___	___
Independent Living Skills			
1. Budgets for household expenses	___	___	___
2. Selects a house on budget and needs	___	___	___
3. Uses public transportation	___	___	___
Math Skills			
1. Pays taxes annually	___	___	___
2. Analyzes and adjusts budget as needed	___	___	___
3. Determines percentage of his or her taxes that goes to police, library, streets, etc.	___	___	___
Science Skills			
1. Can tell from where water for bathing and drinking comes within the city	___	___	___
2. Can find the water and sewage pipes in his or her yard	___	___	___

Source: From *Instructional Methods for Students with Learning and Behavioral Problems* (pp. 340–341), by P.J. Schloss and R.A. Sedlak, 1986, Newton: MA: Allyn and Bacon.

necessary in their community and integrate them into the curriculum. Today's educators cannot get away with merely teaching the content of a selected textbook and believe that information will prepare students for the future. Textbook content (if utilized) must be mixed and molded with real-life experiences. Traditional curriculum areas, including basic academics, vocational readiness and training, study skills, social skills, independent living, and leisure skills, must all be a part of the curriculum as seen through the eyes of a future community member.

Exhibit 3-4 aligns some sample community demands with traditional curriculum areas.

Exhibit 3-4 Community Demands Integrated into Traditional Curriculum

	Traditional Curriculum				
Community Demands	**Health**	**English**	**Math**	**Science**	**Social Studies**
Request utilities turned on		X	X		
Pay utilities		X	X		
Maintain property	X	X	X	X	X
Purchase goods		X	X		X
Maintain health	X	X	X	X	X
Seek assistance	X	X	X	X	X
Obtain employment	X	X	X		X
Communicate with others	X	X	X		X
Select home (rental, etc.)	X	X	X	X	X
Obey traffic rules	X	X	X		X
Raise children	X	X	X	X	X

Source: © Donna Kearns, 1989.

For example, when basic academic skills are taught, the curriculum might include reading, writing, and arithmetic. To integrate community demands within that curriculum, the teacher might use the examples given in Exhibit 3-1 or develop examples more suitable for the students in the community.

Pretesting the At-Risk Youth

The identification of community resources and learner characteristics is extremely important in meeting the needs of youth who are at risk. Once a skill checklist is developed, student pretesting needs to take place. Students will need to perform tasks in a number of settings, including those most natural environments for skill acquisition—the community, the home and so forth. If those settings are in no way accessible, a simulated setting must be arranged in which the student can be assessed for these basic skills. For example, if a student is learning to apply for a job, it is not good enough to bring applications into the classroom for the student to learn to complete. It is more important that the student identify sites within the community that might be hiring, go to those sites, appropriately request an application, complete the form, and go for an interview. If the student is expected to perform responsibly as an adult tax-paying citizen, it is not enough simply to complete tax forms with assistance at school. It is more important that the student learn where in the community to go to get the forms as well as assistance in completing them. For students who need to seek medical care, it is important to enable them to identify appropriate sources of medical care in a number of settings. The same holds true for legal assistance, and so forth. Assessment of the at-risk youth must be ecological.

When students are not able to learn skills required to cooperate in today's society, it is important to identify methods or materials that could enhance their ability to be successful. Some methods might include the use of counseling services, public transportation services, and financial consulting services, to name a few. Adults who have difficulty managing their daily affairs often need the assistance of some of these agencies.

The cost of acquiring skills through a more flexible method needs to be assessed for each student as well. If it is more cost effective to teach some students a skill in the classroom, then it should be considered. If, however, those students cannot generalize to other settings the information presented, it is not cost effective to continue to attempt to teach a task that will not be utilized in the natural environment. If we can structure a situation so that the material is used in some way that has meaning for the learner, then there is a real possibility for improving a student's conceptual learning (Deci, 1989) and maintaining cost effectiveness.

By using the skills checklist for a portion of what is observed in the pretest, it is possible to identify specific curriculum objectives based on deficient skills. Identifying priorities in those deficient skills allows more important skills to be taught, depending on the student's age, interests, community needs, family support, and so forth. These skill deficiencies can then be grouped under traditional curriculum designations. These groupings allow educators to teach the same subjects while becoming much more flexible and creative in the content offered.

Providing Appropriate Instruction

Providing instruction to students who are at risk must be done in a fashion different from the instruction provided other students. At-risk students have experienced failure and have learned few, if any, strategies for solving problems to achieve success. Because their experiences are different, the needs and methods for successful acquisition of new information may also differ. Instruction provided students at risk must (1) be functional, (2) utilize age-appropriate materials and activities, (3) include purposeful drill and practice, (4) develop an executive function, (5) redirect immediately following an error, and (6) integrate skills acquired under traditional curriculum designations. The following paragraphs explain each of these six methods.

Instruction of students who are at risk must first of all be functional. Skills taught in the educational arena must be relevant and important for the student's current and future needs. The skills taught are selected from a myriad of tasks required to function in today's society on a daily basis. Skills must also be future oriented and allow for growth and acquisition later in life. Instead of teaching students about electricity, for example, it is more important to demonstrate the effects of electricity and its uses and dangers. Very few of us actually regurgitate what we learned in our fifth-grade classroom about electricity. Even fewer of us actually remember what we learned about electricity during our elementary or secondary years. The skills we teach today's students must be relevant to their world.

The materials used to teach functional skills need to be age-appropriate. Many students who are at risk are placed in remedial programs. These students often are assigned readings from textbooks at their reading level. Sixteen-year-old sophomores frequently lose interest in the topics found in a third-grade reader, but they may be more interested in the short stories appearing in auto magazines or daily newspapers, or in stories written from their own interviews of several local employees in a job of their interest. The selection of materials for educating young people needs to consider future options if we are going to prepare these students for the future. Today's textbooks are not designed for the student at risk. For these students, creative content that meets their interests must be identified and designed by teachers. This, of course, means more planning time for these teachers. Utilizing a textbook to teach students who understand and learn from a structured approach is much less taxing and requires less planning time for some teachers. A continuous school year (if approved) should allow ample time for teachers to prepare for all types of learners.

If drill and practice are to be used they must be purposeful. Flashcards and worksheets may provide appropriate drill and practice for some students on some tasks. However, for other students, drill and practice must make use of functional skills whenever possible. Teaching students through mathematical calculations how to determine the number of rolls of wallpaper needed to paper a 9-ft by 15-ft room will not be nearly as effective as assigning a student to determine the number of square feet, the number of rolls needed to cover that square footage, the tools to do the job, and the actual task of wallpapering. Teaching students to read a recipe will not be as beneficial as preparing the recipe. Many of these tasks will need to be repeated and the steps checked frequently to better ensure that the student is grasping the concepts while unassisted. Purposeful drill and practice will allow students to learn to be self-reinforcing as well as self-motivating when errors are observed and immediately corrected. Few of us attempt a new task and complete it with no errors the first time. Drill and practice are very important for all of us, but they benefit us most when they are purposeful.

Community participation in the teaching of tasks also provides the most appropriate opportunity for feedback by which to structure future learning tasks.

This type of community input allows for purposeful drill and practice in real-life situations.

While teaching tasks, it is important to enable students to develop an executive function. They must learn strategies for acquiring skills and evaluating the quality of those skills. For many, strategies come naturally. We look at a task and think, "I need to read the directions, lay out all the pieces and put them together beginning with number one and proceeding ahead." For some, there is no process for learning. Tasks attempted represent merely another opportunity for frustration. Strategies must be modeled for students by the teacher so that techniques become obvious. It may be necessary, for example, for a teacher to talk aloud the steps required to apply and prepare for the Armed Services Vocational Aptitude Battery or other postsecondary options. Talking out loud is not a sign of insanity, but rather enables organization! We need to teach students to use the skill of talking aloud to help them organize information effectively.

Education must include not only strategies for acquiring knowledge, but also students' styles of learning. Those who learn best by hearing, seeing, and doing must be given opportunities to use all three modes. Research indicates that many at-risk students have not been taught to use methods and materials that accommodate their learning styles and strengths (Carbo, Dunn, & Dunn, 1986; Dunn, 1988; Hodges, 1987).

As strategies are being taught, students must also learn self-control techniques. In the process of becoming independent learners, it is important to learn when and how to reward oneself intrinsically. Students who have experienced little, if any, success must be taught methods of self-control through goal selection and goal setting. These goals must be attainable and the reward must be predetermined by the student. It is also important to teach students to recognize mediocrity as opposed to excellence in their attempts by using self-monitoring and self-evaluation. Life's daily tasks require self-monitoring and self-motivating. These methods of self-control may alleviate many of the problems students (and teachers) face in trying to remain motivated and actively involved in learning.

In order to function independently, time management is required. Students at risk must be taught the executive function of managing time. Completing a task requires not only a basic concept of the task to be completed, but the strategies to complete it; self-monitoring to know when it is completed satisfactorily; and time management to understand the length of time required to complete the task. It cannot be assumed that students at the secondary level know how to manage time. Experiencing little success in life often results in unmotivated students. These same students have few, if any, ideas of how to motivate themselves. One method is to learn to manage time so as not to become overwhelmed with a lengthy task. Learning to break a task down into its component parts allows one to allot a certain amount of time to each portion of the task and still complete it in a timely fashion. The feeling of successfully meeting time limits is motivating as well as challenging. Time management allows one to gain more self-control.

When developing an executive function, education must utilize cooperative learning. In cooperative learning, students are grouped appropriately to allow the various strengths of each student to be applied to producing a finished product. Many of the tasks required to function independently are actually based on the results of cooperation. Cooperative learning must be utilized in more educational environments if we are to prepare students to function cooperatively in the future (Slavin & Madden, 1987).

Teaching Strategies for Learning

For students receiving a functional education guided by a community assessment and future needs, further development of the curriculum must include planned methods of enabling students to succeed. These methods might be considered "errorless learning." Educators must set the stage for success by constantly evaluating what and how to teach. Although the relevance of the traditional curriculum may be obvious for some students, it may be totally lacking for others. We cannot assume that all of society's members need the same educational background. Adjustments must be made. These adjustments must allow the student to learn without errors in order to result in self-sufficiency.

Setting the stage for success also means analyzing why a student fails certain tasks. If the task is relevant and yet the student fails, questions regarding the need for strategy instruction must be asked. If strategies are being taught appropriately, we must ask whether the student is using the strategy unassisted or whether the strategy fails to meet his or her learning styles. Whenever failure occurs, it is important to question why and to remedy the situation as soon as possible.

Immediately after an error, it is important to redirect the student. Instruction begins again at a point where success can be experienced, and new methods are developed to teach those portions that were not successful. If a student learns a skill only in part or learns it incorrectly, it may be more difficult to use that skill independently in future settings. Errorless learning in the educational program heads off potential problems in the future.

Relevant skills identified through assessment need to be integrated under traditional curriculum designations such as those listed in Exhibit 3-4. This type of integration allows math teachers, for example, to continue to teach mathematics by utilizing a more appropriate content under the same curriculum designations. It also allows the curriculum to become more relevant to the needs of students today and to their adult roles in the future.

Post-Testing the At-Risk Youth

It is not enough to pretest a student and then offer instruction in a natural environment. All instruction must be followed up with post-testing. Four steps to be used when post-testing include

1. reapplying the pretest
2. noting residual deficiencies
3. troubleshooting any identified problem areas
4. planning for the future

After tasks have been taught, it is possible for the student to self-assess his or her skills by using the pretest. The importance of self-testing cannot be ignored, as students must learn to be self-controlling and self-directing. When the teacher has planned for errorless learning, it is easier to identify the point at which the student may be ready to achieve accuracy on a post-test. From the post-test, residual deficiencies can be identified and discussed with the student. Remedies for these deficiencies may come from the student, teachers, parents, or a group of peers working cooperatively toward the same goal. Other troubleshooting methods may be necessary. This troubleshooting may require asking a number of question, such as

- Do any of the goals need to be changed or modified?
- Are the objectives appropriate for this student at this time?
- Are the reinforcers appropriate for this student? If not, what might be more appropriate?
- Are any adaptations needed which might better enable the student to acquire the skills being taught?
- Is the student interested in what is being taught? Is he or she interested in only portions of the skills? What are his or her interests relating to this skill?
- Are strategies being taught along with skills? Are these strategies being generalized to new situations?
- Does the student have the prerequisite enabling skills necessary to acquire the new skills?
- Does the student have the necessary social/interpersonal skills to succeed in this task in other settings?
- What other social skills are required for success in this task?
- What does the student want to do next? What are the next goals to be established with this particular student?

Setting New Goals

If the student is successful in each of the areas above, it is important to plan for the future by helping the student learn to set new goals. Having teachers set goals for students at risk is not practical. Teaching students to set goals and reach them is much more realistic. Cooperative learning offers students an opportunity to set goals and receive feedback through discussion as to why a specific goal may or may not be realistic. Educational settings must allow time for such activities to take place in order to prepare students for the kinds of challenges that lie ahead, when they will have to set goals independently.

SUMMARY

Preparing students at risk for the future requires some major changes in the methods used to educate them. No longer can we rely on the traditional approaches that have been used for years in educational settings. No longer can we assume that the developmentally based curriculum is appropriate for all students and that if each student does not learn, there must be something wrong with the student. We must look at alternative curriculum designs to educate today's students for the future. These alternatives include assessment of the learner and the instructional context, as well as the community. Educators must become more flexible in allowing students to learn in natural settings and to learn relevant information that will be utilized on a day-to-day basis. As educators, we must integrate community demands with traditional curriculum areas and expand these areas to include functional academics, social skills, communication skills, independent living skills, and recreation and leisure skills, as well as strategies for learning in a variety of settings under a number of conditions. Educators today must gain a perspective of the future to be able to prepare all students.

Not only must education change the methods, but those changes must reflect a sound assessment of the true needs students will have as adults. Standardized tests such as the Scholastic Aptitude Test do not give a true indication of the levels of success one might attain, but rather an indication of achievement levels reached based on skills taught in the school—even though they may not be relevant on a day-to-day basis. Instruction must be functional with age-appropriate materials utilized. No longer can we remediate academic deficiencies by holding students back for years, nor by passing them along while continuing to utilize workbooks designed for students 2 to 10 years younger. Students' learning styles must be taken into account along with techniques for learning new material independently.

Finally, we must teach students to assess their skill levels and to troubleshoot any problems that might be identified. This type of learning how to learn is what education is all about. Learning how to learn will prepare students for the future and not simply to answer questions regarding material read yesterday but irrelevant tomorrow.

REFERENCES

Askamit, D. (1990). Mildly handicapped and at-risk students: The graying of the line. *Academic Therapy, 25,* 277–289.

Barbaro, F. (1982). The learning disabled college student: Some considerations in setting objectives. *Journal of Learning Disabilities, 15,* 599–603.

Carbo, M., Dunn, R., & Dunn, K. (1986). *Teaching students to read through their individual learning styles.* Reston, VA: Reston.

Conrath, J. (1984). Snatching victory from the jaws of learning defeat: How one school fought the dropout blitz. *Contemporary Education, 56,* 36–38.

Cordoni, B.K. (1982). Personal adjustment: The psychosocial aspects of learning disabilities. In M.R. Schmidt & H.Z. Sprandel (Eds.), *New directions for student services No. 18: Helping the learning disabled student* (pp. 39–48). San Francisco: Jossey-Bass.

Deci, E.L. (1989). Intrinsic motivation and special education. In J.M. Brown (Ed.), *Programs for at-risk learners in their entry into the workforce.* St. Paul, MN: University of Minnesota, Minnesota Research and Development Center for Vocational Education.

Dunn, R. (1988). Teaching students through their perceptual strengths or preferences. *Journal of Reading, 31,* 304–309.

Finch, C.R., & Crunkilton, J.R. (1989). Curriculum development in vocational and technical education: Planning, content and implementation. Needham Heights, MA: Allyn & Bacon.

Gagne, R.M., Briggs., L.J., & Wager, W.W. (1988). *Principles of instructional design.* New York: Holt, Rinehart & Winston.

Hodges, H. (1987). I know they can learn because I've taught them. *Educational Leadership, 44,* 3.

Kauffman, J.M., & Pullen, P.L. (1989). A historical perspective: A personal perspective on our history of service to mildly handicapped and at-risk students. *Remedial and Special Education, 10,* 12–14.

Posthill, S.M., & Roffman, A.J. (1990). Issues of money management for the learning disabled adolescent in transition to adulthood. *Academic Therapy, 25,* 321–329.

Schloss, P.J., & Sedlak, R.A. (1986). *Instructional methods for students with learning and behavior problems.* Boston: Allyn & Bacon.

Slavin, R. & Madden, N. (1987). *Effective classroom programs for students at risk* (Rep. No. 19). Baltimore: Johns Hopkins University, Center for Research on Elementary and Middle Schools.

chapter **4**

The Vocational Connection

Arden Boyer-Stephens

INTRODUCTION

Students who comprise the "at-risk" category are not a homogeneous group (Baker & Garfield-Scott, 1981). Just as each individual is unique, a student labeled at-risk must also be viewed as a distinct person with particular needs, interests, and abilities. However, a shared characteristic of these students is that they are potential labor-force participants. As future workers, all students need a vocational connection in their lives.

A number of reports and national studies have been published that chronicle the growing challenges of teaching students at risk. More than 1 million youth drop out of school each year. Each dropout earns between $200,000 to $260,000 less than a high school graduate during his or her lifetime. Unemployment rates among dropouts are higher than they are for graduates of high school. In fact, the unemployment rate for dropouts who are black was 47.1 percent in October 1986 (National Collaboration for Youth, 1989). *Making the Grade* also drew the nation's attention to the issues we face in the areas of literacy, juvenile crime, substance abuse, and teenage pregnancy.

FEDERAL PRIORITIES

Former Department of Labor Secretary Elizabeth Dole (1989) clearly recognized the need for a vocational connection when she stated that a major objective of education at all levels is to prepare people for work. Dole views that preparation as encompassing vocational skills necessary for jobs as well as all the skills necessary for independence and adjustment to change. She sees the need for coordination efforts among education programs and other federal, state, and local agencies. This comprehensive perspective is refreshing in light of the need to mobilize a variety of services and programs to meet the challenges of students at risk.

The concentration of efforts in the reauthorization process for both the Carl D. Perkins Vocational and Applied Technology Education Act of 1990 (P.L. 101-392) and the Job Training Partnership Act (JTPA) of 1982 on the needs of disadvantaged students and the future work force also indicates a federal focus on the linkage between vocational education and labor-force demands. Both acts center around the need to infuse high-quality programs into geographic areas that demonstrate high dropout and unemployment rates. A survey of recent Federal Registers attests to the fact that federal priorities lie in funding programs and services for youth most in need. Opportunities abound for vocational education systems to restructure, improve, and expand training programs for students at risk.

It may be helpful here to review the progress made through federal programs for youth. Reingold and associates (1989) reviewed these programs in an excellent reference entitled Current Federal Policies and Programs for Youth. This resource describes many programs that can serve youth. What follows is a summary of these programs.

The United States Department of Education currently provides financial assistance to schools for compensatory education of economically disadvantaged students under Chapter 1. Under Chapter 2, block grants are available for the improvement of elementary and secondary education, such as grants for drug-free schools, teacher training and administrative improvement grants, magnet schools, and innovations in education grants. Special Education and Rehabilitative Services, a section of the Department of Education, provides financial assistance to schools for the education of students with disabilities, as well as specialized grants in the areas of supported employment, demonstration projects, and special education technology. In the postsecondary education realm, Pell grants and other student loan packages are made available to those in need. Special programs for disadvantaged postsecondary students provide funding for support services and outreach that can be accessed through a proposal process. Vocational and adult education projects are administered under the United States Department of Education; funding for these educational programs include the Carl D. Perkins Vocational and Applied Technology Education Act and monies for literacy training in adult education. Recent White House initiatives include recognition awards for schools and teachers.

The Department of Labor provides for a variety of youth programs through the JTPA. Specific programs for youth include work experience programs, summer employment and training programs, the Job Corps, and demonstration projects. Consideration for child care needs is evident throughout all programs. The Department of Labor also supports Youth: 2000 projects, Cities in Schools, and Summer Training and Education Programs (STEP); and it has grants available for recent school dropouts, out-of-school youth, teen parents, and youth offenders.

The Head Start program is administered by the United States Department of Health and Human Services. This department also awards grants to develop or strengthen community-based facilities for runaway or homeless youth. The Department of Justice created the Office of Juvenile Justice and Delinquency Prevention in 1974. This agency provides for research and demonstration grants and technical assistance to communities, and has recently directed its efforts to the issues of youth gangs and drug abuse.

The Department of Labor, through JTPA, has cut across department lines and formed cooperative programs with other departments. This type of coordination and collaboration is emphasized at the federal level. All of these agencies are clearly concerned about youth, and especially youth in need. All are concerned with producing healthy, effective, and independent citizens who will be an asset rather than a drain to the resources of the country. This is the climate at the federal level today. This climate will allow for initiative and restructuring of the educational and training experiences for youth at risk.

VOCATIONAL ALTERNATIVES CONTINUUM

Great possibilities for broadening the traditional scope of vocational education programs exist today. Because of the federal stance toward the holistic approach to the education of at-risk youth and the idea that at-risk students are a heterogeneous group, plus the opportunities for restructuring the image of vocational education and the notion that all students need a vocational connection, vocational education and vocational educators have the support to develop and implement innovative programming. Options and alternatives must be available for students to reach individual goals both during and after their formal school careers. This allows for a redefinition of vocational education to include the concept of career development for all students. Traditional vocational education, that is, specific job training offered within an educational setting, would certainly be a part of the vocational connection continuum. These programs, because they are structured so as to respond to labor market demands, emphasize experiential learning, and include academic skills within the context of real work, are alluring to many of the at-risk youth who stay in school long enough to reach a point of entry into vocational programs. However, many students are disillusioned prior to age 16 and lose the opportunities traditional vocational education programs have to offer. For these students, the vocational connection must take place much earlier.

The vocational alternatives continuum should begin in elementary school with career education concepts and the introduction of roles as a worker (Kokaska & Brolin, 1985). The relevance of academic curricula to life roles must be stressed. Problem solving, creativity, and decision making must be a part of all educational endeavors and their importance must be related to the life roles of students. The middle school years should provide ample opportunities to explore the world of work through every content area. Guidance and counseling, realistic self-appraisal, involvement of parents, and volunteer experiences must be emphasized. Decision making for high school career preparation (4-year plans) should allow for changes and, in fact, encourage youth to continue to explore options and change. Planning should be based on the concept of broadening options for youth. High school preparation ought to offer alternatives for further exploration, vocational training, work experiences, summer employment, after-school employment, parent and employer involvement, and preparation for postsecondary education. It is necessary for schools to be creative in their approaches to the provision of options for individual students. Often services from a variety of community agencies must be coordinated to meet the needs of students at risk.

Vocational connections are networks comprising students, educators, parents, and the community at large. Redefining vocational education to include career development concepts, enhancement of the school curriculum to include these concepts, and the development of a variety of alternative options for career preparation would encourage the interface of traditional vocational education programs and traditional academic programs. This interface would positively affect the K through 12 curriculum, creating a more cohesive, comprehensive, and relevant educational community that is able to provide individualized alternatives to meet the needs of at-risk youth.

CAREER DEVELOPMENT

Career Awareness

Most experts agree that career choice is a developmental process. In reviewing the work of career theorists, Healy (1982) noted that all believe in a developmental process, although the stages and names of each stage may differ by theorist. Most would concur that career awareness is an initial stage in the development process. Young children are often in a fantasy stage and have no realistic concept of work. Most could not tell you what their parent(s) do(es) on the job. Some children at risk live in poverty and may have no parent(s) who works; therefore, their ideas about work are very limited. The environment in which they live may value neither educational nor occupational aspirations (MacLeod, 1987). Children need information about the world of work and also information about themselves. Exploring individual values, interests, and abilities necessary for various types of work is a primary objective for any elementary school curriculum. Students require structure and guidance to understand the relationship between school and the rest of their lives. The basic work habits demanded for success in school are similar to those required for success on a job. Competencies such as following directions; working independently; using appropriate social and interpersonal skills, decision-making skills, and problem-solving skills; and applying critical thinking and self-care skills are prerequisites for successful living and working. Business leaders surveyed by the Committee for Economic Development (1987) stressed the need for more attention to the "invisible curriculum" in the education of disadvantaged children (p. 43). Employability skills such as work habits, honesty, self-reliance, teamwork, and perseverance were considered by business leaders as the foundation of both educational and occupational success.

Elementary school teachers may feel ill-prepared to infuse employability skills or career education concepts into their already full curriculum. However, the vocational connection only requires looking at the present curriculum and relating it to the world outside of school. This is not to say that the present curriculum does not need review and perhaps changes, but that, for this purpose, the elementary school teacher needs to look at the total curriculum through a different framework. The basic demands of successful academic work can easily be related to various jobs (following directions, working independently, etc.). All content areas have potential for teaching about careers. A guidance counselor, parent, or community person could supply information in these areas to the teacher or the students, or both. Basic academic skills (reading, math, science concepts) are generalizable to a multitude of careers or to independent living. The trick is to be able to relate the academic skill being taught to the student's present or future life. For example, teaching fractions can be related to preparing food, building a house, sewing, using tools, or making change. More time and effort will be necessary to structure the curriculum to include activities designed to foster creativity, problem-solving skills, and decision-making skills. Children can be involved in the development of classroom rules and consequences. Cooperative learning groups can be formed for the purpose of solving a problem of interest to the class, as well as for developing appropriate interpersonal and social skills.

Although all children need career awareness programs, career education activities, and basic work habit development, children at risk need these skills taught explicitly in the curriculum. The "invisible curriculum" may be imparted implicitly to many children, but children at risk may have no reinforcement or opportunities for practice of these skills other than in the school environment. At-risk children need concrete exposure to various careers and the tasks within those careers. Different cultural impacts on these children outside of school often have more influence than the curriculum. If teachers understand the context of the environment that children bring with them to school, then the experiences of the children can be used to develop the structured activities necessary to impart decision-making and critical thinking skills. The involvement of the community, and especially of parents, is essential in attempting to teach these career education concepts. For inclusion of a parent as a partner in education to be effective, teachers must be aware of the cultural background of that family and be interested in learning more about the perspective of that family. Since a majority of teachers are white and have middle-class backgrounds, their understanding of other cultures tends to be, in most cases, limited. Teacher training must take place prior to any efforts to involve parents actively in the education of children at risk. Schools must be cognizant of and sensitive to the needs of parents as well as the educational needs of the child.

The National Commission for Employment Policy undertook a case study approach to the programming efforts of schools in relation to career education and at-risk children. Their report chronicles the paucity of information and programming for late elementary, middle, and junior high school students (National Commission for Employment Policy, 1988). Examples of exemplary programming include recreational and social programs, peer tutoring programs, exposure to career activities, special rewards for attendance and performance, counseling, and family involvement/intervention. Elementary school-age children at risk are often involved in Chapter 1 programs for academic remediation, but the exemplary program characteristics listed in the above report also stress career information and social/recreational activities as well as family involvement.

Career Exploration

Career exploration is essential to moving individuals from the fantasy stage into a more realistic perspective of themselves in relation to work. The middle school or junior high school years are critical ones for youth at risk. The entry into adolescence itself is turbulent for many individuals, but for students at risk, these years are crucial. During these years, students are encouraged to develop 4-year plans for high school. Decisions about college, postsecondary vocational training, and life style expectations must all be addressed. Certainly if students have not had the advantage of structured career education in elementary school, the middle school years become another catch-up time. However, there are too many career development tasks for students in this age group to allow for effective remedial work in career awareness. For students who are prepared with good work habits; employability skills; awareness of a variety of jobs; self-awareness of interests, values, and skills; and a basic repertoire for decision making, the career exploration and choice level required at junior high is still a formidable task. For underprepared students, these tasks may become insurmountable and result in disillusioned students, behavior problems, or dropouts from school (Hallahan, 1986).

Bhaerman and Kopp (1988) present a wide variety of program options for use at the middle/junior high school level. Among these options, career planning is paramount. Schools must increase their efforts to involve all segments of the community in providing exploration activities for students. Curriculum can also express the importance of career exploration, both by infusion of activities into each content area and the establishment of courses uniquely designed to address the developmental career tasks of this age group. Both classroom-based experiential learning and community-based learning are possible options. An occupational orientation class would give students a semester or a year to concentrate their efforts on realistic self-appraisal and exploration of various occupations. Curriculum laboratories across the nation develop and distribute curricula designed for occupational orientation at the middle school or junior high school level. The *ACCESS Skills: Employability and Study Skills Assessment and Curriculum Guide* (Flanagan & Johnson, 1987) is just one of these types of materials, as is the Youth Employment Curriculum and Competencies, a guide developed by a multiagency task force for use with economically disadvantaged youth (Izzo & Drier, 1987).

Another career exploration strategy that can be used at the junior high school level is that of job shadowing. The existence of a school/business partnership is helpful to designing this type of activity. All ninth graders are required to spend one day with an adult who is working in a field in which the student is interested. This culmination activity follows a month of guest speakers and career information infusion into all content areas. For students who may be at risk, special efforts are made by the school to ensure the opportunity for choice in occupational fields, provision of transportation, and special contacts made to the business community if necessary. Following the job shadow, students have several activities to complete that are designed to allow for reflection on the job tasks and their own abilities and interests. Some of these students may even procure volunteer employment as a result of the job-shadowing experience. These volunteer experiences can be used by the students to explore their interests, values, and abilities. Students can share these experiences with other students, thereby helping others gain a deeper understanding about the world of work. Employers involved in providing volunteer or paid work experience can be offered assistance and training in supervising students and developing work tasks that are conducive to high-quality learning experiences. Employers can be encouraged to relate the job task to necessary academic skills to bring relevance to classroom assignments. They also should be involved in evaluating the student's ability to perform the tasks. A school/business partnership agreement would make this task easier. No work experience should be overlooked as a means of helping students evaluate their work attitudes and skills. Babysitting, chores at home, paper routes, lawn care, and the like all have skills associated with quality work. Students can assess their likes and dislikes of different parts of the jobs they have done and arrive at a better understanding of themselves.

For students whose opportunities to work in the community are limited by transportation or other barriers, in-school work experiences can introduce them to various occupational tasks. If their work is evaluated, these types of experiences can provide teachers, counselors, parents, and students with invaluable information regarding interests and abilities. Often, in-school work experiences such as office or library helper are given to the "best" students. However, with a little effort, rotating job assignments could be developed as part of an occupational orientation class or an extracurricular activity for which students sign up, much as they would for a club. During the summer, a work experience program may be initiated in cooperation with JTPA to provide exposure to community job sites and real jobs. These programs can be combined with academic remediation activities when necessary.

In many middle and junior high schools, the industrial arts curriculum is changing to include technology education (Bhaerman & Kopp, 1988). Exploratory cluster areas such as communications, construction, manufacturing, and transportation emphasize career orientation, problem solving, and adaptation to changing environments. These courses are striving to create relevance and intellectual challenge while using a hands-on approach to learning. Successful demonstration programs are detailed in *Technology Education: A Perspective on Implementation* (International Technology Education Association, 1985). Courses such as these allow students to explore interest areas while integrating the development of academic and vocational skills.

During the middle school or junior high school years, teachers and counselors must continually be aware of the strengths and weaknesses of students at risk and aid these students in self-discovery of strengths and weaknesses. Unless there is a systematic method for keeping track of students' experiences, many abilities of at-risk youth may be overlooked. Checklists, competency profiles, work experience portfolios, and individual educational planning forms have all been used to keep track of a student's progress in skill development, interests, and abilities. Cumulative records that include career planning information and vocational assessment information are helpful in developing a 4-year plan for the high school years. These records should contain information related to the student's career interests, achievement/academic levels, physical skills, health/medical information, paid/volunteer work experiences, personal/social skill levels, learning styles, future goals, work behaviors, motor coordination and dexterity skills, and the like (Sarkees & Scott, 1985). A form developed by Missouri special educators to compile such information is shown in Exhibit 4-1.

Career Preparation

A third stage in career development begins after a decision has been made regarding a career goal. Preparation for achieving that goal begins in earnest for

Exhibit 4-1 Informal Vocational Assessment Summary

CONFIDENTIAL
INFORMATION

Student's Name _____   Age _____   Sex _____

Home School _____   Grade _____   DOB _____

Parent's Name _____   Address _____   Phone _____

I. GOALS

   A. Vo-tech training interests

      1st choice _____

      2nd choice _____

   B. Goals/interests for after high school graduation

      1. _____

      2. _____

      3. _____

   C. Parent's comments _____

      _____

      _____

   D. ATTACH COPIES OF STUDENT'S 4-YEAR PLAN AND TRANSCRIPTS

II. BACKGROUND/READINESS

   A. Prior training/experience

      1. Work experience

         a. Paid _____

         b. Volunteer _____

         c. Other (school jobs, etc.) _____

         _____

   B. Coursework

      1. Practical arts classes and grades

      _____   _____

      _____   _____

   C. ACCESS SKILLS (attach checklist)

      _____ Adequate   _____ Lacking in some areas

   D. Physical characteristics

      1. Height _____

      2. Weight _____

      3. Vision _____   Glasses _____   Contacts _____

      4. Hearing _____

      5. Medications _____

      6. Physical limitations _____

   E. Attendance

      1. Number of days missed: This year _____ Last year _____

      2. Suspension/detention: This year _____ Last year _____

      3. Excessive tardies _____

      Reasons _____

      _____

Exhibit 4-1 continued

F. Grooming/behavior skills

E = Excellent A = Adequate NI = Needs Improvement	E	A	NI
Wears appropriate clothes			
Clothes neat and clean			
Hair neat and clean			
Takes daily shower/bath			
Brushes teeth daily			
Keeps hands clean			
Uses makeup appropriately			
Peer interactions			
Interactions w/authority			
Reaction to criticism			
Attention to task			
Ability to follow oral directions			
Ability to follow written directions			
Quality of work			
Quantity of work			
Initiative			
Works safely at all times			
Turns in assignments			
Attitude toward school			
Fine-motor skills			
Gross-motor skills			

III. RECENT TEST DATA

A. Intelligence
   WISC-R
   Date _____   Other _____
   Verbal _____
   Performance _____
   Full scale _____

B. Achievement

	Test	Date
Reading		
Math		
Written language		
Spelling		

C. Aptitude (aptitude tests, observations)
   ASVAB Date _____ GATB Date _____
   Other/Date _____
   Strengths   Weaknesses
   _____ _____
   _____ _____
   _____ _____
   _____ _____

D. Interest inventory
   Inventory Used _____
   Area of Interest _____

Exhibit 4-1 continued

E. Preferred learning style

_____	Auditory	_____	Visual
_____	Kinesthetic	_____	Combination

IV. RESOURCE INFORMATION

A. Special services teacher

_____

B. Counselor _____

C. Date of last IEP/IVP review _____

D. ATTACH COPY OF IEP/IVP

V. SPECIAL LEARNING NEEDS

A. Diagnostic category

_____

B. Areas of strength

1. _____
2. _____
3. _____

C. Areas of weakness

1. _____
2. _____
3. _____

D. SPECIAL CONSIDERATIONS NEEDED

(Please check)

_____ Notification of special teacher or counselor concerning

    _____ reading assignments

    _____ written assignments

    _____ math assignments

    _____ tests

_____ Supplemental study guides or handouts

_____ Assistance with note-taking

_____ Needs to use calculator

_____ Sit near front of room

_____ Tests read to student

_____ Additional time needed to complete tests

_____ Adjusted course curriculum

_____ Pass/Fail grading

_____ Use of behavior contracts

_____ Career counseling

_____ Monthly progress reports

_____ Support personnel monitoring/counseling

_____ Parent contact

_____ OTHER (health related, assistive devices, etc.)

_____ _____

Abbreviations: WISC-R, Revised Weschler Intelligence Scale for Children; ASVAB, Armed Services Vocational Aptitude Battery; GATB, General Aptitude Test Battery; IEP, individualized education plan; IVP, individualized vocational plan.

Source: Missouri LINC (1988) with adaptations by Missouri teachers.

many youths while they are in high school. In most schools, vocational and academic educational tracks are viewed as very separate lines of preparation. However, since all students need a vocational connection, any high school class should be an integral part of each student's career preparation. An integrated learning environment is proposed for all secondary education (Fennimore & Pritz, 1988) and comprises three interconnected elements: academic, psychosocial, and vocational. These three elements are essential curriculum components for at-risk youth. Vocational training classes at the secondary level should be uniquely tailored to provide each of the elements. All vocational subject areas include specific vocational skills, academic skills related to the vocational area, and the employability or psychosocial skills necessary to be successful in the world of work. Some vocational classes build work experience into the curriculum, which allows students to connect the relationships between school and work. There are various approaches that schools can use to ensure opportunities for career preparation for students at risk.

Relevant Curriculum

Regardless of the career preparation path chosen by students at risk, the curriculum taught must be relevant to the students and their future. Many students may see no reason to learn geometry, but if they are shown how geometry is used in building a house, they are able to relate these skills to "real life." Even students who do not choose building trades/construction as a career are likely to have some interest in the structures in which they live. This kind of relevance is at the heart of student motivation. If at-risk students rarely have the opportunity to relate subject content to their lives, they tend to become bored, frustrated, and unmotivated. All teachers should understand their subject area well enough to relate it to the world outside the four walls of the school. Being able to bridge the curriculum content to the real-world experience of students is an integral skill that master teachers possess. The importance of a relevant, functional curriculum is addressed elsewhere in this book but is a concept worth repeating in regard to the career preparation of students at risk.

Curriculum materials are available to help teachers demonstrate relationships between the subject matter and real life. *BASICS: Bridging Vocational and Academic Skills* is one such curriculum (National Center for Research in Vocational Education, 1987a). Another is *Applied Mathematics* (Center for Occupational Research and Development, 1988), which allows students to experiment and manipulate concrete items to arrive at mathematical equations and truisms. Use of these types of materials allows students to understand how a concept works, why it works, and when to apply it in various settings. Academic skills are embedded in relevant life skills, thereby enhancing the motivation to learn such skills.

College Preparation

Some students at risk will aspire to postsecondary education. This option may not be open to students without the basic skills usually included in a college preparatory curriculum in high school. However, alternative programs designed to increase basic skills should be offered to students, rather than limiting their aspirations. Many alternative programs have demonstrated effectiveness in raising the basic skill level of students. Some of these programs can be found in *The Learning Bank*, a journal produced by the editors of the American School Board Journal and the Executive Educator (1989). Academic support programs may be necessary for some students so that they are able to reach their full potential as adults.

Work Experience

Work experience or work-study programs have been available in many schools for years. The focus of many of these programs has been to give students not only experience in the world of work and teach specific skills, but to aid them in their transition from school to work. Work experience programs can be either educationally relevant or devoid of educational content, and the former is clearly preferable. The individual needs of students should be considered and selective goals determined or students may just be placed in any available jobs in the community. Wehlage, Stone, Lesko, Nauman, and Page (1982) reviewed research on work experience programs and found that they often did not make a significant difference in the lives of marginal high school students. These authors point out the psychosocial and developmental needs of adolescents and contend that many work experience programs do not account for these needs. They offer five principles on which experiential education should be built. The implementation of these principles within a work experience program may be difficult, but it would result in higher-quality education for participating students.

The first principle Wehlage et al. (1982) propose is that students be provided with optimal challenges. The community job placement should challenge but not frustrate the student. This means that the teacher must know the student well, and also know the job tasks required in the business. It may also mean changing placements to allow the student to learn more complicated tasks. The relationship between the school and the community is important in being able to provide challenging job placements.

Work experience programs should require students to show responsibility and initiative. Students must have some input into the placement and must indicate an interest in obtaining the job. Once on the job, an effective employer requires the student to continue to demonstrate responsibility and initiative. The third principle promoted by Wehlage et al. (1982) relates to the students' perceptions of the job. Students view different jobs as valuable. Some jobs are not highly valued, either by students at risk or by society in general. Students must see the job as important or as a stepping stone to a job that is valued. Placement in a fast-food restaurant or seasonal employment in parks may be seen by some at-risk youth as "confirming their lower status" (p. 203). Teachers with responsibilities for work experience programs recognize these perceptions and attempt to find other types of employment for such students.

The fourth principle of experiential education is that it must provide the opportunity for the student to acquire a sense of competence and success. This principle is related to the first one. If a job is found that challenges, but does not frustrate the student, the environment is conducive to the student's gaining skills and success on the job. The fifth principle is the necessity for the student to reflect on his or her experiences in order to learn to resolve conflicts and contradictions. This critical-thinking component in the work experience program is essential. It gives students practice in higher-order thinking skills and allows them to develop accurate perceptions about their involvement with the environment in which they operate.

The development of excellent work experience programs is a difficult but worthwhile task. To incorporate the five principles outlined above, teachers must know their students and their community well, have administrative support and time provided to search for appropriate jobs, and be able to help students process experiences that lead them to a deeper understanding of the work world and their place in it.

Community service programs (or other types of volunteer work programs) should also be cultivated with the above five principles in mind. These experiences can help students at risk develop adult roles, work habits, and social skills (Fennimore & Pritz, 1988). Again, the ability to process these experiences is crucial to the existence of a high-quality educational experience for students at risk.

Vocational Education

For many students at risk, vocational education is an option that includes many model dropout program characteristics (Weber, 1988). Vocational teachers have more control of their curricula and fewer students, spend more time counseling individual students, use small group instruction along with active learning and individualization, reinforce basic skills, relate learning to the world of work, and recognize students more often for their performance than do teachers in nonvocational classrooms. These characteristics of the vocational education classroom tend to nurture success in students who have had difficulty with the more traditional academic classroom. The five principles for experiential education noted above are exemplified in model vocational education programs. These programs challenge students, individualize instruction when necessary, require student responsibility and initiative, foster competence and success, are valued by students as "real work," and encourage problem solving and critical thinking.

The American Association of School Administrators (1989), in their recent report, *Students at Risk: Problems and Solutions*, acknowledge that vocational education is a crucial ingredient in keeping potential dropouts in school. In reviewing model programs, vocational education is viewed as a major component at the secondary level. For example, in Missouri, Centers for At-Risk Youth (CARY) have been established at more than 30 of the 58 area vocational schools in the state. These CARY centers are a cooperative funding effort among the Missouri State Department Divisions of Employment and Training and Vocational Special Needs and Guidance and the local education agencies (school districts). Students at risk of dropping out may be eligible for Carl D. Perkins funds or Job Training Partnership Act dollars to participate in an at-risk center program. In each area vocational school with a CARY program, various academic alternatives are offered as well as training in a vocational area and cooperative work experience programs. Academic programs include the preparation for a general equivalency diploma or instruction by a basic skills instructor in core academic areas so that the student can obtain credit for high school graduation. This credit is awarded by the student's sending high school; the basic skills instructor works with the teacher from the high school in setting competencies in the area for student mastery. Basic skills instructors also offer tutoring in basic skill areas needed by the student to master the competencies required for the vocational class. Students have many vocational choices at the area vocational school. Most vocational schools nationwide offer business and office education, agriculture, health occupations, vocational home economics, trade and technical areas, and marketing and distributive education. Some vocational classes have opportunities for cooperative work experiences also. These types of alternative programs are on the increase in every state across the nation as one solution to the needs of many students at risk.

Vocational education does help some students stay in school and find better paying employment upon leaving school according to the National Assessment of Vocational Education (NAVE) study (Technical Assistance for Special Populations Program, 1989). This study recommended that vocational education also improve its ability to recruit students at risk, increase the use of cooperative work experience programs, and expand placement and follow-along activities (Hayward & Wirt, 1989). Follow-along activities are more intensive than follow-up activities; students are contacted more frequently and over a longer time period. Employers are encouraged to call the program coordinator if problems arise and intervention is provided as needed. Broussard and Wulf (1983) made similar recommendations, but also included the involvement of business and industry in the search for solutions to problems encountered by students at risk. Vocational education, through the use of its mandated community advisory committees, is in a unique position to collaborate with business and industry in expanding the opportunities for students at risk in the labor market. In conjunction with the required review for state-of-the-art equipment and curriculum, vocational educators can encourage and aid community employers to assess their needs and develop various alternatives to enable students to enter the labor pool and to advance.

THE SEARCH FOR IMPROVEMENT

All educational endeavors can be improved. Vocational education has made great strides in flexibility and curriculum enhancement to meet the needs of at-risk students. Competency-based education, open entry/open exit programming, supportive basic skills instruction, integration of academic skills into the curriculum, enhancement of linkages between vocational education and other educational experiences, expansion of cooperative work experiences, in-depth assessment, counseling and guidance for students, articulation with postsecondary vocational education, and cooperation and collaboration with business and industry are all examples of the changes sustained and advanced by innovative vocational educators and administrators. Continued improvement is suggested by the NAVE study (1989). Weber (1987) recommends that exploratory courses be offered at younger ages in order to allow the high school years to be spent in occupationally specific coursework. The need for child care alternatives and parenting instruction continues to increase. Vocational education personnel continue to search for better instructional methods and programmatic improvements for students limited in English proficiency, as well as strategies for substantial involvement of parents in the vocational education process. All of these solutions will help students at risk stay in school, learn a saleable skill, develop employability skills, and learn appropriate roles for adult life.

SUPPORT SERVICES

Students at risk often need an assortment of support services to gain success in school. The Learning Bank (American School Board Journal and the Executive Educator, 1989) and other sources of exemplary programs and services can provide educators with ideas to supplement already existing programs or to replace ineffectual programs. Some students will need continuous support throughout their academic careers, while others will need minimal targeted help at various junctures in school. This section briefly reviews some of the support services that might be considered when working with at-risk students in regard to their career development.

Tutoring

Most students, at some time during their school years, need tutoring. Often this is provided by parents in helping with papers, studying for tests, drill and practice, and review of skills. At-risk students may not have this kind of support available at home. Other methods have been used by schools to provide these students with the necessary tutoring. Some schools employ older students or honor society students as tutors. Sometimes these students are available to assist anyone during the day. Other schools assign students to help other students. Teachers often assign "buddies" to work with one another in the classroom. Cooperative learning techniques are used to help students at risk keep up with others. Learning centers are established in some schools and students who are failing are assigned 1 hour a day for help in certain subject areas. Assistance in establishing such programs is provided in Technique for Remediation: Peer Tutoring (National Center for Research in Vocational Education, 1987).

Some schools have established hotlines that students can call after school hours if they need help with homework. Neighborhoods have initiated after school study halls where small groups of students can get together for help; parents are often involved in such endeavors. Some schools send computers home with students after an orientation with them and their parents. Software is provided in the areas of student weakness.

Vocational education provides for tutoring through the use of vocational support personnel as well as the use of buddy systems, individualized curricula, and cooperative learning techniques. Vocational support personnel are charged with monitoring and assisting the student at risk. They can provide a variety of services to both the student and the teacher. Tutoring is only one of the strategies employed by vocational support personnel in creating environments that lead to success for at-risk students.

Counseling

Counseling plays a large role in the success of a student at risk. These students need to know that someone cares about them as persons. The counselor is in a prime position to make a difference in the lives of such students. However, most counselors with very large caseloads find themselves unable to meet the continuing needs of students at risk. Schools have attempted to resolve this problem in various ways. Making a large school environment appear smaller has been utilized in many urban schools. Cities-in-Schools and school-within-a-school approaches break down the student body into cohesive, manageable parts, with teachers and counselors assuming responsibilities for smaller numbers of students. Teachers are advisors for 10 to 15 students in some larger schools, and work with the counselor to help students with significant problems.

Developmental guidance programs have been initiated in some schools that enable counselors to work with small and large groups of students on psychosocial and career education competencies (Starr & Gysbers, 1989).

In some states, vocational education funds vocational special needs counselors who are designated to work only with special needs students. These counselors are responsible for the guidance needs of these students and work with them on vocational planning and personal issues; they also advocate for these students. Some of these specialized counselors also help students obtain employment and serve as a liaison with community agencies and services. Provision of vocational assessment services is also incorporated into some of these counselors' job duties.

Students at risk often have overwhelming counseling needs. Counselors can have significant impact on the career development of all students if they begin at the elementary level and utilize the concepts of career development throughout the students' school years. A systematic approach must be implemented for students at risk prior to the secondary level if these students are to be expected to make sound decisions regarding career goals. Schools must address the needs of these students with increased numbers of counselors and lower counselor/student ratios.

Parental Support

The importance of parental support is addressed elsewhere in this book. It should be reinforced here, though, that the support of parents in the career development of their children cannot be taken for granted. Parents can influence their children positively in regard to staying in school and building career aspirations. Again, many schools have implemented programs designed to encourage more parental involvement. These programs should begin in the elementary years and should change in focus as the student ages. Teachers must be aware of their power to intimidate parents and, instead, strive to encourage parental input. As students enter the career exploration and preparation stages, parents can provide experiences outside of school to help their children become more aware of the roles needed in adult life and the world of work.

Community Support

The vocational connection for at-risk students requires close communication with the community. Business, industry, and service agencies must understand the needs of these students; educators have the responsibility to inform them of these needs. At-risk students need to explore the community; in doing so, they will become more aware of the diversity of career options open to them. These students often see a very different "community" than teachers see. Programs can be implemented that allow students to broaden their perspective of the community. Students can begin to see the needs of the community as well as how their interests and skills can fit into those needs. Developing community linkages can bring the community into the classroom as well. It provides an easier way to bridge the academics in the curriculum to the "real-life" world of the student.

Vocational education has natural links to the heart of the community. Vocational educators work with business and industry leaders to update curricula and equipment, develop jobs for students, and provide employers with well-prepared workers. These natural links are helpful to the student at risk by providing the opportunity to see the relationship between school and work. In supporting cooperative work experience programs, employers are able to work closely with schools, teachers, and students and come to understand the challenges facing all of them. Employers know, perhaps better than anyone else, where the workforce of the future stands and how important the vocational connection is to all students, and especially to students at risk.

Staff Development

Although often overlooked, staff development is an essential element in the effort to offer quality career development activities for students at risk. Few teachers have the expertise they feel they need in order to help students explore the world of work. They have few contacts with the business community, and yet they need to provide students with career exploration options. Vocational teachers must constantly update themselves in their field of expertise as well as in the field of instructional strategies. Teachers need guidance and support in order to provide quality educational experiences for their students at risk. Counselors can help in this respect by providing teachers with information about the world of work and helping to design activities for classroom use. They can also contact employers in the community to provide exploratory experiences or jobs for students, as well as searching out potential guest speakers in a variety of fields.

Counselors cannot do it all, though. Administrators must be supportive of training related to career development objectives. Teacher release time for in-service training, visitation of exemplary programs, and perhaps even teacher exchange programs would help teachers and employers understand each other better. Vocational teachers need support and encouragement to update themselves in their fields as well as learn more about students at risk and instructional methodologies that are effective with such students. They need release time for job development, employer contacts, and follow-up with students who already have jobs. Needs assessment for staff development programming should be conducted each year to develop long-range planning for in-service, release time, travel, and exchange programs. Without well-founded plans to support teachers in their efforts to work with students at risk, programs for these students will falter and fail.

Support after High School

Students at risk need help to transit smoothly into the adult world. Career development planning efforts can help in this transition process if begun early. Students going on to postsecondary educational institutions must explore financial aid forms, scholarships, agency funding, and so forth early in their high school years. These students may need someone to contact them during the summer months to provide encouragement to follow through with their plans. Students entering the world of work from a general education track may have significant problems, because of few specific skills and an inability to transfer the skills they have into a work setting. These students may need help with interviewing skills and placement. Students leaving school from vocational education programs have a better chance of employment as a result of specific skill training and access to trained job placement personnel.

Many students leaving high school proclaim they want a "break," and the prospect of going directly to work is distasteful to them; parental support is needed in these cases. For example, some students who are allowed to stay home, with no rent charges, are more likely to remain at home rather than look for work! Vocational placement personnel should be aware of these feelings. Sometimes it helps to give the student a short "vacation" prior to placement.

Students involved in a cooperative work experience program may have a job prior to graduation. Those who do not may need help in locating similar employment possibilities. The role of schools in the transition of at-risk students is as intense as its role in providing in-school programs for them. Preparation for transition through the use of vocational connections and career development concepts will decrease the need for intensive services after graduation.

BUSINESS/LABOR/EDUCATION PARTNERSHIPS

If schools are to produce healthy, productive workers, teachers must know what skills employers look for in employees. Carnevale, Gainer, and Meltzer (1989) report seven areas of competence that employers value. These are:

1. learning to learn
2. basic skills (reading, writing, and computation)
3. communication (listening and oral communication)

4. creative thinking/problem solving
5. self-esteem/goal-setting/motivation/personal and career development
6. interpersonal skills/negotiation/teamwork
7. organizational effectiveness/leadership

Career development is specifically mentioned in this listing as well as the familiar basic skills. The list also contains higher-order thinking skills and psychosocial skills, so the vocational connection that schools must strive to achieve includes the broad spectrum of skills to which Fennimore and Pritz (1988) allude in their concept of the integrated curriculum. Business and industry leaders know the skills they want employees to possess, and with the increasing numbers of business/education partnerships, employers are becoming more knowledgeable and more involved with the challenges faced by schools today. A survey in 1988 indicated that 40 percent of schools were involved in a partnership, whereas only 17 percent of schools had such involvement 5 years ago (Walker, 1988). Fifty-one percent of urban schools, compared with 31 percent of rural schools, were collaborating with business/industry. Walker surveyed 1,500 principals to determine what types of support they wanted from partnerships. Fifty-two percent of the principals stated that scholarships, student awards, and other incentives were needed. Forty-five percent were looking for donations of equipment, computers, or books; the third priority was the need for guest speakers and the use of the partner's facilities. Academic tutoring and work experience/summer jobs were other frequently mentioned needs.

Identifying Potential Partners

Schools should develop a needs assessment to determine the support they might desire from a partnership with business and industry. By using a career development framework, an outline of core competencies might guide the needs assessment. For example, in elementary schools, the greatest need may be access to guest speakers in a variety of occupations and openness to tour facilities. In middle schools or junior high schools, the needs may be geared more toward allowing students to shadow employees for a day to learn more about job tasks or to have job stations set up for students to experiment with different types of jobs. Adult mentors and tutors might also be a need at this age as well as at the high school level. High schools might also want summer employment opportunities and work experience opportunities for their students. Guest speakers in nontraditional jobs might also be sought, as well as apprenticeship and volunteer opportunities. Teachers, parents, administrators, and students might all be surveyed as to their perceived needs and ideas about how best to utilize a partnership within their community.

Once these needs have been determined, businesses or industries in the community or region can be tapped for their resources. Some schools have personnel already involved with community leaders through memberships in community organizations. Others will need to promote their desire for partnerships through other channels. Knowing what the needs are and being able to articulate those needs to business and industry leaders are essential to developing a partnership. It is also wise to include some benefits for the businesses that enter the partnership. These benefits might include publicity, award recognitions, access to volunteer workers, assistance in training employees, worker exchange programs, and personal involvement in the lives of youth at risk. Any partnership must include an understanding of responsibilities on the part of the school and the business. Both long-range and short-range goals should be negotiated and written into an agreement. Each of the goals should have an evaluation component so that the partnership can systematically determine the extent of its achievement. The initiation of a partnership takes planning; but, once established, the goals become a part of each organization. Partnerships with business and industry can aid schools in the provision of activities and services to strengthen the vocational connection for students at risk.

Mentorships

Many students at risk have no access to role models in various occupational arenas. Their knowledge of the world of work is extremely limited. Through partnerships, business and industry can provide mentors to students in need of a personal relationship and exposure to career opportunities. In addition, some mentors can provide tutoring, recreation/leisure activities, work experience, and referral for employment.

The mentor role has been defined by Ward (1988) as multifaceted. A mentor is a role model, a supervisor, an instructor, a counselor, and an evaluator. It may be that these various roles are allocated to different individuals within some partnerships. Mentorship programs can be developed to meet the needs of one student, or they can become institutionalized as a part of coursework. Ward describes a program in Cincinnati in which students can enroll in a 6-week class that consists of seminars and direct work experience with a mentor in the area of their career interest. Students must spend at least 18 hours in the workplace with their mentor, maintain a career journal, attend three career education seminars, and write a summary of their experiences. This program links the school and community, links academics with careers, and provides students at risk with a strong vocational connection.

Entrepreneurial Support

Small businesses are the fastest growing sector of American business today. Schools need the help of the business community in developing curricula for such enterprises. Many rural districts with few business/industry resources have initiated entrepreneurial activities that involve students with the community. Examples of such activities include the training of students in woodworking skills and the sale of products, the production and sale of tourism products, and student-formed businesses in lawn care, house painting, and seasonal maintenance. One school developed a courier service for the community (Schwartz, 1987).

In urban areas with greater resources, schools have entered alliances with community service agencies as well as business and industry to form small businesses. Partnerships with small businesses could include vocational training on the job through internships, the placement of vocational instructors and other school personnel during the summer months, or the hiring of proprietors to develop and perhaps teach a class on entrepreneurship. The possibilities are limited only by the creativity of the people involved in initiating such partnerships.

Work-Site Use

The most obvious use of business/industry partnerships lies in the work experience arena. Certainly, students would have access to a variety of jobs for shadowing, volunteer experiences, work experience, after-school jobs, and placement on graduation. Such experiences should be developed in accord with the principles given above for quality experiential education. However, students are not the only beneficiaries of such partnerships. Internships for teachers, counselors, and administrators within the business community would allow for their continued growth in awareness of work environments, worker requirements, and career opportunities and allow them to return that knowledge to students in the classroom. These experiences would help teachers feel more comfortable teaching the tenets of career development and creating activities through which students can master the competencies. The interaction between school personnel and business/industry in the context of the world of work would enhance each group's understanding of the other (Vocational Education Counseling and Placement Services, nd).

Other Uses of Partnerships

Depending on the needs of students in each school district, partnerships are utilized in a variety of ways. Employers serve on advisory committees and task forces and have input into programs, services, and curriculum development. Some businesses have agreed to operate homework hotlines for advanced math and science classes. Some community partners provide scholarships and financial aid to students, while others provide equipment. Teacher exchange programs between high schools and community college instructors highlight one partnership (Shelton, 1986). A monograph produced by Izzo and Drier (1987) contains summaries of 19 programs that provide career guidance services to students at risk. Among these are seminars for parents to help their children arrive at career goals, employer mentoring programs, summer enrichment programs either in the community or at college campuses, and teen parenting and child care programs.

Business and industry leaders have demonstrated their interest in helping schools and youth. Opportunities abound for innovative programs to increase the vocational connection necessary for students at risk. School personnel need only to delineate their needs, be willing to communicate and cooperate with other agencies and organizations, and expend time and energy in developing the services and programs needed by youth at risk. Partnerships can provide so much more than a school system alone can do. This "extra" component is vital to students at risk who are the workers of tomorrow.

SUMMARY

Schools must make the vocational connection happen for students at risk. Broadening the concept of vocational education to include career development is an essential first step in creating a vocational connection. The linkage of school and work begins early in the elementary years and continues even after graduation. Infusing career education concepts throughout the curriculum and providing for career exploration activities and career preparation programs can be accomplished in a variety of ways. Support services can be developed both within the school and throughout the community, depending on the needs of students at risk in particular school districts. These students can be successful, healthy, and productive both in school and as adults if schools and communities work together to ensure that the vocational connection is strong, flexible, and continuous throughout the curriculum and that students at risk are exposed to and have the opportunities to experience their relationship to the world within the context of work.

REFERENCES

American Association of School Administrators. (1989). *Students at risk: Problems and solutions.* Arlington, VA: Author.

American School Board Journal and the Executive Educator. (1989, August). *The learning bank: A treasury of terrific ideas for instruction.* Baltimore: National School Boards Association.

Baker, M.E., & Garfield-Scott, L. (1981). Cognitive style of disadvantaged students. *Journal for Vocational Special Needs Education, 4,* 23–28.

Bhaerman, R.D., & Kopp, K.A. (1988). *The school's choice: Guidelines for dropout prevention at the middle and junior high school.* Columbus, OH: National Center for Research in Vocational Education.

Broussard, V., & Wulf, K. (1983, April). *Some solutions to vocational education problems of minority, disadvantaged and handicapped students.* Paper presented at the meeting of the American Educational Research Association, Montreal, Canada.

Carnevale, A.P., Gainer, L.J., & Meltzer, A.S. (1989). *Workplace basics: The skills employers want.* Alexandria, VA: American Society for Training and Development.

Center for Occupational Research and Development. (1988). *Applied Mathematics.* Waco, TX: Author.

Committee for Economic Development. (1987). *Children in need: Investment strategies for the educationally disadvantaged.* New York: Author.

Dole, E. (1989). Preparing the work force of the future. *Vocational Education Journal, 64,* 18–20.

Fennimore, T.F., & Pritz, S.G. (1988). *A guide for dropout prevention: Creating an integrated learning environment in secondary schools.* Columbus, OH: National Center for Research in Vocational Education.

Flanagan, M., & Johnson, J. (1987). *ACCESS skills: Employability and study skills assessment and curriculum guide.* Columbia, MO: University of Missouri Instructional Materials Laboratory.

Hallahan, K.M. (1986, May/June). Why so Violent? *Foundation News, 27* (3), 29–31.

Hayward, B.J., & Wirt, J.G. (1989, August). *Handicapped and disadvantaged students: Access to quality vocational education.* Washington, DC: National Assessment of Vocational Education, U.S. Department of Education.

Healy, C.C. (1982). *Career development: Counseling through the life stages.* Boston: Allyn & Bacon.

International Technology Education Association. (1985). *Technology education: A perspective on implementation.* Reston, VA: Author.

Izzo, M.V., & Drier, H.N. (1987). *Career guidance within JTPA for high risk populations: Programs, methods and products.* Columbus, OH: National Center for Research in Vocational Education. (ERIC Document Reproduction Service N. 278 869)

Kokaska, C.J., & Brolin, D.E. (1985). *Career education for handicapped individuals* (2nd ed.). Cincinnati, OH: Charles E. Merrill.

MacLeod, J. (1987). *Ain't no making it: Leveled aspirations in a low-income neighborhood.* Boulder, CO: Westview.

National Center for Research in Vocational Education. (1987a). *BASICS: Bridging vocational and academic skills.* Columbus, OH: Ohio State University.

National Center for Research in Vocational Education. (1987b). *Technique for remediation: Peer tutoring.* Columbus, OH: Ohio State University.

National Collaboration for Youth. (1989). *Making the grade: A report card on American youth.* Albany, NY: Boyd.

National Commission for Employment Policy. (1988). *Another ounce of prevention: Education and employment interventions for 9 to 15 year olds.* Washington, DC: Author.

Reingold, J.R., & Associates. (1989). *Current federal policies and programs for youth.* Washington, DC: Commission on Work, Family, and Citizenship.

Sarkees, M.D., & Scott, J.L. (1985). *Vocational special needs* (2nd ed.). Springfield, IL: American Technical.

Schwartz, P. (1987). *Rural transition strategies that work.* Bellingham, WA: American Council on Rural Special Education.

Shelton, C. (1986, April). Community colleges join in partners. In *Pipelines* (p. 4). Seattle, WA: PIPE, Private Initiatives in Public Education.

Starr, M., & Gysbers, N. (1989). *Missouri comprehensive guidance: A model for program development, implementation and evaluation.* Jefferson City, MO: Department of Elementary and Secondary Education.

Technical Assistance for Special Populations Program. (1989, August). *Vocational education and the at-risk student.* Berkeley, CA: National Center for Research in Vocational Education.

Vocational Education Counseling and Placement Services. (nd). *Partnerships with business and industry: Local internship program.* Big Rapids, MI: Ferris State College Center for Occupational Education.

Walker, R. (1988, November). Principals seek links with businesses to provide scholarships and materials. *Education Week, 8,* 15.

Ward, M.L. (1988, Spring). *Career mentorships in a suburban community. CEActionotes, 5,* 4.

Weber, J.M. (1987). *Strengthening vocational education's role in decreasing the dropout rate.* Columbus, OH: National Center for Research in Vocational Education.

Weber, J.M. (1988). The relevance of vocational education to dropout prevention. *Vocational Education Journal, 63,* 36–38.

Wehlage, G., Stone, C., Lesko, N., Nauman, C., & Page, R. (1982, September). *Effective programs for the marginal high school student: A report to the Wisconsin governor's employment and training office.* Madison, WI: Wisconsin Center for Educational Research.

chapter 5

Cooperative Learning

Carl T. Cameron

In the preceding chapters, effective strategies for dropout prevention are examined from several perspectives. The content of those chapters provides the reader with a background on who are at-risk youth, what is the issue related to dropout prevention, and what program planning is necessary to develop effective programs and strategies. In Chapters 3 and 4, the content of instructional programs is also examined from a variety of perspectives. In this chapter, we turn to the process of instruction, and more specifically to the exploration of an exciting area of instructional application—cooperative learning.

The term *cooperative learning* has been used in an informal manner and has been applied in the past to instructional activities that refer, in some general way, to developing cooperation among various students, groups, or classes of students; or in a field such as vocational education, the term might refer to instruction that takes place both in school and at the workplace. In recent years, however, *cooperative learning* has been used specifically to define a set of activities or learning experiences completed by a group of students in which a group goal is assigned and the group is rewarded on the basis of its combined performance. Cooperative learning is based on the belief that teaching democracy and independent learning is essential for students to become fully participating members of modern society. While cooperative learning techniques have been used in a wide variety of settings, only recently has attention been focused on their use with at-risk youth. This chapter examines the following aspects of cooperative learning:

- components of cooperative learning
- effectiveness of cooperative learning
- benefits of cooperative learning for at-risk youth

- cooperative learning models
- innovative cooperative learning strategies
- instructional activities
- role of the instructor

COMPONENTS OF COOPERATIVE LEARNING

The term *cooperative learning* describes a process whereby learning is facilitated through a group or team effort to complete a task successfully. This process normally involves

1. assignment of learners to a working team
2. assignment of a goal to the team
3. measurement of attainment of that goal by a criterion-referenced evaluation system
4. evaluation of each member of the team individually
5. reward of team members on the basis of their group performance

This definition contains four essential points that have been included in almost all definitions of cooperative learning: assignment of a team goal, criterion-referenced evaluation system, individual evaluation, and group reward (Slavin, 1989).

Assignment of Learners to a Team

Before a team goal is assigned, the team itself should be selected. The instructor, or learning manager, should select a team whose members are diverse in experience, exposure, and abilities. This selection provides an ideal opportunity to include at-risk youth with team members of various strengths and weaknesses. The teams should be reassigned periodically to provide an opportunity for students to work with a variety of individuals. The actual length of time a team works together is dependent on the task, the environment, and the needs of individual students; the team should work together, however, until a task or subtask is completed.

Preparing a team to work together requires specific instruction in how to work cooperatively (Schultz, 1990). Specific social skills for working together include the following:

- making eye contact when speaking

- praising others' responses
- disagreeing without hostility
- depending on others to complete a task (Smith, 1987)

It is important to keep in mind that students do not automatically have skills for learning in a cooperative manner, particularly when most students have been taught to learn competitively—to compete with classmates for status as a form of demonstrating skills and knowledge. This training, although provided in the initial stages of cooperative learning, must be reinforced continually and taught throughout the learning activities.

Assignment of Team Goals

Once teams are selected and trained to work together, they are assigned tasks with goals that can be completed only by working as a cohesive unit, and including all members of the team. Each team should be encouraged to develop solutions to the problem by using a variety of expedients, including instructions from the teacher, outside resources, and the experiences of all group members.

Cooperative learning experiences for at-risk youth may include such activities as a construction project that requires team members to share construction responsibilities and decisions, or the development and implementation of a small business operation. Other examples include:

- developing new alternatives to using toxic chemicals in various materials
- developing alternative communications for workers in noisy environments
- proposing new alternatives to saving the rain forests

It is important that the instructor play a key role in monitoring the team activities, and he or she should be prepared to intervene with additional instruction of cooperative learning skills.

Criterion-Referenced Team Evaluation and Individual Evaluation

The evaluation of team efforts should be based on a measurable criterion, not on the relative performance of the participating teams. In addition, each member of the team should be evaluated individually in meeting performance goals; any change or improvement on the part of the member should be of equal weight to all others on the team. The inclusion of criterion-referenced evaluation provides an equal opportunity for all teams to meet the performance standards—even if, in some situations, all students in the classroom earn perfect scores. This may be a rather difficult concept for instructors who are used to grading students by assuming a normally wide distribution of scores or grades or who use the competition between individuals as a primary classroom motivator.

Reward of Team Members

The use of a criterion-referenced evaluation system for both team members individually and the team as a whole allows the reward to be based on completion of the task, not on the team's relative status to others. The team that meets the minimal performance criteria must be rewarded equally among team members. It is possible to have both group rewards for the team members and individual rewards for team members who meet a specified high level of individual contribution.

EFFECTIVENESS OF COOPERATIVE LEARNING

The effectiveness of cooperative learning has been well-documented in the professional literature. According to Slavin (1990c), cooperative learning is "one of the most thoroughly researched of all instructional methods" (p. 52). The effectiveness of cooperative learning has been examined from a variety of perspectives, including academic achievement, intergroup relations, gains in self-esteem, and other outcomes.

Academic Achievement

There is wide agreement that cooperative learning methods have a positive effect on student academic achievement (Davidson, 1985; Johnson & Johnson, 1990; Johnson, Maruyama, Johnson, & Skon, 1981; Newmann & Thompson, 1987; Slavin, 1983; Slavin, 1989; Slavin 1990c). Johnson and Johnson (1974) report that mastery of learning, retention of information, and transfer of information are all higher in cooperatively structured learning than in competitive or individually structured learning. Slavin (1990c) reports that achievement effects are not found in types of cooperative learning, but apparently depend on two features: the establishment of group goals and individual accountability. Newmann and Thompson (1987) suggest that results indicate the importance of not only group assignment and individual accountability, but inclusion of group competition.

Relatively fewer studies have examined cooperative learning for adolescent students. At the college level, even fewer studies exist; however, there are several reports of positive achievement in high school and college programs (Fraser, Beaman, Diener, & Kelem, 1977; Sherman & Thomas, 1986).

There is some evidence that, as the age of the student or level of student education increases, the effectiveness of cooperative learning changes. For example, in a study examining secondary school learning, Newmann and Thompson (1987) question whether cooperative learning is effective in senior high school (grades 10 to 12).

Central to the issue of effectiveness in adolescents and college-age students is the appropriateness of cooperative learning for higher-order conceptual learning (Slavin, 1990c). Most current research has focused on basic skill development, but several studies report success in teaching higher-order skills such as creative writing, identification of main ideas and inference in reading (Stevens, Madden, Slavin, & Farnish, 1987), and social studies (Sharan, Hertz-Lazarowitz, & Ackerman, 1980; Smith, Johnson, & Johnson, 1981). Radebaugh and Kazemek (1988) suggest that literacy is a social phenomenon and describe the importance of cooperative learning in teaching higher-order literacy skills.

It is not clear whether the implementation of group goals and individual accountability is necessary for college student achievement (Davidson, 1985); however, it is apparent that for high-risk students, cooperative learning offers one avenue for student achievement. Achievement of students at-risk in high school and college environments may be influenced strongly by a number of other factors related to achievement, such as high social interaction, more individual involvement, mutual support, emotional involvement, sense of independence, self-esteem, risk taking, and awareness of the social nature of academic activities (Johnson, Johnson, Holubeck, & Roy, 1984).

Intergroup Relations

"When students of different racial or ethnic backgrounds work together toward a common goal, they gain in liking and respect for each other" (Slavin, 1990c, p. 53). Madden and Slavin (1983) and Johnson et al. (1981) have reported a consensus on the positive effects of cooperative learning on relationships between racial and ethnic groups and between students of different functioning levels. The social acceptance of mainstreamed academically handicapped youngsters by their classmates, which is a primary goal of the Education of All Handicapped Children's Act and the Carl D. Perkins Vocational Education Act, has been demonstrated to be a positive effect of cooperative learning (Madden & Slavin, 1983; Johnson, Johnson, & Maruyama, 1983). The friendships of students in general are also reported to be a positive effect (Slavin, 1990a).

Gains in Self-Esteem

Gains in the self-esteem of a wide variety of students engaged in cooperative learning have been reported in the literature (Slavin, 1990a). In addition, at-risk populations of mainstreamed youngsters have been described as making great strides in self-esteem (Augustine, Gruber, & Hanson, 1990).

Other Outcomes

Slavin (1990c), in *Research on Cooperative Learning: Consensus and Controversy*, describes a wide variety of other positive effects on children and youth as a result of cooperative learning experiences. These effects include a positive attitude toward school and specific subjects, increased amounts of time spent on tasks, and increased school attendance. Sharan et al. (1984) report an increased ability of students with extended experience in cooperative learning to work effectively with others. Sarkees, West, and Wircenski (1988) report that students demonstrate more positive interpersonal relationships, self-concept, motivation toward school, and social development than do students in competitive or individually structured learning.

BENEFITS OF COOPERATIVE LEARNING FOR AT-RISK YOUTH

Of major importance to the issue of instruction of at-risk youth is the necessity not only to provide specific academic and vocational skills, but to provide an experience that will enhance each student's perception of his or her own self-worth and his or her ability to work cooperatively with a wide variety of individuals who may be encountered in school, at work, or in many other situations.

A New Way of Thinking

In a recent article in *Educational Leadership*, Crowell (1989) states that "the greatest challenge facing education is not technology, not resources, not accountability—it is the need to discover with our students a new way of thinking. This quest does not require merely different information, but rather a whole new way of viewing the world" (p. 60). There is a growing body of evidence that at-risk youth view the world as complex and chaotic. This viewpoint is supported by the complexity of events that appear to "happen," and that support a perception of lack of control over the environment on a day-today basis. This chaotic viewpoint is not unique to at-risk youth, but it may be shared by most youth in our society. Crowell asked students to describe the world in which they live, and they used words such as "complex," "dynamic," "hectic," "stressful," "fast-paced" and "chaotic." The perception of lack of control and confusion about the rules of the society in which at-risk youth find themselves may be a function of lack of specific skills and, more important, lack of skills needed to organize and operate in that world. The goal of cooperative learning not only is to provide those skills to deal with the world at large, but to provide a method for confronting the world and its changing demands.

A Process for Learning To Think

Pogrow, in a recent article, "Challenging At-Risk Students: Findings from the HOTS Program" (1990), suggests that the lack of knowledge of at-risk students is not the fundamental problem. The fundamental problem is that at-risk students do not understand "understanding" or the process of thinking. According to Pogrow, thinking skills are based on four general thinking techniques:

1. *metacognition*—consciously applying strategies to solve problems
2. *inference from context*—figuring out specific information from surrounding information
3. *decontextualization*—generalizing ideas from one context to another
4. *synthesis of information*—combining information from a variety of sources and identifying the key pieces of information needed to solve a problem

Pogrow suggests that learning problems cannot be remediated by traditional remedial services; in fact, they may actually exacerbate learning problems. His solution is to develop a curriculum focused on the process of thinking, rather than on curricular objectives. This solution can radically alter the relationship between teacher and student, from a source of information to a guide and a model for problem solving.

COOPERATIVE LEARNING MODELS

The cooperative learning models that have been developed in the United States have emanated from two major research and development efforts: that of Robert Slavin and his colleagues at Johns Hopkins University (Student Team Learning) and that of David and Roger Johnson and their colleagues at the University of Minnesota (Learning Together).

Student Team Learning

The design of Student Team Learning, developed by Robert Slavin and his colleagues, has components of both cooperation and competition. The success of this approach is based on the requirements that all team members participate, that rewards for successful completion are focused on the group, and that each individual's contribution is evaluated and necessary for team success. The team members are encouraged to assist each other in completing the task, but each member of the team is assessed individually with members from other teams who have a similar level of skill. The results of individual performances are added together to compose team scores.

Learning Together

David and Roger Johnson and their colleagues have developed an equally well-known methodology called Learning Together. Learning Together is a less specific methodology that relies on teachers' using differential methods that will result in five elements the authors describe as positive interdependence, face-to-face interaction, individual accountability, social skills, and group processing. A major focus of this process is the interdependence of group members in solving a problem before asking the teacher for assistance. The group works on a group assignment and is rewarded as a group for performance. Neither individuals nor groups compete with one another.

INNOVATIVE COOPERATIVE LEARNING STRATEGIES

The use of cooperative learning strategies has been shown to be effective both for educational achievement and for a myriad of other skills important to the success of at-risk youth. Some of the innovative cooperative learning strategies that have been used with, or are recommended for, at-risk youth are described below.

Future Problem Solving Program Method

The Future Problem Solving Program was developed by E. Paul Torrance in 1974 (Crabbe, 1989) to assist students in developing creative talents and to address issues that will affect the students as adults. This method uses an adapted version of the creative problem-solving process developed for business and industry by Osborne (1976) to examine problems related to the future. In the

Future Problem Solving Program, teams of four complete the following sequence of activities:

1. research and learn as much as possible about the general topic
2. brainstorm problems related to the specific situations presented
3. identify the major underlying problem from the list of brainstormed problems
4. brainstorm solutions to the underlying problem
5. develop a list of criteria by which to evaluate the solutions
6. evaluate the solutions according to the criteria to select the best solution (Crabbe, 1988)

The products of these activities are practice booklets that are sent to trained evaluators to be scored and critiqued. There is a competitive aspect to the cooperative learning approach, with both state-level and national-level competitions.

Student Teams Achievement Divisions

Student Teams Achievement Divisions (STADs), an approach to Student Team Learning developed by Robert Slavin at Johns Hopkins University (National Center on Effective Secondary Schools, 1988), is currently being implemented at Southern Senior High School in Harwood, Maryland, by Elaine Preston. The STADs are implemented in tenth- and twelfth-grade history classes in which students are divided into teams and provide oral examination to individuals within the group. Each group member contributes to the team total, with rankings of the group being assigned as "super, " great, " or "good." The heterogeneous teams are selected by the instructor, and the students are taught how to work as a team. One important aspect is that the STADs are used in conjunction with other types of instruction, and STADs are usually developed to expand previously acquired knowledge into higher-order thinking.

Cooperative Learning Teams

The Cooperative Learning Teams strategy was developed at Eastern Washington University in Cheney, Washington, by Radebaugh and Kazemek (1988). The teams were developed to assist students who were labeled " high-risk" or to assist students who did not do well in high school and who may have difficulty in college. The rationale for the development of cooperative learning teams was to provide cooperative and supportive endeavors to reduce exacerbation of reading problems and subsequent student isolation. Nelson and Herber

(1982) report that "high-risk" and underachieving college students in reading/study skills classes most likely have emphasized the individual aspects of the reading process while ignoring the social aspect. Literacy is perceived by the program as a social process, and in order to improve literacy skills, cooperative learning must be central to the program. The Cooperative Learning Teams approach focuses on the following activities:

1. beginning the cooperative learning at the beginning of the academic term so students can learn how to work with others
2. developing permanent, heterogeneous study teams to provide support and friendship as well as a vehicle for collaborating on academic assignments
3. sharing study habits such as note taking to provide alternative strategies and to develop confidence as students realize they possess many of the skills required
4. preparing for examinations and tests in conjunction with individual study
5. developing a positive environment as students learn to listen to each other and themselves, thus providing encouragement and self-confidence

Group Investigation

Group Investigation was developed by Sharan and Sharan (1990) from earlier work by Thelen (1960), "which attempts to combine in one teaching strategy the form and dynamics of the democratic process and the process of academic inquiry" (Joyce & Weil, 1972). Students involved in Group Investigation take an active part in planning what they will study and how. Students form cooperative groups according to a common interest or topic. All group members help plan the exploration, and they divide the work among themselves. Each group member carries out his or her part in the investigation, and the results are synthesized, summarized, and presented to the class. The stages of activity are as follows:

1. identifying the topic to be investigated and organizing students into research groups
2. planning the investigation in groups
3. carrying out the investigation
4. preparing a final report
5. presenting the final report

The particular advantage of this model is the emphasis on the students' control over their learning, and the model allows the students to choose subjects that interest them the most. During the past 12 years, effectiveness studies of this model have demonstrated that academic performance is greater and that language use is at a higher level, even for non-native speakers. Positive social interactions were shown to increase, and teachers also were more satisfied and provided more personal and intimate assistance to students (Sharan & Sharan, 1990).

Computer-Supported Cooperative Learning Environment

The Computer-Supported Cooperative Learning Environment (Dede, 1988) has developed as a result of changes in the workplace as it develops toward an emphasis on group task performance and problem solving. Information technology tools increasingly are being designed for team use, rather than for individuals working in isolation (Gorry, Burger, Chaney, Long, & Tausk, 1988), and new types of interpersonal skills will be needed (Dede, 1989). Dede has developed a scenario for a sophisticated "learning-while-doing" and computer-supported cooperative learning environment.

Team-Assisted Individualization

Team-Assisted Individualization (TAI) (Slavin, Leavy, & Madden, 1984) is a cooperative learning system that combines cooperative structured learning with individualized instruction. In this model, heterogeneous groups of individuals work as a unit to master individual assignments. Team members work on their own assignments and assist other group members in completing their assignments. Group members are rewarded if their team's performance exceeds a pre-established criterion (Salend & Washin, 1988). Salend and Washin found that TAI is an effective method of increasing on-task and cooperative behaviors of handicapped adjudicated youth. These results were found to be long-lasting, and students strongly preferred TAI to working independently. TAI also was found to improve significantly the students' cooperative behaviors and their attitudes toward fellow students. The successes of cooperative learning processes such as Positive Peer Culture with at-risk youth in correctional programs and TAI (Salend & Washin, 1988) with handicapped adjudicated youth have supported the belief that cooperative learning strategies offer effective intervention for at-risk youth.

Structural Approach to Cooperative Learning

One of the most promising strategies is not a single strategy at all but an approach to cooperative learning that focuses on the organization of cooperative learning through the application of what Kagan (1990) calls "structures" or content-free ways of organizing social interaction in the classroom. Structures are more than activities; they are parameters that allow almost any subject matter to be used in a variety of ways. In addition, these structures can be combined to form multistructural lessons in which each structure provides a learning experience on which subsequent structures expand until the learning objective has been met. It is important to note that a variety of structures is necessary because the structures have different functions or domains of usefulness. Kagan categorizes functions, or domains of usefulness, into the following (examples are given under each domain of usefulness):

- team building
    1. expressing ideas and opinions
    2. participating equally
- class building
    1. meeting classmates/getting acquainted
    2. identifying alternative hypotheses
    3. clarifying values
    4. identifying problem-solving approaches
- communication building
    1. knowing and respecting different points of view
    2. developing vocabulary
- communication mastery
    1. role taking
    2. reviewing
    3. checking for knowledge
    4. comprehending
    5. memorizing facts
    6. practicing skills
    7. tutoring
    8. helping others
- concept development
    1. praising
    2. sharing personal information, developing reactions
    3. forming conclusions
    4. generating and revising
    5. reasoning inductively
    6. reasoning deductively
    7. applying concepts
    8. analyzing concepts
    9. understanding multiple relationships
    10. differentiating concepts

• multifunctional skills
   1. applying combinations of above examples

Major structures are defined and exemplified by Kagan (1989) in *Cooperative Learning Resources for Teachers* and include the following:

- *Roundrobin*—Each student in turn shares with his or her teammates an example of how drugs can be abused.
- *Corners*—Students move to the four corners of the room, each corner representing a different way to get a job. Students discuss within corners, then listen to and paraphrase ideas from other corners.
- *Match Mine*—Students attempt to match the assembly of a brake drum on a workbench of another student, using only oral directions from the other student.
- *Numbered Heads Together*—The teacher asks a question on the requirements for maintaining a credit card. Students consult to make sure everyone knows the answer, then one student is called on to answer for the team.
- *Color-Coded Co-op Cards*—Students memorize different combinations for making change, using a flashcard game. The game is structured so that there is a maximal probability of success at each step, moving from short-term to long-term memory. Scoring is based on improvement.
- *Pairs Check*—Students work in pairs within groups of four. Within pairs, students alternate—one locates a place on a local or regional map while the other coaches. After every two problems the pair checks to see whether it has the same answers as the other pair.
- *Three-Step Interview*—Students interview each other in pairs in relation to their existing job skills, first one and then the other. Each student shares with the group information he or she learned in the interview.
- *Think-Pair-Share*—Students are asked to think about how they would react in case of an assault; each pairs with another student to discuss reactions; they share their thoughts with the class.
- *Team Word-Webbing*—Students write simultaneously on a piece of chart paper, drawing main concepts, supporting elements, and bridges representing their solutions to eliminating the killings in large cities.
- *Roundtable*—Each student in turn writes one answer to a series of computations related to estimating a construction project, as a piece of paper and a pencil are passed around the group. With simultaneous Roundtable, more than one pencil and one piece of paper are used at once.

- *Inside-Outside Circle*—Students stand in pairs in two concentric circles. The inside circle faces out; the outside circle faces in. Students use flashcards or respond to the teacher's questions on basic principles of the procedure for apartment rental; each student then rotates to a partner.
- *Partners*—Students work in pairs to create or master the process for reconfiguring a piece of public-domain software. They consult with partners from other teams. Each partner then shares his or her products or understanding with the other partner on the team.
- *Jigsaw*—Each student on the team becomes an "expert" on one sport by working with members from other teams assigned to the corresponding sport. Upon his or her return to the team, each student in turn teaches the group. All students are assessed on all aspects of the topic.
- *Co-op*—Students work in groups to produce a completed business plan to share with the whole class; each student makes a particular contribution to the group.

INSTRUCTIONAL ACTIVITIES

Instructional activities for at-risk youth are, and should be, as varied as the population they serve. The focus of this section is to provide some creative suggestions as to what kinds of activities can be used with at-risk youth in a cooperative learning setting, with the knowledge that instructors will be able to generate a wide variety of other activities for the students they serve and the curriculum content being taught.

Group Authorship of Résumés and Application Materials

The cooperative learning team can be assigned the responsibility for developing a résumé or other written employment application materials for one or more members of the team, with specific activities assigned to each group member. One team member may be responsible for locating sample résumés, another member may be responsible for locating format requirements, a third may be responsible for locating word-processing programs, and so forth. The group determines the appropriate format, style, and information to be included and time to completion of the final product. Each team member should be assessed on the background research completed and the written materials produced based on a criterion-referenced model. Each team that meets the established criteria should be rewarded appropriately.

Small Group Research Teams

The cooperative learning team is charged with resolving an issue, such as dealing with one aspect of environmental pollution in the workplace. Each student researches the background information on one aspect of the problem, interviews experts on the topic, and generates a solution to his or her individual component of the problem. The team convenes to identify individual solutions to each segment of the problem and to synthesize the individual solutions into a global response to the entire problem.

Weekly Group Meetings

Weekly meetings of the cooperative learning teams are integrated into a variety of classroom instruction and are scheduled to resolve problems of classroom operations, select rewards for teams who meet criteria, plan the focus of instruction for the following week(s), or assess the knowledge gained during traditional instructional periods. Of particular importance to some groups of at-risk individuals is behavior management. Weekly group meetings offer an opportunity for teams to discuss problems of behavior in classrooms and to set goals for the group for the following week. The setting of goals requires each member to work on individual goals; total performance is rewarded by the instructor. This is a good example of a situation in which some members of the team may find that their individual goals are more difficult to accomplish than those of other team members; all team members may support the member with the most difficult goal.

Mixed-Ability Groups

One of the major tenets of cooperative learning is the strength of a heterogenous cooperative learning team. When groups are the most diverse in terms of verbal abilities, leadership qualities, skills in specific tasks, ethnic and cultural makeup, gender, disabilities, and enthusiasm, a broader range of ideas and solutions is possible. Weaver and Prince (1990) suggest that creative problem solving is most effective when there is a mixture of the following three types of individuals:

1. *appositive thinkers*—individuals who limit their problem solving to material that is closely relevant to the problem
2. *divergent thinkers*—individuals who search for widely divergent, often seemingly irrelevant, solutions to problems

3. *generative thinkers*—individuals who search for the connection between widely divergent ideas that make the solution more workable

Practice Teams/Periodic Change

A system should be developed for periodically changing the members of the cooperative learning teams to reinforce the concept of cooperation with a wide variety of individuals and to expose students to a more diverse population of creative thinkers. For instance, a construction laboratory may develop separate teams to solve heating and cooling, roofing, and framing problems. The group members may be rotated and each group given a different assignment in order to develop several solutions to each construction problem.

Vocational Education Programs

Vocational education programs offer opportunities for cooperative learning for students preparing to enter the workplace in roles that have existed traditionally and in roles that represent a variety of new options. As Dede (1989) points out, "During the next two decades, major changes in the technological base of American society will alter the knowledge, skills and values we need to be capable workers and citizens" (p. 23). The two most important types of skills in the coming years will be the ability to manipulate computer-based technological machinery and the interpersonal skills required in occupations in computer-mediated communication (Kiesler, Siegal, & McGuire, 1984). Valuable experience in communication with other team members may be gained easily by formation of teams that develop specific aspects of a project, such as development of the budget on a spreadsheet, the design on computer-assisted design/computer-assisted manufacturing (CAD-CAM), the financial plan on a word processor, and the requirements to integrate components from all other groups into the team product. Specific instructional activities in vocational education must integrate both of these skill areas in order to produce capable and effective graduates.

Cooperative Education

Involvement in cooperative education programs within vocational education has been demonstrated to be effective in learning about the real world of work. Cooperative education provides the perfect opportunity to develop the cooperative learning strategies needed to participate in the evolving workplace. As Gorry et al. (1988) suggest, as the workplace shifts to an emphasis on group task performance and problem solving, collaborative learning will become increasingly important. New types of interpersonal and communications skills will be necessary, and individuals who lack these skills, with both coworkers and machines, will be at a disadvantage in the workplace (Reder & Schwab, 1988).

Creating a cooperative education program based on cooperative learning activities provides an opportunity for team problem solving in traditionally individually performed activities such as sales, marketing, advertising, and display. In reality, many of these activities are already team efforts in the workplace, but few students are being prepared for them through the acquisition of team decision-making skills.

ROLE OF THE INSTRUCTOR

Slavin (1990b) suggests that cooperative learning, when instituted in a classroom or laboratory, "makes life more pleasant for teachers as well as students" (p. 1). The level of comfort with cooperative learning is also dependent on an instructor's knowledge and implementation of the following activities.

Selecting Appropriate Instructional Goals and Objectives

The selection of appropriate instructional objectives obviously is a high priority for all instruction. Instructors using cooperative learning techniques must select not only appropriate curriculum objectives, but those that foster the objectives of cooperative learning. Kagan (1990) provides an approach to cooperative learning that identifies learning structures that are independent of the content and that attempt to address skills in cooperative learning, such as team building, class building, communication building, communication mastery, concept development, and multifunctional skills. These structures provide cooperative alternatives to more typical competitive structures, such as the "whole-class/question-answer" structure, in which students vie for the teacher's attention and praise, creating negative interdependence among them (Kagan, 1990). In contrast, cooperative structures are suggested, such as Jigsaw (Aronson, Blaney, Stephan, Sikes, & Snapp, 1978), in which each student on the team becomes an "expert" on one topic by working with members from other teams assigned the corresponding expert topic. Upon returning to the original team, each one in turn teaches the group; all students are assessed on all aspects of the topic.

Selecting Team Members

Selecting a cooperative learning team should depend on factors such as verbal abilities, leadership qualities, skills in specific activities, and enthusiasm. Select the group size most appropriate for the lesson or activity. The optimal size of a cooperative learning group will vary according to the resources needed to complete the task, the cooperative skills of group members, and the nature of the task. If the task is selected after the groups are formed, it may be necessary to reorganize or modify the makeup of the group in order to maximize the unique requirements of the activity.

Structuring Environment

The environment in which cooperative learning teams operate may provide a very influential role for at-risk youth. Cluster the teams so that they do not interfere with other teams that are also working. Within the teams, students should be able to see and examine the relevant instructional materials and converse easily with each other. The use of alternative environments is certainly appropriate for periods of time, but arrangements for monitoring the activities are important for successful group interaction.

Teaching Concepts of Cooperative Learning

It cannot be assumed that students, of any age, are aware of the rules for working cooperatively. Conditions that are necessary for successful cooperative learning include positive interdependence, face-to-face (promotive) interaction, individual accountability, social skills, and group processing (Johnson & Johnson, 1990). Johnson and Johnson suggest teaching the following steps:

1. have students get to know each other and trust each other
2. demonstrate the need to use these skills
3. demonstrate what the skill is, and when it should be used
4. provide opportunities for practice of the skills
5. provide feedback to students so that they know how frequently and how well they are using the skill
6. provide continuing opportunities to practice the skill

It is very important that students be taught specifically the steps in the cooperative learning process; the goal, the process, and the materials to be used; and the evaluation and the reinforcement (reward).

Providing Appropriate Instructional Materials

Instructional materials must be provided that allow for maximal team independence. Affording access to materials that promote innovative problem solving may involve movement outside the traditional confines of the instructional situation. It is important that the teacher anticipate the material demand and not inadvertently impose a competitive environment through competition for inadequate materials.

Managing Group Activities

The monitoring of group activities is crucial to the success of cooperative learning activities, because learning the process of cooperating is equally as important as learning the curriculum content. For instance, when an impasse develops in the problem solving of a team, the instructor must be in a position to observe the cause of this impasse. If the impasse is a function of a breakdown in the ability of the group to learn cooperatively, then intervention by the instructor is necessary to remind the group of the skills that should be used and to have the group demonstrate a solution.

Observing Individual Student Performance

The ability of a student to function as a member of a cooperative learning team should be one of the instructional objectives for each student. Observation of each student as he or she attempts to work on both the curriculum materials and the process is necessary to provide feedback on individual students.

Evaluating Individual Student Progress

Each student should be evaluated on his or her knowledge or performance of the assigned activity. It is the basis of cooperative learning that individual students be measured in their progress toward a pre-established criterion.

Evaluating Group Products

The product evaluation of a cooperative learning team is based on a composite of the individual performance of each student and the demonstration or presentation of the team as a whole. It should not be possible in any assignment for a team to meet the criterion of the activity without having met both levels of performance—each student demonstrating successful completion at a minimal level of competence, and the team sharing that knowledge with others.

Applying a Criterion-Referenced Evaluation System

The evaluation of both individual students and team demonstrations should be based on an objective, or criterion-referenced, standard. All teams should have an opportunity to meet the standards, and all should be rewarded if they do.

Reinforcing Group Products

All reinforcement or reward for successful completion should go to the group. It is important that the members of the group recognize that the team functions as a unit and that their participation is important not only in individual performances, but in assisting and supporting other group members as they pursue their contributions to the team.

CONCLUSION

Involvement in cooperative learning offers real promise to the educational community to resolve long-standing concerns over the performance of at-risk youth. The cognitive and behavioral issues of at-risk youth are addressed directly in cooperative learning by focusing on activities that develop skills in working together and in communicating and problem solving through the use of a variety of resources. It is no secret that most employers and others who deal with problems of efficiency in the workplace believe that the single most important factor in maintaining a high-quality product is the ability of employees to problem solve together in an efficient and effective manner. The at-risk student requires more specific and intense training in these important cooperative learning skills. The successes already reported in the professional literature suggest that the real promise of identifying additional roles for cooperative learning lies in the transition of at-risk youth from an educational environment to independent, adult living.

REFERENCES

Aronson, E., Blaney, N., Stephan, C., Sikes, J., & Snapp, M. (1978). *The jigsaw classroom*. Beverly Hills, CA: Sage.

Augustine, D.K., Gruber, K.D., & Hanson, L.R. (1990). Cooperation works! *Educational Leadership, 47*(4), 4–7.

Crabbe, A.B. (1988). *Coaches guide to the future problem solving program* (2nd ed.). Laurinburg, NC: Future Problem Solving Program.

Crabbe, A.B. (1989). The future problem solving program. *Educational Leadership, 47*(1), 27–29.

Crowell, S. (1989). A new way of thinking: The challenge of the future. *Educational Leadership, 47*(1), 60–63.

Davidson, N. (1985). Small group learning and teaching in mathematics: A selective review of the research. In R.E. Slavin, et al. (Eds.), *Learning to cooperate, cooperating to learn*. New York: Plenum.

Dede, C. (1988). Emerging information technologies of interest for postsecondary occupational education. In K.M. Back, C.J. Dede, P.R. Fama, & O.W. Markley (Eds.), *Education planning for economic development* (Vol. 11, pp. 1–68). Austin, TX: Coordinating Board, Texas College and University System.

Dede, C. (1989). The evolution of information technology: Implications for curriculum. *Educational Leadership, 47*(1), 23–26.

Fraser, S.C., Beaman, A.L., Diener, E., & Kelem, R.T. (1977). Two, three or four heads are better than one: Modification of college performance by peer monitoring. *Journal of Educational Psychology, 69*(2), 101–108.

Gorry, G.A., Burger, A.M., Chaney, R.J., Long, K.B., & Tausk, C.M. (1988, September 26–28). Computer support for bio-medical work groups. *Proceedings of the Conference on Computer-Supported Cooperative Work, Portland, OR* (pp. 39–51). New York: Association for Computer Machinery.

Johnson, D.W., & Johnson, R.T. (1974). Instructional goal structure; Cooperative, competitive and individualistic learning. Review of Educational Research, 44, 213–240.

Johnson, D.W., & Johnson, R.T. (1990). Social skills for successful group work. Educational Leadership, 47(4), 29–33.

Johnson, D.W., Johnson, R.T., Holubeck, E.J., & Roy, P.A. (1984). Circles of learning; Cooperation in the classroom, Alexandria, VA: Association for Supervision and Curriculum Development.

Johnson, D.W., Johnson, R.T., & Maruyama, G. (1983). Interdependence and interpersonal attraction among heterogeneous and homogeneous individuals: A theoretical formulation and a meta-analysis of the research. Review of Educational Research, 53, 5–54.

Johnson, D.W., Maruyama, G., Johnson, R.T., & Skon, L. (1981). Effects of cooperative, competitive, and individualistic goal structures on achievement: A meta-analysis. *Psychological Bulletin, 89*, 47–62.

Joyce, B., & Weil, M. (1972). *Models of teaching*. Englewood Cliffs, NJ: Prentice-Hall.

Kagan, S. (1989). *Cooperative learning resources for teachers*. San Juan Capistrano, CA: Resources for Teachers.

Kagan, S. (1990). The structural approach to cooperative learning. *Educational Leadership, 47*(4), 12–15.

Kiesler, S., Siegal, J., & McGuire, T.W. (1984). Social psychological aspects of computer-mediated communication. *American Psychologist, 39*, 1123–1134.

Madden, N., & Slavin, R. (1983). Mainstreaming students with mild academic handicaps: Academic and social outcomes. *Review of Educational Research, 53*, 519–569.

National Center on Effective Secondary Schools. (1988). *Cooperative learning: Two views on how it is implemented in secondary classrooms* (Resource Bulletin No. 4). Madison, WI: School of Education, University of Wisconsin-Madison.

Nelson, J., & Herber, H.L. (1982). Organization and management of programs. In A. Berger & H.A. Robinson (Eds.), *Secondary School Reading*. Urbana, IL: National Council of Teachers of English.

Newmann, F.M., & Thompson, J. (1987). *Effects of cooperative learning on achievement in secondary schools: A summary of research*. Madison, WI: University of Wisconsin National Center on Effective Secondary Schools.

Osborne, A.F. (1976). *Applied imagination* (3rd ed.). New York: Charles Scribners.

Pogrow, S. (1990, January). Challenging at-risk students: Findings from the HOTS Program. *Phi Delta Kappan*, 389–397.

Radebaugh, M.R., & Kazemek, F.E. (1988). Cooperative learning in college reading and study skills classes. *Journal of Reading, 32*(5), 414–418.

Reder, S., & Schwab, R.G. (1988, September 26–28). The communicative economy of the workgroup: Multi-channel genres of communication. *Proceedings of the Conference on Computer-Supported Cooperative Work, Portland, OR* (pp. 354–358). New York: Association for Computing Machinery.

Salend, S.J., & Washin, B. (1988). Team-assisted individualization with handicapped adjudicated youth. *Exceptional Children, 55*(2), 174–180.

Sarkees, M.D., West, L.L., & Wircenski, J. (1988). *Vocational education programs for the disadvantaged* (Information Series No. 329). Columbus, OH: National Center for Research in Vocational Education.

Schultz, J.L. (1990). Cooperative learning: Refining the process. *Educational Leadership, 47*(4), 43–45.

Sharan, S., Hertz-Lazarowitz, R., & Ackerman, Z. (1980). A group investigation method of cooperative learning in the classroom. In S. Sharan, P. Hare, C. Webb, & R. Hertz-Lazarowitz (Eds.), *Cooperation in education*. Provo, UT: Brigham Young University Press.

Sharan, S., Kussel, P., Hertz-Lazarowitz, R., Bejarano, Y., Raviv, S., & Sharan, Y. (1984). *Cooperative learning in the classroom: Research in desegregated schools*. Hillsdale, NJ: Erlbaum.

Sharan, Y., & Sharan, S. (1990). Group investigation expands cooperative learning. *Educational Leadership, 47*(4), 17–21.

Sherman, L.W., & Thomas, M. (1986). Mathematics achievement in cooperative versus individualistic goal structured high school classrooms. *Journal of Educational Research, 79*, 169–172.

Slavin, R.E. (1983). When does cooperative learning increase student achievement? *Psychological Bulletin, 94*, 429–445.

Slavin, R.E. (1989). Cooperative learning and student achievement. In R.E. Slavin (Ed.), *School and classroom organization*. Hillsdale, NJ: Erlbaum.

Slavin, R.E. (1990a). *Cooperative learning: Theory, research and practice*. Englewood Cliffs, NJ: Prentice-Hall.

Slavin, R.E. (1990b). Here to stay—or gone tomorrow? *Educational Leadership, 47*, (4), 1.

Slavin, R.E. (1990c). Research on cooperative learning: Consensus and controversy. *Educational Leadership, 47*(4), 52–54.

Slavin, R., Leavy, M., & Madden, N. (1984). Combining cooperative learning and individualized instruction: Effects on student mathematics achievement, attitudes and behavior. *Elementary School Journal, 84*, 409–422.

Smith, K., Johnson, D., & Johnson, R. (1981). Can conflict be constructive: Controversy versus concurrence seeking in learning groups. *Journal of Educational Psychology, 73*, 651–663.

Smith, R. (1987, May). A teacher's views on cooperative learning. *Phi Delta Kappan*, 663–666.

Stevens, R.J., Madden, N.A., Slavin, R.E., & Farnish, A.M. (1987). Cooperative integrated reading and composition: Two field experiments. *Reading Research Quarterly, 22,* 433–454.

Thelen, H. (1960). *Education and the human quest.* New York: Harper & Row.

Weaver, W.T., & Prince, G.M. (1990). Synetics: It's potential for education. *Phi Delta Kappan,* 378–388.

chapter 6

Parents and Schools:
Partners in Prevention

John Gugerty

TYPES OF INVOLVEMENT

Parental involvement in education is complex and multifaceted. Joyce Epstein categorizes parental involvement into five types (Jennings, 1990, p. 24):

1. basic obligations of parents, such as providing for their children's health and safety and creating a home environment that supports learning
2. basic obligations of schools, such as communicating with parents about school programs and their children's progress
3. parental involvement at the school site, for example, by attending sports events or student performances or by working as volunteers
4. parental involvement in learning activities at home
5. parental involvement in school governance and advocacy

Ascher (1987) notes, however, that

> two quite specific kinds of parent involvement characterize the recently renewed interest in the issue. Greatly minimized are advocacy and decision making, and even attendance at school functions. Instead, parent involvement means "what parents do naturally in the home to socialize their children," and "what schools can do to help parents be more effective in the home." Policy statements, program descriptions, and even the growing bulk of research now focus on both parental socialization for schooling and home learning more than any other type of activity. (p. 5)

FAMILY CHARACTERISTICS

Complicating the situation further is the fact that the terms *family* and *parent* include a much broader range of options than in the past. For example, Linder (1988, pp. 6–7) notes that the family with a husband who works and a wife who stays at home is not typical. The single-parent family and the family with two working parents are the norms statistically. Linder goes on to describe the major family types as follows:

- *Single-parent families.* Nearly 15 million children under age 18 live in single-parent families, most of whom are headed by women and most of whom are near, at, or below the poverty line as defined by the federal government. Single parents often have less time to work with the schools because they must juggle so many demands alone.

- *Noncustodial parents.* Ninety percent of American children whose parents are divorced are placed in the sole custody of their mothers. Most noncustodial parents are men, and they complain that they are often overlooked, or purposely ignored, by the school. School officials, on the other hand, may find themselves caught in the middle of a conflict between two parents.

- *Families with two wage earners.* Nearly 70 percent of married mothers with school-age children are employed. In 1970, 24 percent of all married mothers with children 1 year old or younger were working or looking for work. In 1986, half of those mothers were in the workforce.

- *Two-parent families with one wage earner.* Only 7 percent of today's school children come from such families, although some schools continue to deal with parents and to schedule events as if this were the norm.

- *Joined or blended families.* Within 5 years after divorce, four of every seven white children and one of every eight black children are in blended families. This quadruples the problems for schools, which may find they have four parents to contact for one child.

- *Homeless families.* Half a million homeless persons are children. The fastest-growing group of homeless are children under age 6.

- *Teenage parents.* More than 1 million teenage girls become pregnant each year. Approximately half will give birth. Of these, half fail to complete high school. This means that schools must help these girls work through their difficulties as parents if they expect to keep them in school.

- *Minority families.* If current demographic patterns and birth rates continue, one-third of the American population will be nonwhite by the year 2000. Racial and ethnic minorities are represented in all of the above family structures, but they also exhibit some different characteristics. Traditionally, racial and ethnic minorities in the United States have less power, wealth, social status, and education than do other Americans. For these reasons, and because of cultural and (sometimes) language differences, minorities may have trouble working with schools dominated by whites.

RESEARCH FINDINGS AND ISSUES

Research has shown that parents contribute directly to the levels and types of aspirations of their children (Auster & Auster, 1981). In addition, the family structure heavily influences the career aspirations, maturity, and expectations of children (Dillard & Campbell, 1981) and is a key ingredient in developing academic excellence (Briston, 1987; Coleman et al., 1966; Epstein, 1987; Mehran & White, 1988).

In contrast to these researchers, however, some proponents of the effective schools movement argue that achievement differences among students from various family backgrounds result not from those backgrounds but from the schools the students attend (Edmunds, 1986). As described by Scott-Jones (1988):

> Parent involvement was not among the variables found to distinguish effective from ineffective schools; some effective schools had low parent involvement and some had high levels of involvement. Distinguishing variables were strong instructional leadership from the principal, clearly articulated instructional goals, safe and orderly school climate, clear teacher expectations for at least minimum mastery of basic skills for children of all races and social classes, and evaluation and modification of school programs on the basis of standardized test scores. (p. 69)

Part of the reason for the diametrically opposite conclusions drawn by researchers who are ostensibly focusing on the same variables may lie in the fact that researchers seldom evaluate the same thing in the same way (Ascher, 1987). Ascher lists four additional obstacles that stand in the way of saying anything clearly about the effect of parental involvement with schools:

1. Studies of parental involvement have almost uniformly linked the success of various strategies and programs with the achievement of the children as measured by grades and standardized test scores.
2. In examining the impact of low-income parents' involvement in the school, it is difficult to isolate the effect of social class on the involvement and on the achievement of their children.

3. The total body of research on parental participation is relatively small, and the populations studied are demarcated very differently (e.g., grade level, grade bands, whole schools, or districtwide). There are also few studies focusing on the involvement of parents of middle and secondary school students.
4. It is not clear how strong an impact various kinds of parental involvement have in comparison to other types of intervention, such as compensatory education programs, tutorial assistance, or school lunch programs. Parental participation in school meetings or even in learning projects at home may have relatively weak value in comparison to other interventions, family background, and socialization. (pp. 7–9)

Ascher does, however, go on to say that some studies of preschool and elementary school children overcome these objections, and have generally found that the more parents participate in a sustained way—in advocacy; decision making and oversight roles; and as fund-raisers, boosters, volunteers, paraprofessionals, or home tutors—the better for student achievement.

INTENSITY LEVEL OF PARENTAL INVOLVEMENT

Research has shown that the level of meaningful parental involvement in the education of children is low. Louis Harris & Associates (1989) interviewed 1,000 parents of children with disabilities. Although 77 percent of these parents were satisfied with the special education system, 61 percent knew little or nothing about their rights in special education and were not as involved in their children's education as the law intended. It is possible that this low level of knowledge and involvement has a bearing on the 36 percent annual dropout rate of secondary students with disabilities and their 15 percent participation rate in postsecondary education programs, and the fact that 66 percent of all persons with disabilities between the ages of 16 and 64 are not working (National Council on Disability, 1989, as cited in "Update: A Compendium," 1990).

In a study of 1,702 randomly selected parents (69.5 percent of whom were black, 27 percent white, and 3.5 percent other racial/ethnic backgrounds), Yanok and Derubertis (1989) found that 23 (n = 1,539) percent of regular education parents were asked by school officials during the past year to participate in an educational activity, while 33.1 percent (n = 163) of special education parents were asked. Nearly 10 percent of the regular education parents served on a school committee during the past year, while 11.7 percent of the special education parents did so. The authors conclude that P.L. No. 94-142 has not significantly altered the participation levels of parents of exceptional children even though the law has existed for 13 years, and that educators must "redouble their efforts to increase the involvement of parents in school planning and decision making. Parents of the handicapped and nonhandicapped alike must be persuaded to become active participants rather than passive observers of their children's education" (p. 198).

In a study commissioned by *Newsweek* ("Education in America," 1990) for the National PTA and Dodge, the ICR Survey Research Group contacted a national sample of adults in 538 households with children enrolled in grades K through 12. (The telephone survey was conducted between December 29, 1989, and January 7, 1990. The results have a margin of error of ± 4.5 percentage points.) Fifty-seven percent of those surveyed said that the parents' role was an extremely important influence in their children's learning. Sixty-nine percent said they discussed school topics with their children every day; 17 percent did so two or three times a week; and 36 percent helped their children with their homework nearly every school day. Twenty-one percent said they helped with homework two or three times a week. However, 56 percent of the respondents said they had not attended a single back-to-school night since the school year started, and 54 percent said they had not gone to a single meeting of the PTA or other parent organization. Thirty-three percent said they never attended meetings of any committee at their children's school, even though most felt that their children's schools encouraged them to get involved. Fifty-eight percent said their children's school was extremely or very encouraging, and 20 percent said they were somewhat encouraged to participate. Only 8 percent said their children's school did not encourage them at all to participate in school activities.

BARRIERS TO PARENTAL INVOLVEMENT IN THEIR CHILDREN'S EDUCATION

In addition to lack of pertinent information about educational programming and procedures (Brantlinger, 1987; Louis Harris & Associates, 1989), other barriers exist that prevent meaningful participation by parents in the education of their offspring. These barriers can be classified as "personnel," "organizational structure," "policy," and "personal." Lehmann, Deniston, and Grebenc (1989) describe personnel and organizational structure barriers. The authors state that "there may not be a systematic process in place that lends itself to incorporating parents into transitional planning. Frequently, no one has been designated . . . as liaison to families needing assistance accessing adult services for their children" (p. 17). McLaughlin and Shields (1987) describe both organizational structure and policy barriers to parental participation. The authors state that "most strategies for parent involvement have not been carried out as they were intended. Parent advisory councils have been pro forma, giving parents little genuine involvement in the decision-making process. . . . Low income parents have shown themselves unwilling to serve on 'paper councils' or to spend time in nonsubstantive roles" (p. 157). These authors also attribute the low involvement of poor parents to a "fundamental design problem." They further state that "parent advisory structures and other strategies aimed at promoting parent/school partnerships have typically defined the content, the structure and the scheduling of parent-involvement activities on the school's terms. Such school-based programs have tended to engage the participation of advantaged parents, but not of low income parents" (p. 157).

Wiswell (1989) describes a typical school policy that frequently exacerbates problems faced by students with learning disabilities and other special needs:

> They have to fail before they can be identified as learning disabled and receive the help they need.... The patterns are fairly predictable: academic difficulties, behavior changes, and difficulties with interpersonal relationships.... By the time he/she is identified...the child not only has the stress of the special education program but must try to keep up with the regular grade level instruction. They have the catch up syndrome all through their school careers. (p. 3)

"Personal" barriers also hinder meaningful parental participation in their children's education. In addition to general perceptions that the school's advisory committees and other avenues of parental involvement are more pro forma than meaningful, parents may face a number of problems that make it difficult for them to be involved with school-related functions. As reported by Cotant (1989), a door-to-door survey of minority families whose children attended one elementary school in Madison, Wisconsin, was conducted by the Madison Metropolitan School District. The interviewers found that 47 percent of the parents did not receive forms requesting them to volunteer, because the parents had moved recently and did not report an address change to the proper persons at school. These parents did not know that their help was wanted. Of the survey respondents who said that they did receive the forms, only 5 percent said that they would not volunteer. However, 11 percent said that they did not read the forms because they did not understand what the forms said, because the forms did not mention minorities, or because few were events targeted toward minorities.

The Madison Metropolitan School District survey also asked parents why they did not volunteer. The main reason given was "lack of time." In addition, 32 percent said "commitments to other children who would be alone at home," 13 percent said "working," and 13 perecnt said "medical reasons."

As Cotant (1989) states, "Often neither parents nor teachers understand what is being said and are afraid to question each other for fear of being thought ignorant or uneducated. . . . The teacher may use a tone of voice that unknowingly causes the parent to feel inferior, and communication breaks down" (p. 17 and 20). Other factors identified by the survey include:

- predominance of nontraditional households
- inadequate child care or transportation
- children in the household attending two, three, or sometimes four different schools
- personal problems in the home
- belief that their children's performance is OK
- school meetings and events held at inconvenient times
- no personal appeal to get parents involved

In a 1988 study entitled "Barriers to Home-School Collaboration," Leitch and Tangri studied 60 black families, of whom 19 were two-parent nuclear families, 14 were single-parent nuclear families, 14 were single-parent extended families, 1 was a blended family, 9 were two-parent extended families, and 3 were institutional or foster families. The 60 school age-children ranged in age from 12 to 17. Slightly more than 50 percent of the mothers worked outside the home, and nearly half the parents had not completed high school. Approximately one-third had attended or finished college. Among personal barriers to school involvement, respondents cited health problems, economic differences between themselves and teachers, and work responsibilities. Parents also said that they felt that teachers looked down on them for not being as successful as the teachers. More than a third of the parents said that they had not been asked by the school personnel to do anything.

Leitch and Tangri (1988) also examined whether or not there was any measurable relationship between parents' own unpleasant school experience and their lack of involvement with their children's school. The researchers "asked parents about their own school experience, and a majority described it as positive. These parents said they liked school, liked and obeyed the teachers, and many said they did well. Those who were not as positive about their own experience mentioned lack of motivation and interest. We found no reliable relationship between the parent's own experience in school and either the child's experience or the parent's involvement" (p. 72).

Parents whose primary language is Spanish face an additional personal barrier to involvement with schools: misunderstandings between themselves and the teachers. The report of a 3-year study of 42 projects designed to bring Hispanic parents into the schools (released in April 1990 by the Hispanic Development Project), concluded that misunderstandings between Hispanic parents and teachers—not a lack of concern—have caused Hispanic parents to be uninvolved in their children's education. As stated in the report, entitled "Together is Better:

Building Strong Partnerships Between Schools and Hispanic Parents," low-income Hispanics care deeply about their children's education, but they do not know what American schools expect of them. As described by Olson (1990), most low-income Hispanic parents are unaware of specific practices that could lay the basis for future learning. In addition, many look upon school officials as experts whom they have no right to question.

A significant personal barrier arises as children move into middle school and high school. The children themselves often discourage their parents from active involvement in school, especially involvement that results in the parents' physical presence in the building. Adolescents often feel "embarrassed" if their parents "hang around" school, and communicate that in no uncertain terms to their parents.

A final personal barrier is faced especially by parents of children with disabilities—"grieving." As usually thought of, grieving is associated with the death of a loved one or with the loss of abilities due to onset of disability. In this instance, however, grieving refers to an intermittent process that parents of children with disabilities experience because their children have disabilities. Moses (1983) describes grieving as a constellation of feeling states (denial, anxiety, depression, anger and guilt) that facilitates a personal reorganization, thereby fostering dramatic changes that permit serious loss to become a life-enriching occurrence. To truly help in the growth process of a child, the professional must attend to the grief struggle experienced by the parents.

Moses (1983) notes,

> The grieving process is far from a one-time occurrence. Parents of... disabled children repeat and rework the feeling states as the child matures. All parents seem to grieve at the point of initial diagnosis. In addition, each time the child comes to a major milestone that impacts the parents in a new way, grief will once again be experienced. Common developmental points that reactivate grieving are:
>
> 1. when the child reaches "regular" school age, for that is a time when comparison between children occurs;
> 2. when the child reaches puberty, and offers all the dilemmas of adolescence, plus the complexities of the handicapping condition;
> 3. when the child reaches high school graduation age and the disability negatively affects the child's ability to move on to a more independent manner of functioning;
> 4. when the child reaches an age where the expectation is that he or she will indeed live totally independently (working, getting married, and so forth);

5. when the parents reach retirement age and the nature of the disability is such that the child might interfere with their retirement and require that arrangements be made for the time after their death. (pp. 30–31)

As a parent described in the PAVE Pipeline (Trujillo, 1989), "For me, and for most parents, milestones are really hard. The baby's first birthday, the first day of school, and Christmas. They are all tough. Tough because our very special kids are different from other kids and these dates really point it out" (p. 1).

A key transition that often revives the parental grieving process is the period surrounding completion of high school by students with disabilities. This transition period makes it very clear to parents that "their kid is different." Most of his or her peers are making plans for college, careers, or other rites of passage into adulthood. Meanwhile, the parents of students with disabilities worry that their offspring will not survive in the post–high school world, will not have sufficient or timely support from adult service agencies, and may not be able to strike out on his or her own for some time. The unemployment rates of adults with disabilities bear out the realism of these parental fears.

School staff must realize that the constellation of feelings (fear, anger, guilt, and uncertainty), coupled with the parents' emotional investment in their children, may color the parents' viewpoint of the school in general and the individual staff in particular. As Redfield (1979) expressed it,

Parents feel that teachers and administrators hold tremendous power over their children and that such individuals are best dealt with obsequiously. As a parent gets to know an individual teacher, these attitudes may change, but only if the teacher is approachable.

Because of the teacher's powerful position, parents often hesitate to ask important questions for fear of being branded as troublemakers or that reprisals will be taken against their children. While these fears are usually not borne out by fact, they nonetheless exist. Many good and concerned teachers who read this may find it hard to believe, but I have yet to meet a parent who did not express this concern. . . .

It is far easier for a parent to talk with another parent about his/her personal feelings and concerns than it is to discuss these issues with the child's teacher. The other parent with a backlog of similar experience can relate to feelings and problems . . . .

So, teachers, please bear with us. Let us blow off steam. Don't take it as a personal affront. Recognize that exposing and talking about the old hurts and grievances are first steps toward purging them from our systems. (pp. 15–16)

STRATEGIES TO OVERCOME BARRIERS AND IMPROVE PARENTAL INVOLVEMENT IN THEIR CHILDREN'S EDUCATION

Strategies to develop parental involvement, sustain it, and make it as productive as possible can be classified as policy, organizational, personnel, teacher-specific, and parent-specific. Regarding policy issues, McLaughlin and Shields (1987) suggest that policy cannot mandate the things that really matter:

In general, mandated parent advisory councils have not been implemented as their advocates intended. In most locales, such councils have functioned primarily as window dressing, merely rubber-stamping the decisions of school administrators.... Partnership models have likewise been implemented unevenly. Such models as are in place tend to reflect the interest of an individual administrator or teacher, not an institutionalized or systematic concern for parent involvement in the schools. (pp. 158–159)

Role of Policy

What role then, should policy have in fostering parental participation in the education of their children? McLaughlin and Shields (1987) point out that since the literature on planned change indicates that behavior often changes before beliefs, an effective policy approach combines both pressure and support:

Norm-based pressures include such things as information about the success of various parent involvement activities, incentives to try new practices, development efforts by professional peers, and the expectations for professional behavior within a given school or school district.... Pressures rooted in the norms of the profession have consistently been the most effective in changing the behavior of educators. Specific and credible information about the value of parent involvement activities, clear statements from opinion leaders and organizational leaders about the need for and the merits of parent involvement, and detailed and believable descriptions of successful parent involvement activities are more likely than rules or mandates to move educators to try something new to foster parent involvement.... If normative pressures succeed in nudging educators to consider new practices, these inclinations require support in the form of materials, training, networks, mini-grants, and the like. Of particular importance are the dissemination of information on and the provision of financial and logistical support for successful parent involvement strategies. (pp. 159–160)

In their publication *Turning Points: Preparing American Youth for the 21st Century*, the Carnegie Council on Adolescent Development (1989) recommends that schools offer families meaningful roles in their child's education and in the life of the school by asking them to serve on schoolwide building governance committees. As the Carnegie Council states,

> The building governance committee affords parents a meaningful opportunity to help define the mission of the school and to join in the decision making process concerning building-wide issues and problems.... Parents on school-wide governance committees who work effectively and cooperatively with school staff become models of such behavior for their young adolescents and other students.... The only places where many young people, particularly in low-income communities, see their parents in important roles are in the school or the church. Even if students do not see their own parents in meaningful roles in school, they benefit from seeing parents of other children in those roles. (p. 67)

Organizational Options

Organizational strategies that have proven effective in developing and sustaining productive parental involvement in the education of their children include the Parents as Teachers project started 9 years ago by the Missouri school system. As described by Baker and Elam (1989), the goal of the program is to deal with the fact that "poor children, once they start school, often lag behind their classmates—and never catch up.... Every six weeks specially trained teachers come into homes to tell parents what to expect at each stage of a preschooler's development; they also recommend toys and games that stimulate learning" (p. 28).

Project Involve, the Madison, Wisconsin, Metropolitan School District effort for which the door-to-door survey described earlier was conducted, also "included parent workshops, and examination of the issues of tutoring students, providing education for parents, and establishing partnerships between home, school and community" (Cotant, 1989, p. 20). This $16,000 project also laid the groundwork for creating a new parental liaison position at the grade school serving parents in the original survey.

Personnel-Specific Strategies

A third example of a promising strategy to involve parents in the education of their children is the approach taken by the Corporate Community School (CCS) in Chicago. As columnist George Will described the school in *Newsweek* (October 9, 1989),

> In a neighborhood where 80 percent of the children are born to single women, the school struggles to help family environments approximate the clear, orderly environment of the school.... The school elicits parental involvement by providing services such as adult education that lead to high school diplomas, or at least help parents keep pace with their children's reading skills.... In this the school's second year, 50 new students were chosen by lottery from 1,400 applicants. Social agencies are enlisted to get the least motivated parents to apply. Soon the school will be giving free education to 300. By then the cost per pupil will be approximately what it is in Chicago's public schools. The CCS's teachers are paid about 10 percent above the public school level. However for CCS teachers the psychic income is incalculably higher.... The CCS is funded by about 60 corporations, including some of Chicago's heaviest hitters.... They know their choice is: pay now or pay later—support competent schools or run remedial education. (p. 118)

As the above examples imply, it is crucial that school administrators assign staff to work with parents, both in one-to-one settings and group activities. These assignments cannot be treated as "add-on's" to current duties, or as "after-thoughts" that will be taken care of when (if?) everything else is completed. Teachers and other school staff must have both the responsibility and the authority to work with parents, using a systematic and continuing process. This includes reallocating duties to make time available, adding staff as necessary, providing resources such as travel reimbursement for both teachers and parents, "coffee and rolls" money for group meetings, and other logistical support.

The Carnegie Council (1989) also recommends

> assigning each student an advisor who meets and comes to know the youth's family over the entire period of enrollment in middle school. This sends a clear signal that the school considers strong linkages with home vital. The advisor should communicate with parents regularly, not just when crises occur. Advisors should contact parents when something good happens, or ask for help in understanding the youth as an individual. In turn, parents should be encouraged to share their con-

cerns with advisors before problems arise and to make advisors aware of special circumstances that may influence their child's behavior.... Parents should understand that communications between advisors and students are confidential and that advisors are not free to pass along information they receive from students. (p. 68)

Specific communication techniques include in-person home visits conducted at least once every 1 to 2 months; live phone calls; tape-recorded phone calls; tape-recorded hotlines that the parent can call to learn about school assignments, events, or other information; live "homework hotlines" that parents or students can call for help on homework subjects; and videotapes for use by individual parents or for broadcast on local-access television channels or on network affiliates as a public service.

In setting up an advisor-advisee program, school administrators should strongly encourage voluntary participation by school staff—not just teachers, but administrators and support staff also. Advisors should meet with their advisees (no more than five advisees per advisor) on a weekly, although informal, basis, and focus on issues of concern to the student at his or her particular stage of development. The advisor's role is not to serve as a professional counselor, but as a mentor, adult role model, and concerned individual. These meetings can be arranged for mutual convenience: before school, during study/preparation periods or lunch, between classes, or after school. Classroom teachers who have served as advisors have found that they are most effective when their advisees also take at least one of their classes during the week. In addition, advisor-advisee programs that paid staff to work with individuals before or after school, or both, found that the level of staff participation was much higher, and the impact on the advisees greater.

Organizational factors can also enhance or hinder communication between school and parents. Rich (1985) suggests that the following will enhance communication:

- Be sensitive to parents' scheduling difficulties, and announce meetings and other events far enough in advance for parents to attempt to arrange time off from work.
- Create a more accepting environment for working and single parents, as well as those undergoing separation, divorce, or remarriage, or acting as a custodial parent. (See suggestions by the National Committee for Citizens in Education (1989) below for specifics about how this might be done.)
- Schedule teacher-parent-counselor meetings in the evening, and provide child care and transportation as needed.

- Allow open enrollment so that children can attend schools near parents' workplaces.
- Provide before-school and after-school day care.
- Be very careful about canceling school at the last minute because of weather conditions, thus leaving working parents with no way to take care of their children.
- Form and facilitate teen, single, working, and custodial parent peer-support groups.
- Provide both legal and custodial parents with regular information on their child's classroom activities, and any assistance they may need to become and remain involved with the child's learning.

Although it is obvious that a school should offer a warm and accepting environment for parents, such an environment is developed only as the result of very concrete actions on the part of school personnel. As described by the National Committee for Citizens in Education (1989), a school that takes the following actions will improve the likelihood that it will develop effective communication and partnerships with parents:

- Publish a clear policy welcoming parental involvement, publicize it, and post it in the school buildings in an obvious place for all to see.
- Organize the staff so that at least one person knows each student well—how he or she is doing in all subjects; whether he or she is making friends; whether he or she is anxious, afraid of failing, and so forth.
- Make sure that the school office is friendly and open and that parents are treated with respect and are not kept waiting.
- Sponsor parent-to-parent events so that parents can get to know one another and develop common standards for their children's behavior and social life.
- Hire a full-time parent contact person whose job is to help parents understand how they can help their kids learn at home and understand the school structure. The parent contact person should also talk to teachers about parents' concerns and make home visits.
- Set up a parent room in the school building. Equip it with comfortable places to sit, a telephone, books about school age-children and what they need, and access to a copying machine. Some schools have even included a kitchen, laundry room, sewing machine, computer, and typewriter.
- Ensure that parents and school staff work together to determine parents' needs and provide necessary services. Sometimes parents will need things that do not seem directly related to their children's education, such as help

in understanding the immigration laws or in getting their electricity turned back on.

- Provide in-person contact with parents whose primary language is not English, and be sure that translators are involved in all parent-teacher interaction as needed.

Teacher-Specific Strategies

If teachers are to be effective, they must (1) believe that parents can contribute in important ways to the education of their children, (2) develop an understanding of what it is like to be the parent of a child experiencing difficulties in school, and (3) devote the sustained effort necessary to involve parents productively.

Teacher-specific strategies and behaviors have a significant influence on the degree to which parents become and remain productively involved in the education of their children. "The Effective Middle Schools Program of the Center for Research on Elementary and Middle Schools at Johns Hopkins University found that teachers' practices, rather than education, marital status, or workplace situation, make the greatest difference in whether or not parents and teachers cooperate in helping students succeed" (William T. Grant Foundation, 1988, p. 36).

Understanding Parents' Experiences with Educational Institutions

A key element in developing a complete understanding of parents' experiences with educational institutions is learning about parents' perceptions. The following is a description of how one parent, Frances Smith (1989), described that experience:

Looking back over 30 years as the mother of a daughter with multiple disabilities and a son with cerebral palsy, I feel again the pain and the joy of my life. I have also been a "professional advocate" and have worked with hundreds of parents who have sensitized me to professional approaches that build trust with parents. I expect that the lessons learned can be of use to others traveling down a similar path.

In spite of encounters with professionals who patronized me, discounted my intelligence and feelings, or openly worked against what I was trying to achieve for my own or other's children, I remain convinced that people who work in early intervention, special education, and residential and vocational services want to do good things for children and adults with disabilities. The following comments are offered in the interest of reducing barriers to open, trusting parent/professional relations.

Respect. Services and professionals come and go throughout the life of a person with a disability, but parents remain. Their role is to assure that their son or daughter will receive the best, most appropriate services possible, while never being sure just where those services are, or which services are the best and most appropriate. This task will be easier when parents are respected for doing their jobs and when the information and opinions they possess, as the person closest to their child, are respected and incorporated into the development of service plans.

Affirmation. Telling a parent that he or she is doing a good job builds instant rapport between a professional and a parent. It was seven years before anyone told me that what I wanted was right and that I have done an outstanding job as a mother of two youngsters with severe disabilities. Those few words of praise bonded me forever to that professional and also got me through lots of rough times in the following years.

Professional Objectivity. Almost every professional discipline instills the notion that the best professionals remain objective about their work—and about the person receiving the services. However, parents are not objective about their child. I always trusted the professionals who not only talked to and smiled at my children, but touched them and actually seemed to like them! Professional objectivity is generally misunderstood by parents because it appears to be cold, uncaring aloofness on the part of the professional.

Predictions. Most parents want reassurance that things will somehow, someday get better. Telling parents, with certainty, that their child will never be able to do this or that may be a way to stop unrealistic thinking, but it is also a way to kill hope. Children need the support of someone who believes in them, perhaps against all odds. There were so many things that my daughter accomplished, things that I was told with certainty she would never do, that I have learned to keep my mind open to possibilities. Until we have crystal balls which can show us the future with 100% accuracy, let's err on the side of optimism and hope.

Teamwork. In a successful team, everyone is committed, knows their role and has the skills to do the job. Newcomers, however, may feel intimidated and may not play their role very well. Parents are newcomers to the service delivery team. Professionals should support and encourage parents to participate effectively as knowledgeable, skilled team members. The team will function best when there is an atmosphere of trust in which parents feel respected, heard, and supported as equal members of the team. (p. 4)

Building Trust

The importance of building trust cannot be overstated. The first step is to behave in a trustworthy manner. As Margolis and Brannigan (1986) state,

> To build trust you need to a) cultivate a cooperative rather than a competitive or dominating mind set; b) make your involvement with parents understanding and concerned; c) be open about your objectives; d) subtly demonstrate expertise without being oppressive or signaling superiority.... Building trust cannot be rushed. It is an interactive process, involving the sharing of information, ideas, and feelings. The operative word in trust building is reciprocity.... It is important to share rather then conceal your feelings. Thoughts, however, should be expressed in ways parents can understand and appreciate. Estimate the parents' level of sophistication regarding each topic on the agenda so that you do not patronize or overwhelm them with information they cannot comprehend. (p. 71)

Below are some specific strategies and behaviors that educators can use to initiate trust-building with parents (Margolis & Brannigan, 1986):

1. Accept parents as they are and do not try to induce fundamental changes. Trying to change parents in some basic way communicates that something is wrong with them.... In conflict situations especially, the less you try to change broad-based philosophical beliefs of people, the greater your ultimate chance of influencing them. Later, when trust is high, parents may demonstrate their readiness to change by asking for assistance in learning new concepts or skills.
2. Listen carefully and with empathy for the cognitive and emotional content of the parents' message.... Give parents your complete, undivided, uninterrupted attention, and communicate that you understand.... Your statements should be short and to the point, using fresh words to summarize the parents' thoughts and feelings.

3. Help parents feel comfortable and share information and resources with them when legally permissible. Small talk about mutual interests or experiences unrelated to the issues of contention and a symbolic "cup of coffee" frequently help parents feel more comfortable. Providing help and requesting legitimate assistance from parents establishes natural trust-building opportunities. Sharing information, resources, and ideas is a powerful process in building trust. On the other hand, evading requests for information or obscuring pertinent facts immediately creates the impression that you are hiding something important. This heightens distrust and defensiveness.

4. Prepare for meetings by studying pertinent materials beforehand, so that a high level of knowledge will be apparent at the right moments. Parents need to trust not only your objectives for their child but also your knowledge and professional competency. It is critical that you share relevant information at natural opportunities without lecturing, dominating, or conveying the slightest attitude or superiority. A few well-chosen comments or questions, devoid of technical jargon, will usually suffice. A lack of correct technical information or relevant details will create doubts about your competency and interest.

5. Focus on the parents' hopes, aspirations, concerns, and needs. Parents' negative feelings toward school personnel usually arise from fear that their child's welfare is being jeopardized. Unilaterally setting agendas for parents, rather than focusing on their concerns, only intensifies distrust and resistance. It is natural to like someone who is interested in you and your concerns. Attending to parents' concerns communicates caring.

6. Keep your word. This is simple, but often forgotten. If you promise to return a telephone call by two o'clock, do so. Making the call promptly communicates respect and reliability.

7. Allow parents' expertise to shine. Parents are knowledgeable about many aspects of their child's development. Asking for their opinions, inviting them to comment on whether or not the student's behavior in school is representative of his behavior at home, asking if your viewpoints or suggestions appear to make sense to them ... facilitate trust and help establish you as someone who values them. Providing knowledgeable answers in response to questions is desirable if it does not take the form of pontificating, intimidation (e.g. through the use of jargon such as "perceptual problems," "haptic," "scaled scores," or "stanines"), or unnecessary complexity. Asking parents to share their particular expertise communicates respect as long as they perceive the request to be both legitimate and timely.

8. Be there when needed. If parents have a legitimate need to see you, do everything reasonable to meet them as soon as possible even if it creates a slight inconvenience. (pp. 71 to 74)

Parent-Teacher Conferences

Parent-teacher conferences are one of the primary formal contact points between instructors and parents. In addition to the steps outlined above to build trust, teachers can use certain procedures that will facilitate productive conferences and build working relationships between school staff and parents. Academic Therapy Publications (1987) suggest the following tips that instructors have used to conduct productive conferences:

1. Mail a written note...or call the parents to establish a firm conference date.... Setting a time during the school day may be difficult. If so, check...to determine policies on after-school or evening conferences.
2. Request a confirmation of the time, place and date if you have used a written, mailed communication.
3. Read the student's cumulative folder thoroughly. Be familiar with the vast array of tests that have been administered to the child. Double check. Are there any gaps that require updated testing in specific areas...? If so, determine who will do the testing and when. You will need that information prior to your appointment with the parents.
4. In addition to test results, set aside a folder showing school assignments from the start of school through the conference date. Point out the ways in which these illustrate the student's strengths and weaknesses.
5. Be positive. Start the conference with a description of an area in which the child has excelled. Then move into ongoing needs.
6. A desk can become a barrier. Try to sit in a cluster, for example, around a utility table, so that test results and work samples can be comfortably shared. Keep your language simple and nontechnical. It is a kindness to say to parents "please interrupt me if I use a term or make a statement that you do not understand."
7. The conference should be a two way dialogue. Engage the parents as much as possible. Get their observations on how their child reacts to school, learning, homework, friends. Listen! Be sure to let them know how much you value their opinions. Parents have much to

offer and sometimes need to be reassured about the contribution they make to their child's well being.

8. A conference should not last longer than one hour. Allow time to summarize and make recommendations for the coming year as well as suggestions for summer activities.
9. If possible, provide refreshments (coffee, soda, rolls) to help set a warm, friendly tone. (pp. 411–412)

Involving Parents in Helping Their Children Learn at Home

Epstein (1987) listed 16 techniques that teachers can use to help parents enhance their children's learning at home. Those techniques are as follows:

1. Ask parents to read to their children regularly or listen to the children read aloud.
2. Lend books, workbooks, and other materials to parents.
3. Ask parents to take their children to the public library. (Provide the necessary information about how to get there, how to get a library card, and so forth as needed.)
4. Ask parents to get their children to describe (in detail, daily) what they did in school.
5. Give an assignment that requires children to ask their parents questions.
6. Ask parents to watch a specific television program with their children and discuss it afterward.
7. Suggest ways for parents to include their children in any of their own educationally enriching activities. (These could be as commonplace as shopping for groceries, working on the car, taking care of the house, making minor repairs, working in the yard/garden, tending animals, and so forth.)
8. Suggest (and demonstrate in person whenever possible) games or group activities related to the children's school work that can be played by either parent and child or by child and siblings.
9. Suggest (and demonstrate) how parents can use home materials and activities to stimulate their children's interest in reading, math and other subjects.
10. Establish a formal agreement whereby parents supervise and assist children in completing homework tasks.
11. Establish a formal agreement by which parents provide rewards or penalties (or both) based on children's school performance and behavior.
12. Ask parents to come and observe the class, not help.
13. Give a questionnaire to parents so they they can provide feedback about their children's progress.

14. Explain certain techniques for teaching, making learning materials, or correcting mistakes appropriately.
15. Ask parents to sign homework to ensure its completion.
16. Ask parents to provide spelling practice, math drills, or other practice.

Parent-Specific Strategies

The demands on today's parents are greater and more complex than ever. Many parents operate from a state of chronic exhaustion, wondering where the energy will come from to cope with any new demands that might, inevitably, arise. Much of their energy goes into attempts to ensure a better future for their children and to help them learn what they need to launch themselves successfully into adulthood. It is unrealistic for schools to throw up their hands and lay student failure at parents' doorsteps. Likewise, it is equally unrealistic for parents to abdicate their responsibility to schools, even when it is very tempting to do so. Parents can do much to improve their children's chances of success, whether or not school personnel ever talk to them, make a home visit, ask them what they think, or request their involvement in school activities. In other words, the parent can have a great deal of impact on the child's performance even in the absence of effective school-parent partnerships. This impact can be obtained by focusing on three areas: academics, helping the children say no to alcohol and other drugs, and helping the children develop healthy self-esteem.

Helping Your Children Succeed in School

Require your children to bring their homework assignments, and the books/materials necessary to complete those assignments, home daily. Require your children to finish their homework daily, and work on longer projects at a steady pace. Shut off the television, cancel cable service, remove the tape player, and turn off the radio/music player as needed. Check homework for completeness, and check longer projects for progress.

Insist that your children go to bed on school nights at a reasonable time. Unless your family needs the money for survival (as opposed to extra cars, stereos, televisions sets, phones, and designer clothes), school-age children should not be working at jobs that require their presence beyond 9:00 p.m., nor should they be working more than 10 to 20 hours total per week during the school year.

Insist that your children get up early enough to get ready for school. This includes eating a reasonably healthful breakfast, not just doughnuts and soda pop. Set an example yourself.

Develop a strategy to help your children budget their time so that longer projects are completed without a panic at the last minute. Help your children establish a regular study time and place, which will be used for a set period each day. When no assignments are given that need to be worked on at home, have your children use the study time for review or preview. You may have to check with the children's teachers to verify the absence of homework or projects, or both.

Get library cards for yourself and your children. Use the library at least once a week. Make it a family outing. Many libraries have play areas for very young children, as well as educational computer software and other audiovisuals in addition to books.

Read to your children, or have them read to you, every night for 5 to 15 minutes. If you have several children, alternate the rotation of reading order and who selects the reading material, or have them pair off and read to each other. Consider a group discussion of what one individual reads aloud. Remember to focus on and point out successes.

A Special Consideration: Interracial Children

As described by Ladner (1985), children in biracial families need the same things that any other child needs—love, support, and acceptance, and the opportunities to grow into well-rounded adults. As they progress through the school system, however, children with a multiracial/multicultural heritage will benefit from actions on the part of both parents and teachers that acknowledge and build on these children's backgrounds. For example, Linder (1988) suggests that both teachers and parents provide the following:

- opportunities for the child to develop a clear sense of both, or all, parts of his or her identity, including knowledge and involvement in the cultural heritages of both parents
- an atmosphere of openness in which racial issues can be discussed, including questions about skin color, hair texture, and the complexities of cultural identification, and especially the child's feelings and reactions
- accurate information—discussed in age appropriate ways—about racism in society and how it may affect the child (Topics might include name-calling, prejudice, stereotypes, discrimination, hierarchies based on appearance/skin color, and exclusionary group behavior.)
- help so that the child understands that he or she is good and beautiful and that anyone who is hostile or disapproving on the basis of appearance or background has a problem
- on-going experiences in multiracial/multicultural environments in which many cultural/racial heritages are celebrated (This area should be interwoven into curricula, not treated as an add-on or an afterthought.)

- role models who are proud to be from interracial families
- books that portray interracial families, and materials that enable children to role-play their own families or see their family situations reflected in the narrative

Teachers should also discuss in person with parents of interracial children the parents' feelings about the children's cultural and racial heritage, how the parents support the children's heritage at home, and how they would like to see this heritage supported at school. If the teachers are sufficiently skilled and multiculturally sensitive, they can also help the parents develop effective ways to support all aspects of the children's heritage at home, help them deal with the children's questions about racial identity, and teach the children how to respond appropriately to derogatory comments.

Saying No to Alcohol and Other Drugs

One of the most crucial decisions in a child's life is whether or not to experiment with the gateway drugs of alcohol, marijuana, and tobacco. Research has shown that these drugs are almost always the first ones that a young person experiments with. Retrospective studies of people whose lives were severely affected by drug abuse have demonstrated that nearly 100 percent started by experimenting with tobacco, alcohol, and marijuana. Parents have a major role to play in helping their children understand the lifetime consequences of this decision, as well as a crucial role to play in helping their children say no, when the inevitable opportunity to experiment arises. Much has been written about the topic, and parents are encouraged to seek information from school counselors, drug/alcohol information agencies, and other local sources. Your public library is a good place to start.

One excellent national source is the National Clearinghouse for Alcohol and Drug Information, P.O. Box 2345, Rockville, MD 20852; telephone (301) 468-2600. This government-funded agency distributes a booklet prepared by the National Institute on Alcohol Abuse and Alcoholism (1986) entitled *Ten Steps To Help Your Child Say No: a Parent's Guide.* This booklet, a short summary of a larger publication entitled *Ten Steps To Help Your Child Say No: A Leader's Guide,* is designed to help parents guide their children away from using alcohol, tobacco, marijuana, and other drugs, while enhancing the parent-child relationship. The short brochure provides a broad overview of prevention, while the longer version is an ideal tool for parenting workshops and for those who wish to explore the subject in more detail. To obtain a copy of either publication, contact the National Clearinghouse at the address above.

The ten steps addressed in these publications are as follows:

1. What shall I say to my child about alcohol and other drugs?
2. How can I encourage my child to turn to me for guidance?
3. How can enhanced self-esteem help my child say no to alcohol and other drugs?
4. Will the values taught at home make it easier for my child to say no to peer pressure to use tobacco, alcohol, or other drugs?
5. How do my own attitudes toward alcohol and my drinking patterns and smoking habits affect my child?
6. What are "peer pressure" skills?
7. How important are family policies concerning alcohol and other drug use?
8. How can I prevent my child from focusing on alcohol or other drugs out of boredom or idle curiosity?
9. What are other parents doing to fight alcohol and other drug use among youth?
10. What if, in spite of my efforts, my child drinks or does drugs anyway?

Each of the above topics is covered in a direct way, using many concrete examples and nontechnical language.

SUMMARY

As Joyce Epstein argues, "involving more parents more often and more productively requires changing the major location of parent involvement from the school to the home, changing the major emphasis from general policies to specific skills, and changing the major target from the general population of students or school staff to the individual child at home" (Jennings, 1990, p. 29). There are no shortcuts or panaceas. Developing and sustaining productive working relationships with parents takes commitment, time, and resources. Expectations govern actions. Without the expectation that parental involvement is valuable, time and resources will never be found.

REFERENCES

Academic Therapy Publications. (1987, March). Parent-teacher conferences, the professional's point of view. *Academic Therapy, 22*, 411–412.

Ascher, C. (1987). *Improving the school-home connection for poor and minority urban students.* New York: Columbia University.

Auster, C., & Auster, D. (1981). Factors influencing women's choices of nontraditional careers: The role of family, peers and counselors. *Vocational Guidance Quarterly, 30*, 253–263.

Baker, J.N., & Elam, R. (1989, September 11). Programs that make a difference. *Newsweek*, p. 28.

Brantlinger, E.A. (1987). Making decisions about special education placement: Do low-income parents have the information they need? *Journal of Learning Disabilities, 20*, 94–101.

Briston, V.J. (1987). But I'm not a teacher. *Academic Therapy, 23*, 23–27.

Carnegie Council on Adolescent Development. (1989, June). *Turning points: Preparing American youth for the 21st century.* New York: Carnegie Corporation of New York. (Report prepared by the Carnegie Council on Adolescent Development's Task Force on Education of Young Adolescents)

Coleman, J.S., Campbell, E.Q., Jobson, C.J. McPartland, J., Mood, A.M., Weinfeld, F.D., & York, R.L. (1966). *Equality of educational opportunity.* Washington, DC: U.S. Office of Education.

Cotant, P. (1989, November 13). Schools reach out to minority students. *Capital Times*, pp. 17, 20.

Dillard, J., & Campbell, N. (1981). Influences of Puerto Rican, black and anglo parents' career behavior on their adolescent children's career development. *Vocational Guidance Quarterly, 30*, 139–148.

Edmunds, R. (1986). Characteristics of effective schools. In V. Neisser (Ed.), *The school achievement of minority children: New perspectives.* Hillsdale, NJ: Erlbaum.

Education in America: A new look. (1990, March 12). *Newsweek*, special advertising section, p. 6.

Epstein, J. (1987, January). What principals should know about parent involvement. *Principal*, pp. 6–9.

Jennings, L. (1990, August 1). Parents as partners. *Education Week*, pp. 23–32.

Ladner, J. (1985, March). What do interracial children need? Suggestions for parents and teachers. *CIBC Bulletin*, p. 8.

Lehmann, J.P., Deniston, T., & Grebenc, R. (1989). Counseling parents to facilitate transition. *Journal for Vocational Special Needs Education, 11*, 15–18.

Leitch, M.L., & Tangri, S.S. (1988, Winter). Barriers to home-school collaboration. *Educational Horizon*, pp. 70–74.

Linder, B. (1988, August). *Drawing in the family: Family involvement in the schools.* Denver, CO: Education Commission of the States.

Louis Harris & Associates. (1989). *The ICD survey III: A report card on special education.* New York: ICD Education and Training Department.

Margolis, H., & Brannigan, G.G. (1986). Building trust with parents. *Academic Therapy, 22*, 71–74.

McLaughlin, M.W., & Shields, P. (1987, October). Involving low-income parents in the schools: A role for policy? *Phi Delta Kappan*, 156–160.

Mehran, M., & White, K.R. (1988). Parent tutoring as a supplement to compensatory education for first-grade children. *Remedial and Special Education, 9*(3), 35–41.

Moses, K.L. (1983) The impact of initial diagnosis: Mobilizing family resources. In J.A. Mulick & S.M. Pueschel (Eds.), *Parent-professional partnerships in developmental disability services.* Cambridge, MA: Academic Guild Publishers.

National Committee for Citizens in Education. (1989, Winter Holiday). Parent involvement in middle school—Your young adolescent needs you more than ever. *Network for Public Schools, 15*(3), 7, 8–9.

National Institute on Alcohol Abuse and Alcoholism. (1986). *Ten steps to help your child say no: A parents's guide*. Rockville, MD: Author.

Olson, L. (1990, May 2). Misreading said to hamper Hispanics' role in school. *Education Week, 9*, 4.

Redfield, J. (1979, September/October). Reflections of a parent. *ACLD Newsbriefs*, No. 128, pp. 6, 16.

Rich, D. (1985). The forgotten factor in school success. In *The family —A policymaker's guide*. Washington, DC: Home and School Institute.

Scott-Jones, D. (1988, Winter). Families as educators: The transition from informal to formal school learning. *Educational Horizons, 66*, 66–69.

Smith, F. (1989). Do's and don'ts for professionals: Advocating vocational outcomes for young adults with disabilities. [Special Issue] *Parents and Families, 5*, 4.

Trujillo, S. (Ed.). (1989, December). Christmas at our house. *PAVE Pipeline, 9*, 1–2.

Update: A compendium of special education news. (1990, Winter). *Teaching Exceptional Children, 22*(2), 92.

Will, G.F. (1989, October 9). A school for families. *Newsweek*, p. 118.

William T. Grant Foundation. (1988; November). Commission on Work, Family, and Citizenship. *The forgotten half: Pathways to success for America's youth and young families* (Final report). Washington, DC: Author.

Wiswell, J. (1989). Why must they fail? *LDA Newsbriefs, 24*, 3.

Yanok, J., & Derubertis, D. (1989). Comparative study of parental participation in regular and special education programs. *Exceptional Children, 56*, 195–199.

chapter 7

Strategies for Dropout Prevention

Jerry L. Wircenski

Strategies for dropout prevention. The topic sounds so simple, yet the task is very complex. The information provided in earlier chapters shows that the dropout problem is compounded by a wide variety of social, emotional, environmental, economic, and educational issues that affect at-risk students who leave school before graduation. As a result, there is no single or simple solution to the task of suggesting strategies for dropout prevention that will be effective with all at-risk students.

There is a strong link between the problem of student dropout and the educational environment of the school (Fennimore & Pritz, 1988). The educational environment or school climate incorporates a number of elements. Teachers, administrators, counselors, peers, curriculum emphasis, physical facilities, philosophy, and geographic location are just a few. Ironically, the concern about school climate is not new. In 1960, Kvaraceus stated that the imbalance in the curriculum in the public schools today favors the " academically talented middle-class child and is highly prejudicial to both the non-academic and the lower-class youngster" (p. 204). Thirty years later this is still the case in more schools than we care to admit. Education needs to come face to face with the nature of the problems at hand. Who are the clientele that the schools are designed to serve? Is the current educational system meeting the needs of these students? Is the educational system meeting the needs of the community it serves? Is the educational climate fair and open? Is the system holding students or is it forcing students out? Unfortunately, the answers to many of these questions are less than desirable.

LOCAL DROPOUT APPRAISAL

Before a discussion of suggested strategies for dropout prevention can be instituted, it is important that each school or district conduct a complete appraisal of its dropout problem. The cause or causes of the problem must be identified before possible solutions can be determined. Why are students dropping out of school? The nature of the school or district's dropout problem is critical to the strategy selected. A homogeneous grouping of at-risk students might profit from a single strategy, whereas a heterogeneous group would probably require a wide variety of dropout prevention strategies.

If students are dropping out to seek employment opportunities, then the school might consider establishing a cooperative vocational education program whereby students could receive a coordinated academic and vocational education under the supervision of a teacher-coordinator. Perhaps students are late or absent from school on a regular basis because of poor or inadequate public transportation. The school or district might seek assistance from volunteer community agencies or church groups to assist with van pools or car pools to help at-risk students get to school. If the school dropout rate has increased as a result of an increase in teenage pregnancies, the school or district might need to incorporate a sex education or sexual awareness program to address this problem. Another solution might be to establish an in-school child care assistance program or to provide some assistance in conjunction with a local community agency for child care services while the mother or father attends school. If students are leaving school before graduation as a result of poor academic performance in the classroom, the school or district might consider the formulation of a tutoring program to assist students with improvement in the basic skills of reading, writing, or mathematics. Another alternative might be to establish a study skills program to teach students how to take notes and to study.

Perhaps a complete re-examination of the school's curriculum is in order to determine whether it is meeting the needs of the students currently enrolled. Demographic changes, such as the influx of non–English-speaking families, have changed many districts or schools within a district; yet often the curriculum direction has remained unchanged. If students are leaving school because they feel that the educational system is forcing them out, then perhaps the district might reassess its philosophy on student retention, provide staff development opportunities for the faculty and staff on techniques for working with at-risk students, and design a more effective personal guidance and counseling program. Some of these strategies might be incorporated into a redesigned alternative curriculum for at-risk students.

When are students leaving the educational system? If it is at age 16, then dropout prevention programs in the middle school (grades 7 and 8) or the first year of high school (grade 9) need to be established. If students are dropping out in grades 10, 11, or 12, the establishment of an alternative curriculum may better assist at-risk students to stay in school until graduation. If students have already left school, dropout retrieval strategies must be structured to attract them back into the educational environment, as opposed to retaining them or keeping them from joining the dropout roles in the first place.

What types of staffing changes need to be made or what staff retraining needs to be conducted in order to accommodate the proposed changes? Does the current faculty need to receive in-service staff development to incorporate the proposed changes? It is unrealistic to think that all members of an existing school staff are going to approach the problems of reducing the dropout rates of at-risk students with the same vigor. Many will be concerned that they have not been trained adequately through their degree or certification programs to address these new, nontraditional learners in the classroom. Identification, assessment, motivation, instructional strategies, curriculum modification, and evaluation of at-risk students are examples of subjects that should be addressed in an ongoing staff development program if a school or district is to implement strategies for dropout prevention.

What financial resources are needed? The issue of money always seems to surface in any conversation regarding the implementation of new programs. Changes very often warrant the review of financial resources to determine whether adequate funding is available within a district's budget. The lack of adequate funding can undermine the most well-intended program. A school or district's strategy for dropout prevention might be supported through a collaborative effort between the district and a local business or community agency. The local Private Industrial Council (Job Training Partnership Act, JTPA) is an excellent resource to link with the local district. Social service agencies and volunteer groups could be solicited for assistance in human resources. Outside funding might also be secured through a joint effort with a state education agency or through a national grant.

A STUDENT-CENTERED APPROACH

Once the causes for the dropout problem have been identified and all other related issues and concerns have been addressed as much as possible, the next task is to select a dropout prevention strategy that focuses on the individual needs of the student, is student-centered, and is linked to the future. Any program that does not address this concern is doomed to repeat the failures of many of the current educational programs that have not been directed to the needs of at-risk students. A student-centered strategy is one that is competency-based and is individualized to meet the needs of the student. A good student-centered strategy seeks to cultivate each student's strengths and personality. It does not force everyone to conform. This is not to say that a student-centered strategy is a permissive one. A student-centered strategy should contain structure, with established rules, procedures, and organization, but it also should provide some opportunities for making choices and building responsibilities.

As discussed in earlier chapters, at-risk students who drop out of school display no single set of traits or characteristics. As a group, at-risk students are very often like those students who have chosen to stay in the educational system until graduation. The only difference is that some at-risk students have chosen the path of dropping out. In order to be successful, schools must incorporate a student-centered approach that will enable all students to achieve their educational potential.

Dropping out of school very often has its roots in the culmination of experiences related to the school's approach to student's needs. According to data from the United States Department of Education, National Center for Education Statistics (1983), youth who dropped out of school report doing so for various reasons: 33.1 percent dropped out because "school was not for them"; 33 percent, because of "poor grades"; and 15.5 percent, because they "didn't get along with teachers." The best chance for attracting students who have already left and to prevent those who are currently at risk from dropping out lies in a student-centered approach to learning that meets the needs of students who will be active participants in the society of the 21st century. This approach must be one that takes into account the individuality and uniqueness of each student. In the past, schools have put forth their efforts in enticing or attracting school dropouts to return and then to adjust to the same unsatisfactory and unpromising learning environment. If schools continue to offer a curriculum that is perceived as unrewarding and unrelated to the needs of these students, the dropout problem will persist.

Mentoring programs, tutoring assistance, counseling and guidance efforts, parental involvement programs, and alternative curricula are just stopgap measures that will be effective for some at-risk students. The educational system will still be the same old system that has been forcing square pegs into round holes. It is time for schools to come face to face with the needs and concerns of all of the students the educational system was designed to serve and not just cater to the needs of those who will further their education by enrolling in college on graduation. If a district or school's curriculum seems to be addressing the needs of most of the students for whom it is intended to serve, then an alternative curriculum that is student-centered might be in order for those special at-risk students who are dropping out before graduation.

DROPOUT PREVENTION STRATEGIES

The selection of a dropout prevention strategy or strategies should be linked to the number of at-risk students in need of assistance. For example, an alternative school generally will not be set up for just a few at-risk students. Perhaps some parental involvement strategies or a mentoring program would better fit the few at-risk students in need of special help. Second, the selection of a strategy must be based on the specific types of assistance that will be required in order to prevent students from dropping out of school before graduation. If students are in need of an alternative class or curriculum, the establishment of better guidance and counseling strategies alone will not solve the dropout dilemma. Each strategy has its strengths and limitations. Although each can function independently, perhaps the best scenario may be a combination of strategies designed to best address the unique needs of students for whom it was designed. For the purposes of this chapter the discussion of strategies for dropout prevention focuses on five principal strategies that have been successful in dropout prevention:

1. mentoring strategies
2. tutorial assistance strategies
3. counseling and guidance strategies
4. parental involvement strategies
5. alternative curriculum strategies

Mentoring Strategies

One dropout prevention strategy that has been used effectively is a mentoring program that links each at-risk student with a mentor. A mentor is an individual whom a student can confide in and look to for assistance. Mentors can assist at-risk students with the difficulties of trying to cope with the everyday problems and hardships that adolescents face. Being an adolescent or a teenager is not an easy experience for anyone. Often at-risk students must face the problems of daily living without much assistance. Good role models may not be readily available in the home or community. Parents, teachers, counselors, senior citizens, community leaders, business leaders, sports figures, ministers, or older students can provide guidance and assistance to at-risk students in a mentoring role. According to Fennimore and Pritz (1988), the "role of the mentor is to aid students in promoting the most essential of all developmental areas—self, or existential, development" (p. 2). Through this role, mentors help at-risk students to clarify their personal and occupational development.

Several different types of skills or qualities are necessary for a mentor to fulfill the responsibilities of promoting a student's self-development (Fennimore & Pritz, 1988). An effective mentor must become a proponent of the student. In the past, at-risk students have had very few individuals who have become their advocates. The traditional schools of the past have forced at-risk students to leave school if they did not conform to the rules and curriculum. A mentor must become the student's advocate and speak up for the student in times of need.

Because of the interpersonal relationship that can develop with a mentor, the mentor is in a unique position to hear the student's side of an issue. Because at-risk students have few role models to follow, the mentor is often looked to for guidance and advice. Often the mentor can assist the student by suitable contacts or by making the first contact on behalf of the student.

Closely linked with functioning as a proponent of the at-risk student is the ability of the mentor to be a good listener. A mentor provides advice and support for the student but must also take the time to listen to the student. The world of the at-risk student is one that has been filled with teachers, parents, and adults who are always providing advice; yet few people may have taken the time necessary to listen to the student's side of the story. Many times students are seeking someone who will listen and understand their thoughts, feelings, and concerns. The mentor may be the first one to hear that the teenage girl might be pregnant and in need of advice and assistance. The mentor may be the person who can encourage the student to have the appropriate tests conducted at a clinic or will go along with the student when she speaks with her family.

The mentor must have good networking skills to help at-risk students link with available community or school resources. For example, a mentor could help the at-risk student locate employment opportunities in the community, to prevent the student from dropping out because of economic constraints. In addition, the mentor could assist the student by providing advice and making the initial contact for enrollment in a cooperative vocational education program. The mentor can guide students through periods of low self-esteem by pointing out that they, too, had similar self-doubts. A mentor can share information and help students make the decisions that seem best for them.

Last, a good mentor should be able to motivate others. Vince Lombardi, the famous coach of the Green Bay Packers football team, and Knute Rockne, the immortal coach of Notre Dame, are two names that come to mind when the term motivation is discussed. One quality that each of these individuals possessed was the ability to instill in others the desire to do their very best even when facing the greatest of problems. Many at-risk students tend not to participate in extracurricular activities, which increases isolation and the potential to drop out of school (Texas Dropout Information Clearinghouse, 1989). At-risk students have been exposed to a series of failures—one after another. Many have just given up. A good mentor can encourage and motivate these students to do their very best.

Tutorial Assistance Strategies

A second strategy for dropout prevention is the use of tutorial assistance programs. Tutorial assistance can be provided by paraprofessionals, resource teachers, regular academic teachers, community agency personnel, senior citizens, parents, or other students.

The employment of students as tutors is referred to as peer tutoring. One of the principal concerns of educators and parents has been the problem of failure in the important academic subjects of English, science, social studies, and mathematics. Teachers who have employed peer tutors have seen numerous benefits. Teaching time in the classroom can be reduced because peer tutors can provide the necessary help to those at-risk students who fall behind because of difficulties in understanding the subject matter. In addition, peer tutors can be extremely important in teaching students who have missed school or who have been late to class. Peer tutoring, when used in conjunction with regular classroom instruction, can assist at-risk students in improving achievement scores. Furthermore, tutors themselves benefit because they learn more about the subject they are teaching.

Through the use of peer tutors, teachers have discovered improvement in attitudes toward school of both the tutor and the student receiving special help. Research reported by Pritz and Crowe (1987) indicates that students who had been disruptive changed their attitudes and exhibited more maturity toward school as a result of becoming peer tutors. Furthermore, the relationships established through the peer tutoring process are often less threatening than those established through the use of teachers, resource personnel, or other individuals who are not of the same age level. Students generally feel that the peer tutor "talks the same language" as they do and can make many of the more difficult tasks seem easier.

The first step in establishing a peer tutorial program is to determine the types of facilities and equipment that will be needed. For a tutoring program to be effective, adequate space must be provided for the number of at-risk students to be served. The first priority should be a quiet location where students can meet for one-on-one study and instruction. In addition, this area will need adequate storage space to house special equipment, such as tapes, records, and video and other educational equipment.

The second step in implementing a peer tutorial program is to determine the personnel requirements for operating the program. Who is going to coordinate the overall activity? Who will handle the scheduling of tutors and facilities? Who will provide staff development with regard to the teacher's role within the classroom? Who will monitor the tutoring sessions and keep track of records and student progress? These are just a few of the questions that must be addressed by a program coordinator. Planning to implement a tutoring program must encompass the overall operation of the program if it is to be effective.

The third step in establishing a peer tutorial program is to formulate various operational policies. The program coordinator will need to set up a procedure for identifying at-risk students who will be participating in the program. Tutors will need to be identified along with their specific areas of expertise. After identification, a cadre of qualified tutors will need to be trained in tutoring techniques, supervised practice, and strategies for working with at-risk students. Once tutors are trained, student tutors will need to be to matched with students and assigned. Compatibility should be a major consideration in this area.

The last step in establishing a peer tutorial program is to plan for the evaluation of its effectiveness. What criteria will be used to determine whether the program has met its planned objectives? Has the operation gone smoothly? Were all of those involved with the program pleased with the results? Did the scores of the at-risk students receiving instruction improve? Did more at-risk students stay in school until graduation? These and many other questions need to be addressed as part of the program evaluation. Evaluation is an integral part of any tutoring program, and its importance should not be overlooked. The evaluation process requires the development or selection of evaluation instruments and the collection of data by both an in-house review team and a team of outside evaluators. Once the evaluation results have been collected, tabulated, and analyzed, recommendations for program strengths and suggestions for improvement can be made in order to modify the program.

The peer tutoring strategy for dropout prevention can be a no-cost or low-cost approach to helping resolve many of the education-related problems of at-risk students. A plan can be implemented easily, and peer tutors can be trained effectively to assist other students.

Counseling and Guidance Strategies

According to Orr (1987), "Youth dropouts are far less likely to be involved in school activities and generally have a poorer opinion of themselves and their ability than their in-school peers" (p. 26). It is very difficult to know whether these feelings have a significant impact on at-risk students who drop out of school, but counseling programs that stress the important issue of self-concept have been shown to be more effective in keeping students in school (Orr, 1987). Guidance and counseling involvement strategies can establish trust and communication with at-risk students to convince them that someone in the educational system cares. Others concur. Conrath (1986) believes that too many schools are impersonal, threatening, and confusing. Larsen and Shertzer (1987) suggest that, although school counselors cannot alone instill self-confidence and self-worth in all students, they can have a significant impact. Counselors can build self-development through individual and group counseling sessions as well as through the establishment of peer groups or support groups for at-risk students. In addition to self-development, many at-risk students need help with academic and career counseling. Others will need assistance through personal and social counseling.

Any guidance or counseling program that ignores the issue of substance abuse by at-risk students is remiss. Drug or alcohol abuse can affect all aspects of a student's life. Family relationships can become impaired and school achievement affected. Many students under the influence of drugs turn to delinquency, crime, or other deviant behavior. The effects of drugs can also impair a student's ability to cope with the demands of daily life. Counselors should become involved in the prevention of, as well as the rehabilitation process for, substance abuse by at-risk students.

In implementing guidance and counseling strategies for dropout prevention, there are a number of ideas that can be incorporated. The counselor can keep close track of those students who potentially might be identified as at risk. This can be done by keeping a watchful eye on excessive absences from school or classes. When patterns or trends begin to appear, the counselor should meet with the student, teacher, or parent to determine the causes. Low involvement in activities, low or failing grades, and disruptive behavior are early signals that a student may be experiencing difficulties. One-on-one or small-group counseling sessions are recommended first steps in implementing guidance and counseling strategies for dropout prevention. Students can be encouraged to pursue cooperative vocational education programs to develop entry-level job skills along with good work attitudes.

If students do decide to leave school before graduation, counselors can hold exit interviews to suggest community-based support agencies that might intervene on behalf of the student. For example, the counselor might inquire as to whether the student needs assistance in seeking employment, drug abuse counseling, legal assistance, or health care.

Parental Involvement Strategies

A fourth strategy for dropout prevention is the use of parental involvement programs. Parents of at-risk students can encourage and influence their children's success in school. Many parents of at-risk students view education as a means of breaking the cycle of low income and substandard living conditions. Parental involvement can take a number of forms. It can take the form of home visitations, parent-school conferences, the formation of parent education centers, parents-as-tutors programs, or any one of several other strategies. Parents of at-risk students very often do not know what they can do to promote and encourage their children to stay in school. Many times these parents have difficulty in supervising and disciplining their children at home. Parents of many at-risk children have expressed a willingness to be involved actively in their children's education if given the opportunity. Furthermore, research has indicated that working with parents is an effective way to bring about positive behavioral changes and improvement in student achievement (Warner, 1974). The benefits of increased parental involvement are improved student attendance, decreased dropout rates, more positive parent-student communication, and increased parent-community support of the school (Texas Dropout Information Clearinghouse, 1989). Examples of components of parental involvement programs include:

- parent-teacher conferences
- monthly meetings
- training seminars and workshops
- career days
- open houses
- luncheons
- personal and family counseling sessions
- community coffees
- instructional aides
- tutors
- community resource persons
- home visitations
- newsletters
- telephone follow-ups
- parent study groups
- advisory committees

The central idea behind parent involvement strategies is to bring parents, teachers, administrators, and counselors together into a close working partnership for the benefit of children.

Alternative Curriculum Strategies

A fifth dropout prevention strategy is the use of alternative curricula. A few examples of components of alternative curricula include part-time classes, evening instruction, year-round schools, weekend classes, open-entry/open-exit programs, schools-within-a school, and expanded time-on-task programs. An alternative curriculum generally consists of three different approaches (Edison-Swift & Novak, 1981): alternative classes, alternative programs, and alternative schools. One or more of these may be necessary to meet the needs of students that are not being met through the regular curriculum. Students who are experiencing failure in one of their regular classes are good candidates for an alternative class that can provide more teacher-student interaction and individualized instruction. On the other hand, students who are having difficulties and experiencing a number of failures in several classes such as English, science, social studies, and mathematics might best profit from an alternative program. If large numbers of students are experiencing failure and are dropping out, a district might consider the adoption of an alternative school. The latter two options are generally most desirable if students have become disruptive in the regular curriculum and need a fresh start.

Not everyone is enthusiastic about the alternative curriculum approach to reducing the dropout statistics of at-risk students. Many educators view the alternative curriculum as an opportunity to relax some of the school policies or to create smaller specialized classes for at-risk students. Some educators view the alternative curriculum as an opportunity to take at-risk students out of regular classes, thereby reducing class size and, more important, as a means of removing disruptive students from the classroom. Others view the alternative curriculum approach as an expensive approach for taking care of students who do not want to be in school.

Careful consideration should be used before deciding whether the alternative curriculum approach will successfully meet the specific needs of at-risk students. If the strategy is selected just to remove or segregate at-risk students, then the strategy is not correct; it will be only a means of reducing or pushing under the table a justifiable concern that will surface at a later time somewhere else.

The alternative curriculum strategy is a viable means of meeting the needs of certain types of at-risk students because the educational environment can be adjusted to meet the needs of these students. But no alternative can address the needs of all at-risk students. Students who are having problems with drug abuse or severe emotional problems will also have a difficult time succeeding in an alternative curriculum. The alternative curriculum strategy is designed to address certain kinds of needs that at-risk students may have such as:

- remedial instruction in the basic skills of reading, writing, communication, and mathematics
- study skills
- employability skills
- social adjustment skills
- everyday living skills

The alternative curriculum generally has as its central goal the improvement of students' academic skills, self-concept, decision-making skills, employability skills, and everyday living skills so that they can become contributing members of society.

Alternative Classes

Perhaps the least degree of modification to a school curriculum involves establishing alternative classes. Alternative classes can be established to address the needs of students at risk of dropping out by providing special assistance and instruction in a specific area. Alternative classes provide at-risk students with additional time and individualized attention as a result of lower student/teacher ratios. Generally because of the special emphasis that alternative classes place on learning and instruction, students begin to perform much better in their regular classes. As with all special classes, educators must be aware of the labels that students can quickly attach to other students who are receiving specialized instruction.

The alternative class is structured so that the at-risk student participates in all other regular-curriculum classes while receiving more specialized instruction in the alternative class. Let's examine the alternative English class, as an example. Students who have been experiencing failure in a ninth-grade English class would be desirable students for an alternative English class. In the alternative English class, remedial instruction can be provided in a less threatening environment in which individualized attention can be provided by a teacher who has received specialized training in remediation techniques for at-risk students. The development of good reading skills, writing skills, verbal skills, comprehension skills, and study skills can be stressed in the alternative class.

Another example of an alternative class might be a cooperative vocational education program designed for students who are at risk of dropping out because of economic reasons. The focus of the alternative class would be on the establishment of employability skills that emphasize how to seek and retain a job and advance in the world of work. The alternative cooperative vocational education program could also be utilized for the at-risk student who needs special instruction in the development of interpersonal skills such as getting along with others, values clarification, employee-employer relations, personal hygiene, and respecting the rights of others.

An alternative class for at-risk students can be implemented at any grade level. The most successful are those that are implemented when they are first needed. Early intervention keeps at-risk students from experiencing failure after failure in their academic subjects. The value of the alternative class is that it can respond to the specific problems of an at-risk student.

Alternative Programs

Alternative programs are very much like alternative classes except that they consist of sequences of classes that are designed specifically for a larger number of at-risk students. Because alternative programs are designed for a larger number of students, homogeneous groupings of students such as teenage parents, truants, students in trouble with the law, or drug abusers can be made to address the specific needs of the students. Alternative programs can be more comprehensive in scope, since the curriculum can be interrelated and coordinated among teachers and other school personnel who are working with the same at-risk students.

Alternative programs lend themselves to the use of a wide variety of school options. One of these options, often used, is the school-within-a-school concept, which enables a district to use its existing facilities. The concept is to provide within an existing facility a separate program established for at-risk students. Instead of being placed in regular programs, most of these students are instructed under the school-within-a school program. This strategy enables flexible scheduling through the use of part-time classes, evening classes, open-entry/open-exit classes, and extended time on tasks to become the norm instead of the exception.

Alternative Schools

Alternative schools represent the most comprehensive strategy of the alternative curriculum strategies. Alternative schools are usually located in a separate facility and are operated by a separate school staff. Because many components of the alternative school are very different from those of the regular school, the staff are usually well trained in techniques and strategies for working with at-risk students. Alternative schools are usually a district's last effort at resolving the problems of at-risk students. The alternative school separates at-risk students from the regular school population where they mixed on a daily basis with other students. This separation is deemed necessary in many instances to give at-risk students a new start at completing the requirements for graduation. The separation of at-risk students from regular school students prevents the daily conflicts that come from being labeled as different when attending alternative classes or an alternative program. The alternative school can also be a successful option for returning dropouts.

Alternative schools have the advantage of being able to experiment with very nontraditional approaches with at-risk students. One example of a nontraditional approach is the open-schedule concept. With an open schedule, at-risk students may decide to attend classes during daytime hours as well as evening hours. In conjunction with this type of schedule, students have open time blocks between classes and are permitted to leave the school campus between those classes. The regulations under which regular schools are operated, such as requiring permission to enter the hallways, to use the restrooms, and to smoke on school grounds, are very often dismissed. Alternative schools operate very much like college campuses.

Students in need of job skills training may participate in cooperative vocational education programs as part of their educational curriculum. The alternative school provides much more flexibility for on-the-job training because individual classes can be better designed to fit the student's hours of employment. Some alternative schools also enjoy greater flexibility in determining the required curriculum for at-risk students enrolled in a cooperative vocational education program by permitting students to receive academic credits in such subjects as English, science, and mathematics while they are enrolled in the vocational curriculum.

In addition to offering more flexibility and an individualized curriculum, many alternative schools have adopted a student grading system, such as the pass/no pass course option, which eliminates the anxiety that repeated school failures have brought to at-risk students. Many alternative schools award their own diplomas or certificates of graduation. Because of the needs of many of the students who enroll in alternative schools, many provide a variety of other services such as child care, personnel and family counseling, transportation, and various social services for their students.

SUMMARY

The selection of a dropout prevention strategy for at-risk students should be founded on the causes of the dropout problem. Once the causes of the dropout problem have been identified and related issues and concerns have been addressed, the next task is to select a dropout prevention strategy that focuses on the individual needs of the student. This is referred to as a student-centered approach.

The ultimate selection of a dropout prevention strategy will be linked to the number of at-risk students to be served and the specific type of assistance that will be required. This chapter discussed five principal strategies that have been successful in dropout prevention: mentoring strategies, tutoring strategies, counseling and guidance strategies, parental involvement strategies, and alternative curriculum strategies.

REFERENCES

Conrath, J. (1986). Effective schools must focus on potential dropouts. *NASSP Bulletin, 70* (487), 46–50.

Edison-Swift, S., & Novak, J. (1981). Identifying approaches for dropout prevention. In J. Novak & B. Dougherty (Eds.), *Staying in . . . A dropout prevention handbook.* Madison, WI: Vocational Studies Center, University of Wisconsin.

Fennimore, T., & Pritz, S. (1988). *A guide for dropout prevention: Creating an integrated learning environment in secondary schools.* Columbus, OH: National Center for Research in Vocational Education.

Kvaraceus, W. (1960). The status and function of personnel services. *Education, 81,* 202–209.

Larsen, P., & Shertzer, B. (1987). The high school dropout: Everybody's problem. *School Counselor, 34,* 163–169.

Orr, M. (1987). *Keeping students in school.* San Francisco, CA: Jossey-Bass.

National Center for Education Statistics. (1983). High school dropout: Descriptive information from high school and beyond (Bulletin). Washington, DC: U.S. Department of Education.

Pritz, S., & Crowe, M. (1987). *Techniques for remediation: Peer tutoring.* Columbus, OH: National Center for Research in Vocational Education.

Texas Dropout Information Clearinghouse. (1989). *Successful schooling for economically disadvantaged at-risk youth.* Austin, TX: Texas Education Agency.

Warner, R., Jr. (1974). Research in counseling: Consulting with parents. *Personnel and Guidance Journal, 53,* 68–70.

chapter 8

The School At-Risk Team

Michelle D. Sarkees-Wircenski

As the United States moves into the decade of the 1990s and beyond that into the 21st century, one of the critical issues that will have to be addressed is the organization of the nation's educational system and the growing numbers of at-risk students who are unable to succeed in this system. National estimates suggest that approximately one-fourth of the fifth graders who are now in school will not graduate. A variety of factors cause youth to drop out of school, including low grades, grade failure, negative attitudes toward school, pregnancy, need to support their family, and marriage.

Doyle (1985) states that

> Many secondary school students, despite their ability, will not expend the effort to achieve their potential. Underachievement can become a way of life. Once students begin believing they have failed, because they lack ability, they tend to lose hope for future success. They develop a pattern of academic hopelessness and stop trying. (p. 41)

A team effort will be required to decrease the dropout rates in our nation's schools. Flexible programs will have to be developed. Educators must assume that every student has the potential to succeed. Professional collegiality will be necessary to meet this challenge, including support, cooperation, and sharing. The message must be delivered to all students that we believe they can succeed. The educational community must assume that the best way to help students succeed is to start with their strengths, rather than with their limitations. These will be the challenges of the next decade for all educators.

RESTRUCTURING SCHOOLS TO ADDRESS AT-RISK POPULATIONS

The education of our children is the most important investment that the United States can make. Currently, many of the schools in this country stand accused of failing to meet the needs of a large number of youth. Our schools should hold as their mission the responsibility of preparing individuals to assume the rights and obligations of citizenship and to assist them in achieving their full potential.

Since the early 1980s, the current state of public education in our nation has been criticized in numerous reform proposals. These proposals have pointed out the rising dropout rate and the resulting serious problems that can be seen in the social, economic, and moral fiber of our communities.

Educational Imperatives

After reviewing studies and reports on education that have been issued in recent years, the Committee for Economic Development (1985) has identified 10 imperatives to guide our nation's schools in reforming their current practices in order to be successful schools for all students in the future. This committee is an independent research and educational organization of 200 educators and business representatives. The purpose of the organization is to propose policies that will help achieve steady economic growth, to provide greater and more equal opportunities for every citizen, and to increase productivity and living standards. The imperatives that have been proposed for education are as follows:

1. Educational priorities should be better defined, and resources should be invested where the payoffs will be high. As a proportion of total spending, instruction requires a larger investment; administration and bureaucracy need less. Priority should be given to preschool programs for the disadvantaged and to programs that address the special educational needs of junior high school students.
2. Employability should not be confused with vocationalism. Employability requires problem-solving skills, command of the English language, self-discipline, and the ability to acquire and apply new knowledge.
3. The central purpose of education is to develop the potential of every student, regardless of race, sex, or physical handicap.
4. Teachers are professionals. They should be held to high standards and rewarded accordingly.
5. Parents are a critical component of successful public schools.
6. Greater trust should be placed in the initiative of individual schools. Teachers and administrators should have increased decision-making power.

7. States should refrain from excessive regulation, centralization, and control of the schools. But they should set standards, monitor achievement, and intervene if schools fail to perform.
8. A new coalition to support the public schools is needed—one that joins business, labor, and civic leaders with parents, educators, and school boards.
9. Education research and development and its effective utilization should be given greater emphasis. There is a great deal that we do not yet know about education, and much of what we do know is not being applied in the classroom.
10. Business should make a long-term commitment to support the public schools. Companies should provide policy and project support and targeted funding, with the expectation that the schools will improve their performance. But business should not be expected to provide general funding for education beyond the taxes it pays to the community. (p. 3)

Future Challenges for Educators

The imperatives proposed by the Committee for Economic Development (1985) certainly present a tremendous challenge to public schools everywhere. Increased graduation requirements, increasing class sizes, decreasing budgets, declining test scores, teacher shortages, and higher dropout rates will undoubtedly confront educators in the next decade.

In addition, the number of at-risk students who will require assistance in succeeding in school will continue to escalate. Sarkees and Feichtner (1987, p. 22) point out that of the 3.6 million children who entered school for the first time in 1986, the following scenario is predicted:

- one of four will be from poverty homes
- 14 percent will be from single-parent households
- 15 percent will be handicapped
- 15 percent will be limited English-proficient
- 14 percent of their mothers will be unmarried
- 40 percent will come from broken homes
- 10 percent will have illiterate parents
- 25 to 33 percent will be "latch key" children
- 25 percent will never finish school

This certainly has implications for all educators. Creating success for dropout-prone students will mean a drastic change in the delivery of educational services as we now know them.

Effective School Characteristics

In a study of public school teachers asked to describe their school, only 15 to 35 percent selected "imaginative," "adventurous," "intellectually exciting," "curious," or "initiating." Yet, when asked to identify the 10 characteristics that attributed to their own educational growth, "adventurous" and "intellectual excitement" were among those most frequently selected (Heath, 1986). The research on effective schools indicates that some specific factors increase the chances of success for all students. Administrators, students, teachers, and parents from these successful educational settings collaborate on the goals, methods, and curriculum of the school. Effective schools have certain characteristics, including:

- vigorous instructional leadership
- orderly, positive school climate
- emphasis on specifying objectives and expected achievement, and monitoring of these objectives for mastery
- instructional practices that emphasize basic skills and academic achievement
- belief that all students can master basic skills objectives and can learn, accompanied by high levels of expectation for success for students and instructors
- collegiality among teachers in support of student achievement
- assessment as an important component of all programs, with the results used for accountability as well as to make necessary changes
- provision of developmental counseling services for grades K through 12
- establishment of the relevance between the curricula and career goals through such programs as work experience activities, mentoring activities, self-awareness classes, and career development experiences (Lehr & Harris, 1988, p. 16)

In looking beyond the characteristics of effective schools, certain elements serve to improve programs for at-risk students. Sarkees, West, and Wircenski (1988) make several recommendations:

- Consider all factors that affect students' educational programs, including economic, health, cultural, and linguistic factors in addition to academic disadvantages.
- Establish programs that incorporate parents in the educational planning process for at-risk students.

- Establish a better tracking mechanism for dropouts, including outreach.
- Expand programs and services to an earlier age.
- Emphasize generalizable skills in academic and vocational curricula.
- Improve interagency coordination.
- Establish alternative educational delivery strategies for dropouts.
- Publicize and expand instructional strategies and models that work well with at-risk populations.
- Implement a comprehensive career development and employability skills process for at-risk students.
- Use successful individuals who come from at-risk populations as role models.
- Establish a clearinghouse for information and contacts for dropout prevention.
- Expand the support services available to at-risk students. (pp. 35–38)

THE AT-RISK TEAM

Suggested changes for schools and at-risk programs will require the cooperative efforts of a variety of individuals representing different backgrounds and expertise. No one individual can effect all of these changes. The challenge demands a team approach. The philosophy that educators adopt regarding at-risk students will direct the extent and nature of dropout prevention strategies. The at-risk team's role in planning, implementing, and evaluating programs to meet the needs of at-risk students is crucial to the success or failure of these programs.

An example of a philosophy that would help to create successful schools for all students is that of invitational education (Purkey & Novak, 1984). This theory offers an approach to the educational process that attempts to make the schools a place where students want to go, rather than a place they want to leave. Invitational education centers on four assumptions:

1. People are able, valuable, and capable of self-direction, and they must be treated accordingly.
2. The process of teaching/learning is a cooperative activity in which the process is as important as the product.
3. Individuals possess relatively untapped potential.
4. Individual potential is best developed by policies, places, programs, and processes that are designed to encourage success and by people who strive to realize this potential in themselves as well as in others.

TEAM MEMBERS

A single formula does not exist for developing a school at-risk team. The members of the team will depend on the size of the district and the number of responsibilities that people are already assuming.

One quality of many at-risk team members is their leadership potential. They have a strong sense of purpose and are not afraid to make changes that will assist students in succeeding in school. They are persistent and willing to invest whatever time or effort is required to achieve results. They realize their own strengths and abilities as well as their weaknesses. At-risk team members are learners who stay informed of new techniques rather than automatically relying on old ones. These individuals are risk takers and are willing to explore any resource that can accomplish their objectives. Team members practice effective communication techniques with others so that everyone is working together. Finally, at-risk team members are not afraid to fail; they turn each mistake into a valuable learning experience.

Administrators

Administrators represent a key element in determining the success of at-risk students. The educational philosophy of the administrator as a primary leader of the educational process is critical to the success of a dropout prevention program. The effective administrator creates an atmosphere for students, teachers, and support personnel that is encouraging and supportive.

Research indicates that strong educational leaders support innovative educational changes in order for at-risk students to succeed in school. To meet the needs of these learners, administrators help to reshape schools into institutions that are more student-focused and less bureaucratic. They build morale among the teachers. They reduce the administrative tasks assigned to teachers to a minimum, so that they can spend more time with students. They develop community support for the school, its faculty, and its goals (Lehr & Harris, 1988). Some suggested contributions that administrators can make to the school at-risk team are described below.

Policy Development

Administrators can direct or influence the development of a written school policy that communicates the philosophy that all students can succeed. The mission of providing quality programming and cooperative working relationships should be stressed.

Use of Innovative Strategies

Administrators can encourage teachers to use innovative strategies that motivate students to learn. An open-door policy with both students and staff members can facilitate open communication, creative ideas, and a sense of ownership. The learning activities conducted in the school should be tailored to the needs of the students. Flexibility should be exercised in delivering curricula with a blend of active listening and counseling.

Needs Assessment

Administrators can conduct a needs assessment of the school, district, or community to determine the extent of the dropout situation and the kinds of problems that prevent students from staying in school. Data may be collected informally by meeting with teachers, counselors, parents, and others to gain an insight into the problems that need to be addressed. A more formal approach can be conducted by selecting an appropriate instrument so that documentation will be on file.

The information collected from the needs assessment should be used to develop a profile of dropout-prone students at the local level. The profile can then be matched to available resources. A review of available staff, facilities, funding, community agencies, and other resources should be conducted in order to match solutions with problems. This match should form a basic profile of what school and community-based elements will need to be included in dropout prevention strategies.

Model Dropout Prevention Program

Administrators should provide an opportunity for the team to propose a model dropout prevention program based on the results of the needs assessment. The model should address indicators of potential dropouts at the local level (e.g., academic achievement, attendance patterns, and substance abuse) as well as the grade level at which the program will begin to work for students who are at risk of dropping out of school (e.g., middle school grades, grade 9, grade 6).

Program objectives should be established by the at-risk team and should include criteria for referrals of students. Components of the model program should be identified so that each can be developed. Examples of program components might include:

- vocational assessment
- career development
- career counseling
- curriculum modification

- employability skills
- basic skills
- transition plans

Short-term and long-range procedures should be developed to evaluate the program on a continuous basis. Frequent feedback should be collected so that necessary changes can be made to improve the model.

Support Services

Administrators can arrange for necessary support services to be provided on a continuing basis. These services should respond to the changing needs of the model program that is developed for a district. Kolde (1987, p. 358) identified some basic services that should be provided by the administrator. These are described below.

Instructional Support Services. Instructional support services include assistance for the instructor in modifying materials or strategies, monitoring of programs, assistance in identifying and solving problems, direct one-on-one instructional support for the student, and assistance for instructor with setting objectives and evaluating progress.

Counseling Support Services. Counseling support services include initial contact with the student; referral to the counselor for regular, ongoing contact; assistance for the counselor with problem solving; facilitation of transition from school to employment.

Educational Program Direction

Administrators can direct the operation of educational programs in a positive way so that they are success-oriented for at-risk students. An emphasis should be placed on interdisciplinary team teaching, adoption of competency-based programming, flexible pacing of instruction, and linkages with parents and the community.

The direction of educational programs also involves the management and coordination of staff. This includes the assurance that personnel are committed to the philosophy and goals of the at-risk program. Teachers, counselors, and support staff should be willing to establish close relationships with at-risk students who can be very demanding. Teachers and counselors should have a close working relationship. A coordinated transition process should exist between elementary school, middle school, and high school, as well as a smooth transition process between school and postschool experiences. Multidisciplinary teaching should be encouraged. Classrooms should have low teacher/pupil ratios. Programs should be presented with a combination of basic skills and differentiated objectives according to ability, counseling, and supportive services.

Budget Planning

Administrators can incorporate the provision of services for at-risk students into existing and future budget plans. They can also determine the level of support that can be expected for dropout prevention strategies from the local board of education. Proposals and presentations may have to be presented to board members so that adequate support can be obtained.

Some costs that should be considered have been identified by Faddis and Pritz (1988, pp. 19–20) are described below.

Developmental Costs. Developmental costs include those for construction or renovation of facilities; curriculum development or revision; in service for participants (professional and volunteer); equipment purchases or repairs, or both; purchase of texts, software, and consumable supplies; and telephone installations.

Operational Costs. Operational costs include those for running the program, such as staff salaries; release time for instructors and other school staff; equipment repair; purchase of additional texts, software, and consumable supplies; transportation for students to alternative schools or cooperative jobs, or the like (as needed); in-service costs (as needed); program evaluation costs; and heating, lighting, telephone, and maintenance estimates if a separate facility is needed.

Initial Orientation Costs. Organize an orientation event for the coordinators of the program at each site when the dropout prevention program is first introduced. The coordinators should include not only the program coordinators at the schools, but also those persons in community agencies and organizations who are assigned the responsibility of coordinating their services with the program. Once these participants have a solid grasp of the program model, objectives, helping process, and so forth, they can in turn offer in-service orientation to other participating professionals and volunteers at their sites.

Annual Orientation Costs. Organize an annual orientation event (e.g., in service, meeting, or luncheon) for all adult participants (perhaps by school or site) to bring them up to date on the success of the program in the past year, any revisions to the model or procedures, and so forth. This is also a good time to orient new participants and to recognize outstanding contributions of participants from the year before. An unspoken purpose of such annual meetings should be to revitalize the participants' interest and motivation; therefore, provide a catered luncheon or dinner, if possible, to both reward them and spark their sense of mission.

Staff Development Activities

Administrators can make provisions for staff development activities. Information that can assist educational personnel in meeting the needs of at-risk students could include:

- referral procedures for at-risk students
- selection of appropriate instructional materials
- modification of teaching techniques to meet learning styles
- competency-based instruction
- motivation strategies
- counseling strategies
- peer tutoring and mentoring strategies
- cooperative learning
- techniques to evaluate the progress of at-risk students

In addition, other in-service and orientation strategies can be conducted to keep educators updated with regard to strategies that work with at-risk students.

Program Evaluation System

Administrators can provide leadership in designing a system for evaluating the success of dropout prevention strategies. Program components that should be evaluated include identification procedures for at-risk students, staff competencies, staffing patterns, support services, instructional resources, community involvement, parent involvement, and student follow-up.

Some questions that might be included in an at-risk program evaluation (Faddis & Pritz, 1988) are:

- How many seniors in the dropout prevention program successfully earned their high school diplomas or general equivalency diplomas?
- How do the grade averages of the graduating students in the program compare with the averages of other graduating students, both at risk and not at risk?
- How many of the graduating students in the program found jobs (what kinds, at what income levels) as compared with those of other graduating students, both at risk and not at risk?

- How many juniors or younger students in the program successfully completed the year without dropping out of school?
- How do the grade averages of the retained juniors or younger students in the program compare with the averages of other students completing those grades, both at risk and not at risk?
- How did the program affect less measurable student outcomes, such as growth in student self-esteem, career ambitions, ambitions for postsecondary education, and so forth?
- How many students who were enrolled in the program dropped out anyway, and why?
- How many students in the program participated in which kinds of educational and non-educational activities or services provided by the program?

Counselors

School counselors can play a significant role on the school at-risk team. Cunningham, Putzstuck, and Barbieri (1987) state,

> Students who are at-risk have multiple problems. It is important to assist these students in understanding and addressing possible solutions for these problems. At-risk students must learn to decrease or eliminate problems that are under their control, and to effectively manage those which are outside their realm of influence. Counselors can help students move from a position of anger and helplessness to one of self-confidence and independence. (p. 29)

Some contributions that counselors can make to the at-risk team are described below.

Development of Identification Process

Counselors can help to develop a districtwide process to identify potential at-risk students at as early an age as possible.

Development of Support Groups

Counselors can start support groups for students identified as potential dropouts. These groups can be small ones or one-to-one sessions. They will help students to communicate their problems and to develop coping skills, and they will also enable counselors to identify specific support services that could help students succeed in school.

Compilation of Extracurricular Activities

Counselors can compile a file of extracurricular activities, share these with at-risk students, and encourage them to become involved in activities that interest them. This may help the at-risk students to identify with the school.

Information on Work-Study Opportunities

Counselors can provide at-risk students with information about available work-study opportunities, which could be an alternative to leaving school.

Knowledge of Community Resources

Counselors should be knowledgeable of other professionals, agencies, and community resources so that they can refer at-risk students who have problems, and their parents to the appropriate resource (e.g., a mental health center, Big Brothers/Big Sisters, local Job Training Partnership Act (JTPA) programs, or Alcoholics Anonymous).

Parental Counseling

Counselors can meet and talk with parents of at-risk students to discuss their concerns and goals. Parents should be provided with information about vocational program offerings and be assisted in developing realistic perceptions of their children's interests, abilities, and special needs. This would be an appropriate time to interpret vocational assessment results. Counselors can also work with parents to set up a program of activity for the home, with specific suggestions regarding motivation, discipline, career development, and remedial academic skills.

Student Schedule Review

Counselors can review the schedules of at-risk students to determine whether they are manageable. They can use learning-style and teaching-style information to match at-risk students with instructors who will be able to work with them effectively.

Vocational Assessment

Counselors are often involved in administering vocational assessment activities, tests, and inventories to at-risk students. They can lend valuable insight by sharing an interpretation of these results, as well as the implications for educational planning and support services.

Consultation with Team Members

Counselors can consult with other team members regarding vocational programs and other curriculum offerings that will meet the needs of at-risk students.

Provision of Career Exploration

Counselors can take a leadership role in providing career exploration experiences for at-risk students. If these students become interested in a particular vocational area at an early age, their chances of staying in school will increase.

Conducting Workshops

Counselors can offer workshops for at-risk students that focus on developing social skills, communication skills, and employability skills. These workshops can also be conducted on an in-service basis for the school staff.

Creation of Job Clubs

Counselors can create job clubs for at-risk students that can assist them in developing job-seeking and job-retention skills. In addition, counselors can provide much-needed career counseling and information about job opportunities in the local area through these club meetings.

Development of Job Placement Services

Counselors can help other team members to develop job placement services for at-risk students.

Sharing Follow-up Information

Counselors can share with other team members important follow-up information regarding the at-risk students who have graduated as well as those who have dropped out of school.

Conducting Exit Interviews

Counselors can conduct exit interviews for students who decide to leave school, and can make appropriate referrals to community agencies that can provide assistance. Valuable information can be obtained about the students' reasons for leaving and how the school could have met their needs better. Counselors can stress to these individuals that if they regret their decision to drop out, they have options for returning to school.

Teachers

Teachers are critical members of the school at-risk team. They can fulfill a major role in preventing students from dropping out of school. However, not all teachers relate to at-risk learners. Research supports the theory that some teachers treat at-risk students differently from students who are high achievers and relate negatively to learners whom they believe to be less capable.

A study conducted by Gudridge (1980, p. 37) identified the characteristics of an "ideal" teacher. Although it is unrealistic to expect that all teachers will have all of these traits, it is accurate to say that teachers who are successful in working with at-risk students must possess a great many of them.

Characteristics of an Ideal Teacher

Intellectual Stimulation. The ideal teacher provides intellectual stimulation by

- inspiring the students to seek more knowledge
- being an exciting, vibrant person
- being enthusiastic
- sustaining pupil attention and response with activities appropriate to the various pupil levels
- making classwork interesting
- sharing with pupils in the enjoyment of humorous situations

Desirable Out-of-Class Behavior. The ideal teacher exhibits desirable out-of class behavior by

- being a good team worker
- striving for improvement through positive participation in professional growth activities
- assuming responsibilities outside the classroom as they relate to school
- being committed to the primary goal of assisting pupil growth
- using community resources in instruction
- reporting pupil progress to parents effectively

Productive Teaching Techniques. The ideal teacher uses productive teaching techniques by

- asking probing questions for understanding of concepts and relationships and for feedback

- incorporating student ideas in instruction
- using structuring comments, such as examples, to serve as "advance organizers"
- explaining things well and putting ideas across logically and in an orderly way
- using varied teaching strategies and materials that stimulate student learning
- providing opportunities for pupils to learn material on which they will be tested later

Positive Interpersonal Relations. The ideal teacher exhibits positive interpersonal relations by

- showing respect for pupils
- being tolerant of students whose ideas differ from his or hers
- using supportive criticism rather than blame, shame, or sarcasm
- being readily available to students
- being fair, impartial, and objective in the treatment of pupils
- providing opportunities for all pupils to experience success

Organized/Structured Class Management. The ideal teacher manages the class in an organized, structural way by

- monitoring pupil progress constantly and adjusting the pace accordingly
- presenting material in a well-organized fashion in order to use class time efficiently
- having well-defined objectives for pupils and working toward them
- using pupil assignments that are relevant and sufficient for in-depth learning
- being businesslike and task-oriented
- keeping the "difficulty level" of instruction appropriate for each student

Suggested contributions that teachers can make to the at-risk team include those described below.

Student Referral

Teachers should refer students who are having difficulty in their classes as soon as possible so that at-risk learners can be identified and provided with assistance.

Coordination with Resource Personnel

Teachers can coordinate with resource personnel to identify the services that students need and how they can be coordinated with the curriculum.

Cross-Training

Academic teachers, vocational teachers, and support personnel should cross-train in order to gain a full perspective of the total curriculum in which at-risk students are involved. This cross-training should include sharing program competencies, so that the integration of academic skills is emphasized in vocational programs, and vocational/career-related information is infused into academic curricula.

Development of an Interdisciplinary Approach

Teachers can develop an interdisciplinary approach to instructing at-risk students. Each teacher brings a repertoire of strategies and techniques, in addition to subject knowledge. A combination of approaches will increase the chances of success for at-risk students.

Diagnosis of Student Abilities

Teachers can diagnose the instructional levels, strengths, and limitations of at-risk students in relation to program standards and objectives. In this manner, individualized plans can be made for them.

Monitoring Progress

Teachers can use a management and record-keeping system that continuously monitors the progress of at-risk students. This information should be shared with other team members.

Basics Skills Instruction

An emphasis on basic skills instruction should be incorporated into all courses.

Cooperative Meetings

Cooperative meetings should be held periodically to include academic teachers, vocational teachers, counselors, and support personnel to share information, exchange ideas, and make plans for at-risk students.

Involvement in Professional Development

Teachers should become actively involved in ongoing in-service and professional development activities, both as participants and as presenters.

Support Staff

Support service personnel are an integral part of the school at-risk team. This category includes remedial instructors, basic academic instructors, special education teachers, resource room facilitators, diagnosticians, psychologists, therapists, social workers, attendance personnel, bilingual specialists, vocational special needs coordinators, paraprofessionals, work experience/co-op coordinators, community volunteers, and others who provide essential services to at-risk students.

General responsibilities of support personnel, depending on the specific job title, may include

- assisting teachers in adapting curricula and materials
- providing direct instruction to at-risk students
- acting as a liaison between teachers who work with at-risk students
- determining the interests, abilities, and needs of at-risk students
- evaluating and documenting student performance
- counseling students in career planning and transition from school into the community
- creating linkages between the school and the home
- developing individualized plans for specific students
- networking with community agencies that can offer appropriate services for at-risk populations
- providing remedial assistance or related academic instruction to at-risk students
- participating in ongoing, professional development concerning effective at-risk programs, both as participants and as presenters
- assisting teachers in selecting appropriate instructional strategies

The use of support personnel is crucial to the success of any at-risk program. At-risk learners generally have complex problems that require the expertise of more than one professional. Suggested contributions that support personnel can make to the at-risk team include the following:

- Support personnel can consult and work with parents regarding their children's future.
- Support personnel can conduct student assessments, including career assessments.
- Support personnel can act as a liaison for at-risk students within the school setting.
- Support personnel can facilitate consultation with other educators regarding the development of basic skills, social skills, self-awareness skills, and career development skills by at-risk students.
- Support personnel can incorporate career development and counseling experiences in the delivery of their special services to at-risk students.
- Support personnel can emphasize the correlation between school and the world of work as well as the development and use of basic skills, vocational skills, and employability skills of at-risk students.
- Support personnel can incorporate problem-solving and decision-making skills, stress management, and interpersonal skills into their work with at-risk students.
- Support personnel can assist at-risk students in examining their interests, abilities, and attitudes and how these affect their future goals.

Students

Students, both at risk and not at risk, represent the clientele for whom educational institutions have been founded to serve. Therefore, it is inconceivable that a school at-risk team could be successful in meeting the needs of students with no student input. Students comprise an integral part of the school at-risk team.

The contributions of at-risk and non–at-risk students should be considered. One of the primary goals of integrating nondropout-prone students in dropout prevention activities should be to ensure that peer pressure is exerted in a positive manner. Educational personnel can help to nurture a positive attitude by offering activities that allow for cooperative group interaction.

Suggested contributions that can be made by non–at-risk students to the school at-risk team are described below.

Contribution as Peer Tutors

Students can be trained as peer tutors, which promotes a positive relationship with at-risk students. Crucial academic and social reinforcement are important byproducts of this process. At-risk students generally develop self-confidence and feelings of acceptance after working with peer tutors.

Contribution as Mentors for At-Risk Students

Students can serve as mentors for at-risk students. This relationship can help at-risk students to make a smooth transition between educational levels (e.g., from elementary school to middle school, from middle school to high school). Mentors can become advocates for at-risk students and thus can assist them in developing self-esteem. At-risk students can also learn effective social skills, coping skills, communication skills, and study skills from mentors.

Contribution in Student Government

Non–at-risk students can represent the needs and interests of at-risk populations through such vehicles as student government, where school rules and policies are discussed. If at-risk students feel that their needs are addressed by the entire school, they will have a better chance of bonding.

Students who are at risk should also be included as members of the school at-risk team. They are, in fact, the reason the team is initiated. Suggested contributions that can be made by at-risk students to the school at-risk team include the following:

- At-risk students can provide valuable information to other team members concerning their needs and what the schools can do to encourage students to remain in school.
- At-risk students can assist educators and other team members in evaluating innovative changes made to meet the needs of dropout-prone students.
- At-risk students can take advantage of special programs to help them in acquiring basic skills, study skills, note-taking skills, and organizational skills.
- At-risk students who successfully complete high school can volunteer to serve as mentors to other dropout-prone students.

Parents

Parental involvement on the school at-risk team is very important. Parents probably know more about their sons and daughters than does any professional in the school system. They have valid questions and concerns that should be addressed by the school at-risk team. Many schools have established vehicles to communicate with parents. However, many parents feel that the current communication methods are one-way. If parents and schools can begin to communicate effectively, greater trust and understanding can be established.

Research indicates that there is a strong relationship between parental involvement and learner achievement. There are numerous benefits associated with parent participation in local schools, including increased student attendance, more positive parent-child communication, decreased dropout rates, improved student attitudes and behaviors, and increased parent-community support of the local school system (Rich, 1985; Sattes, 1985). These benefits are particularly relevant when dealing with parents of at-risk students. These learners often enter or leave school with low levels of academic ability, lack of vocational goals, and lack of parental support. Parents of these students do not have to be well educated to become involved as a member of the school at-risk team. They just need guidance and training for their specific role on this team (Clark, 1983; Scott-Jones, 1988).

Suggested contributions that parents can make to the school at-risk team include the following:

- Parents can share important information about their children with other team members, including their limitations, needs, interests, styles of learning, goals, and reasons for being discouraged or enthusiastic about school.

- Parents can serve as volunteers for the school district, including service as speakers, tutors, mentors, and workshop presenters or facilitators.

- Parents can spread the word to other parents regarding efforts the school is making to meet the needs of dropout-prone students, as well as resources that are available to students and families.

- Parents can encourage at-risk youth to stay in school and to follow goals that will enhance their futures.

- Parents can coordinate closely with teachers to monitor the progress of their children. Reinforcement can then be offered at home.

- Parents can learn career-development strategies that will help their children see the relevance between school and the world of work, as well as help them to develop realistic vocational goals.

- Parents can become leaders of parent groups in the community to teach parents of drop-out-prone students skills they can teach to or reinforce with their children at home. These skills may include coping skills, problem-solving skills, study skills and work habits.

- Parents can volunteer to serve on advisory committees for specific programs within the school.
- Parents can organize community involvement projects and encourage at-risk students to participate in them.

Community

Membership from the community represents an important part of the school at-risk team. Sources of community assistance can include representatives from business and industry, the Chamber of Commerce, state and community agencies, advocacy groups, adult service providers, postsecondary institutions, employers of graduates, clergy, and local government. An assessment of the needs of at-risk students at the local level should help to determine the team membership. The development of linkages between the community and the schools assists students through the exchange of information and the provision of support services not available within the school.

Taking students into the community and bringing community representatives into the schools can provide at-risk students with excellent learning opportunities. The relevance between school and the working world can be established or reinforced. Suggested strategies that the community can use to make a contribution to the school at-risk team include the following:

- Local business and industry can establish partnerships with schools and work actively with educators to plan effective programs for at-risk students. Advice can be offered about necessary employability and job-seeking skills that should be incorporated into school curricula. Equipment can be donated to schools. "Adopt-a-School" and "Adopt-a-Student" arrangements can be made through which visitations to local industrial sites can be arranged, volunteers can visit students in classes to talk about the world of work, and shadowing experiences can be scheduled.
- Community members can volunteer to act as mentors for at-risk students.
- Volunteer tutorial services can be provided by the community.
- Scholarships, part-time paid employment, and other financial assistance can be provided by the community.
- Information about valuable community resources can be shared with other members of the school's at-risk team.
- Community representatives can volunteer to serve on advisory committees for specific programs in the school system.
- Information about potential job placement opportunities for at-risk students can be provided.

- Volunteers can help with student events, clubs, and other extracurricular activities and encourage at-risk students to become involved in them.
- Members of the community can work in the classrooms as teacher volunteers. This can be an ongoing service throughout the year or can represent a one-time experience.

THE TEAM PROCESS

Dyer (1977, p. 73) states that the major tasks facing any team attempting to establish an effective working relationship include (1) setting goals, (2) solving problems, (3) making decisions, (4) focusing on follow-through and task completion, (5) developing cooperative efforts among team members, (6) establishing open lines of communication, (7) ensuring that team members feel accepted, and (8) allowing for open discussions and nonthreatening disagreements.

Establishing and nurturing a successful, high-performance at-risk team is a developmental process. An effective team does not develop overnight, but rather goes through several stages of growth. Each working team will progress through these phases at its own pace and will exhibit different patterns of interaction at each phase.

Team Development

The three phases of team development identified by Buchholz and Roth (1987) are described below.

Phase 1: Collection of Individuals

Phase 1 brings together a number of individuals who ultimately will form a team. Each of these individuals brings a unique background of professional preparation, educational perspective, and experiences. In this first phase, members tend to be more individual oriented than group oriented. Responsibility is not always shared. Many people will avoid change and avoid dealing with conflict that may arise. It is important during phase 1 that individuals start to define the purpose of the team, recognize the skills of other members, and address ways in which members can work together effectively.

Phase 2: Groups

Individuals begin to form into a group during phase 2 of team development. This occurs when the members establish a group identity, formulate the purpose of the group, and develop a pattern of working together. A leader usually emerges who provides direction, assigns tasks to members, facilitates communication, and oversees group performance.

Phase 3: Team

In phase 3 of effective team development, the team becomes purpose oriented. The whole becomes equal to the sum of the parts. Members understand the goal of the group and are committed to it. All actions and decisions are based on this goal. This is the most difficult end to attain.

A number of factors contribute to the development of a team. Newly established groups start out at phase 1. Even groups that have been together for a long time also may be in the early phases of team development if group dynamics have not developed.

Problems in Team Building

Team building and the effective use of groups is a key ingredient for institutional change. A team is a collection of people who must rely on collaboration if each member is to experience ultimate success and goal achievement. However, there are some common problem areas that make it difficult for people to work together. Dyer (1977, p. 73) identifies the following problems:

1. Even though people are aware that a problem exists, they don't know how to address it.
2. The group members do not have a common goal to which everyone is committed.
3. Some people do not want things to change, while others are actively searching for new methods.
4. Some people never accept their role and responsibilities in relation to the team's goals.
5. Some people are intimidated by the team leader(s) and therefore pretend to know things that they should be asking questions about.
6. Decisions are made by the team, but some people disagree with the decision or procrastinate about following through with the decision.
7. Tension or friction among team members makes it difficult for them to work together.

A variety of reasons cause people to dislike being on a team. Dyer (1977, p. 75) states that the following reasons will decrease the chances of effective team development:

- *Poor leadership.* The team leader does not keep the discussion on the topic, fails to monitor and keep things moving in the appropriate direction, or does not provide activities that are motivating to team members.
- *Unclear goals.* Team members are unsure about what they are to accomplish.
- *Lack of commitment.* Team members do not take their tasks or assignments seriously.
- *Ignored recommendations.* People in decision-making positions disregard recommendations made by the team.
- *Unproductive discussions.* Team members feel that their time is being wasted when discussions lead to no conclusion or decision.
- *Lack of follow-through.* Committee members do not follow through with tasks and assignments.
- *Lack of materials or information.* Materials and information needed by team members to complete tasks are not readily available.
- *Plans with no action.* The team spends time making plans, but no action is ever taken.
- *Hidden agendas.* People often have hidden agendas, and therefore pay more attention to their personal goals rather than to the team's goals.

Characteristics of Effective Teams

Buchholz and Roth (1987, p. 14) report that typically there are eight characteristics of a successful, high-performance team:

1. *Participative leadership.* Members of a team participate in planning and decision making and openly collaborate with others.
2. *Shared responsibility.* The team creates an atmosphere in which all members feel a professional responsibility for the performance of the team.
3. Aligned on purpose. All members share a common purpose regarding the function that the team serves and the reason it was created.
4. *High communication.* The team builds a climate of trust, as well as open, honest communication among team members
5. *Focused on future.* Team members recognize and accept change as an opportunity for growth and improvement.

6. *Focused on task.* Team members keep the focus during team meetings on performance toward stated goals and objectives.

7. *Creative talents.* Team members apply individual talents toward the common goals of the team.

8. *Rapid response.* Team members recognize and act on opportunities that arise that can help to move the team toward successful completion of its goals.

A number of variables increase the participation levels of team members (Dyer , 1977, p. 75). Participation increases

- when there is a clear definition of the team's purposes, including what the goals are and what team members are to do
- when there is careful control of the time commitment necessary for team members; when there is enough time allowed to get the work done
- when team members listen to and respect the opinions of others and are sensitive to their needs
- when there is an informal, relaxed atmosphere rather than a formal environment
- when there is good preparation on the part of the team leadership, so that necessary materials and resources are available
- when team members have an interest in and a commitment to the goals of the team
- when records are kept of team meetings and actions, so that decisions are not lost
- when the team periodically stops and assesses its performance, so that necessary changes and improvements can be made
- when recognition and appreciation are awarded to team members for their efforts, so that they feel they are really making a positive contribution
- when the work of the team is accepted and used by the institution that brought the group together and presented it with a goal to accomplish

School at-risk teams should be aware of both variables that inhibit group cohesiveness and variables that enhance team development, so that members can work effectively to meet the needs of at-risk students.

REFERENCES

Buchholz, S., & Roth, T. (1987). *Creating the high performance team*. New York: John Wiley.

Clark, R.M. (1983). *Family life and school achievement: Why poor black children succeed or fail*. Chicago: University of Chicago Press.

Committee for Economic Development. (1985). Investing in our children. New York: Research and Policy Commission.

Cunningham, D., Putzstuck, C., & Barbieri, M. (1987). *Working together to support at-risk youth*. Denton, TX: University of North Texas.

Doyle, W. (1985). Effective secondary school practices. In R. Kyle (Ed.), *Reaching for excellence: An effective schools sourcebook*. Washington, DC: U.S. Government Printing Office.

Dyer, W. (1977). *Team building: Issues and alternatives*. Reading, MA: Addison-Wesley.

Faddis, C., & Pritz, S. (1988). *The helping process booklet for team members, the helping process booklet for program coordinators, the helping process booklet for administrators/planners*. Columbus, OH: National Center for Research in Vocational Education.

Gudridge, B.M. (1980). *AASA critical issues report: Teacher competency, problems and solutions*. Sacramento, CA: Educational News Service, American Association of School Administrators.

Heath, D. (1986). Developing teachers not just techniques. In K. Zumwalt (Ed.), *Improving teaching*. Alexandria, VA: Association for Supervision and Curriculum Development.

Kolde, R. (1987). Administrator's role in vocational special needs program. In G. Meers (Ed.), *Handbook of vocational special needs education*. Gaithersburg, MD: Aspen Publishers, Inc.

Lehr, J., & Harris, H. (1988). *At-risk, low-achieving students in the classroom*. Washington, DC: National Education Association.

Purkey, W., & Novak, J. (1984). *Inviting school success*. Belmont, CA: Wadsworth.

Rich, D. (1985). *The forgotten factor in school success: The family*. Washington, DC: The Home and School Institute.

Sarkees, M., & Feichtner, S. (1987). Working together: The special needs team. *Vocational Education Journal, 62* (2), 22.

Sarkees, M., West, L., & Wircenski, J. (1988). *Vocational education programs for the disadvantaged*. Columbus, OH: National Center for Research in Vocational Education.

Sattes, B.D., (1985). *Parent involvement: A review of the literature*. Charleston, WV: Appalachia Educational Laboratory.

Scott-Jones, D. (1988). Families as educators: The transition from informal to formal school learning. *Educational Horizons, 16*, 66–69.

chapter 9

Community Resources
and Dropout Prevention

Linda Hudson Parrish

With the publication of *A Nation at Risk: The Imperative for Educational Reform* (National Commission on Excellence in Education, 1983), and the myriad of other reform-related reports of the mid- and late 1980s, America's public schools became participants in a race to achieve educational excellence. This contest has been measured by higher scores on standardized tests, honors curricula tracks, and, most vividly, by the escalating numbers of students who are choosing not to remain in this environment and are becoming known as America's dropouts. Gruskin, Campbell, and Paulu (1987) reported that in the 1985–1986 school year alone, 682,000 American teenagers dropped out of school—an average of 3,789 each day. These authors predicted that up to half of all students entering the ninth grade would fail to graduate 4 years later, and that in later years that figure might even be larger (p. 15). Every indication is that the authors are accurate in this dismal prediction.

Thus, a paradox of immense proportion has developed. On the one hand, we have a national referendum for improving excellence in public education; on the other hand, we recognize the potential crisis that we will face if we equate "excellence" with academic achievement only. Noted educator Dean C. Corrigan (1988) points out that at the same time that almost all states have legislated minimal competency tests for students, only a few states are emphasizing reforms that provide incentives to help students stay in school. He continues by stating that "to achieve the vision of American education for all, we must develop schools based on the firm assumption that every human being has a right to an education" (p. 37).

Just as schools have become a natural extension of, or in some cases a replacement for, the nuclear family, so must the communities become a viable component, or an extension, of the schools. Whether one views the dropout phenomenon from a social, political, or economic perspective, the conclusion is the same. School personnel can no longer afford to work on this problem in

217

isolation. The solutions must be found through joint efforts of individuals, families, agencies, schools, businesses, and industry.

The William T. Grant Foundation (1988) concluded in its report, *The Forgotten Half: Pathways to Success for America's Youth and Young Families*, that

> young people's experiences at home, at school, in the community, and at work are strongly interconnected, and our response to problems that arise in any of these domains must be equally well integrated. Our society cannot expect to deal successfully with just one aspect of a young person's life and hope to bring focus to every other. Efforts to produce success in school—without complementary efforts in families and communities—are unlikely to make a substantial difference for young people. (p. 3)

This national report also boldly underscored the fact that "there is evidence that, by any measure, we invest much more heavily in the future of college bound youth than we do in those seeking work after high school" (p. 41). Another insightful revelation in this report was the fact that there is a tendency to view today's youth as problems in need of solutions, rather than as assets needing development.

Certainly it does not take an economist to determine that we need all of today's youth to be productive in our society, particularly because our society has large numbers of persons in the 65 and over age category. Buccino (1988) reminds us of a historical fact:

> America has always had a surplus of young people. As a result, our economy could function effectively even if a proportion of youngsters were shunted aside into unproductive lives. Now, however, and for the foreseeable future, there is a surplus of old people and a concomitant shortage of young people. (p. 23)

To dramatize this statement, Hodgkinson (cited in Corrigan, 1988) revealed that in 1950 the United States had 17 workers for every retiree needing Social Security benefits. However, by 1992, he postulates that there will be only three workers for every retiree, and one of those three workers will represent a minority ethnic group (pp. 23–24).

Levin (1988), a Stanford University economist, concurs that educational "reforms that create more time in school or higher standards, without salient changes in the schooling process that will increase learning for disadvantaged students will likely increase dropout rates" (cited in Corrigan, 1988, p. 36). He continues to describe the situation as a national economic crisis as well as an educational one in which growing numbers of youth are out of school and out of work, and have no skills to obtain or maintain a job. Refer again to the William T. Grant Foundation study (1988) regarding the 20 million non–college-bound young people who comprise the "forgotten half": The authors submit that a "kindlier society would support the forgotten half; a more gentle people would encourage them, a pragmatic nation would acknowledge that its very future depends upon them" (p. 2).

The world is rapidly changing, and, although schools have continued to "serve" all of America's children, it is time to realize that the schools cannot continue to provide the same service; nor can they do it alone. Schools are, and can remain, the predominant institution in the lives of the students. Schools are well-equipped to be the agency that assesses the needs of the children and then locates, if not provides, that identified curriculum. The schools can become the advocates for their constituents, rather than being defensive about their perceived overwhelming multiple roles and limited resources. The William T. Grant Foundation report (1988) chides us for making "schooling a synonym for education" (p. 3). It supports the notion that schools are essential, but they are not sufficient. Clearly,

> the purpose of all education is to create whole human beings . . . it is time we acted on our understanding that much learning takes place beyond the boundaries of schools (p. 3).
>
> The interplay between youth and community tells much about the development and vitality of both. Young people are simultaneously an asset to, and a responsibility of, the community. Responsive communities, along with good schools and strong families, form a triad that supports youth in their passage to work and adult life. (p. 49)

SUPPORT SERVICES

To determine what support services are needed for students who either drop out or who are considered at risk, one must first know the general characteristics of the population and the specific characteristics of the individuals. Numerous lists have been developed to aid in the identification of these young people, and there are certain common items among the many such litanies. For one, there appears to be consistent reference to the student who has experienced failure in the school process (Texas Education Agency, 1989, p. 42). Therefore, those who are over-age for their educational placement—that is to say older than their academic peers and thus experiencing some problem with academic or social performance—quite often make the lists for potential dropouts.

Other often-mentioned traits, which may or may not be present, are limited English proficiency, low socioeconomic status, and health problems (including substance abuse, disabilities, pregnancy, and trauma associated with dysfunctional families) (Wehlage, Rutter, Smith, Lesko, & Fernandez, 1989). These authors, as well as others, are quick to point out that generic terms such as *at risk* and *dropout* tend to hide the diversity of those they describe. Therefore, it is well to remember that students who comprise this segment of our society are not a homogeneous group. They represent both sexes, all ethnic groups, and all socioeconomic strata, and they often have quite disparate reasons for belonging to this ever-growing group that has the nation alarmed.

It is obvious that while some generic types of support services could be beneficial across all of these described categories, clearly the needs to be met for the young pregnant female student differ substantially from those for the learning-disabled male. It is therefore imperative that school personnel (1) know individuals and their needs very well; (2) be aware of the social service agencies in the community, as well as the eligibility requirements and the services that these agencies can provide; and (3) be able to match those two for a successful reconciliation of the problem.

Another interesting observation is the close parallel among this group of students, those identified as at risk of dropping out of school, and those who are considered disabled in the public schools. Over a decade ago, under the same rubric that states that "American education is for all children," laws were written on behalf of students with disabilities, categories for labeling children were devised to ease administration and funding, support services were defined, and human service agencies were authorized to provide support with inadequate appropriation of funding. As a result there is considerable chaos in service provision today. It is discouraging to think that this pattern will be repeated for another population of students within our society. One way to disallow this is through active, interagency collaboration.

AGENCIES, INTERAGENCIES, AND INTRA-AGENCIES

Within every community in the United States are local public human service agencies that represent larger entities at the state and federal level. Most communities have private agencies as well. Certainly nothing is impossible; but, given the multiplicity of these agencies, it is highly unlikely that a comprehensive listing of them exists for easy reference in one location in the United States. In point of fact, federal offices have directories that encompass thousands of pages of small type just listing the agencies that report to them. Suffice it to say that all of these agencies were initially commissioned to provide some needed assistance for some group of people who qualify for their specific service.

Because of the multiplicity of these organizations, the phrase "interagency cooperation" has emerged as standard rhetoric in the profession. It has been defined by Johnson, McLaughlin, and Christensen (1982) as

> a process through which two or more agencies work together to (a) articulate their services, (b) open communication channels, and (c) build trust among the members. The ideal result of this interpersonal, coordinated and cooperative effort would be in providing optimum service delivery throughout the life cycle of individuals with special needs. (p. 395)

Much has been written about "interagency coordination," which many consider a true oxymoron in the human service profession. And for all the good that many agencies contribute to society, there tends to be far too much duplication of effort, lengthy and confusing application procedures, territoriality, and perpetual self-serving methods. Long ago, these attributes, as well as others, were labeled "barriers within the helping society" (California Advisory Council of Vocational Education, 1977, p. 25). Amid the many barriers present for applicants for human services, it is most disheartening to become aware of barriers created by those very persons and agencies originally authorized to provide assistance.

It is generally understood that although federal initiatives and legislation provide a positive influence and direction for services for persons with special needs, it is at the local level of provision of such services that the idealistic philosophical ideas of human rights become the hard realities of service provision. Therefore, it is the intent of the remainder of this chapter to deal with local-level human service providers, recognizing that this is where people benefit most dramatically through the efforts of others within the same community.

COMMUNITY SYSTEMS

Schools

Public school administrators have often complained about their role of being "all things to all people" while being inundated with paperwork that calls for evaluations, accounting procedures, and the myriad of other responsibilities that fall to public educators. They are right to maintain that their clientele comprise everyone who is of school age regardless of their academic ability or emotional maturity, unlike other service agencies that have extensive screening devices to check for eligibility requirements to obtain their services. However, it is this comprehensive knowledge of all youth in the community that makes school personnel the most logical choice to assume the responsibility for case management of individuals requiring services beyond those normally given to the general population.

Within this premise lies the potential for school personnel to plan with external agencies well in advance of a student's exiting from school so that no interruptions in needed services will occur. This planning is most successful in communities where there are stable relationships with personnel among agencies and trust among the service providers. Schools can no longer be content with the academic preparation of students until they leave the campus, whether through graduation, family relocation, aging out, or dropping out. As an integral component of the long-term planning for students, the responsibility of educators should not stop when the student chooses to leave school but should continue at least to the point of following up on his or her employment status, access to social service agencies, or enrollment in further education or job preparation.

In addition to the roles of school personnel, there are suggestions that the climate of schools also be re-examined. Ducharme (cited in Corrigan, 1988) posits that schools must be more than places to acquire intellectual skills; they must provide humane environments, be inclusive, and cultivate optimism in their students (p. 9). This is difficult to achieve when a large percentage of students who drop out report that they do so because school seems irrelevant or because they can't get along with their teachers or peers, or both. Other reasons for dropping out that were uncovered in this study were fear of gangs, inflexible curricula, uncaring faculty and administration, unfair or unclear rules, language barriers, and social isolation from other students (Texas Education Agency, 1989). Although these are self-reported perceptions and may not include some of the underlying reasons, student perceptions are the basis for decisions to drop out or stay in school.

Programs that foster cooperative, rather than strictly competitive, learning, as promoted by Minnesota researchers Johnson, Johnson, Holeuvez, and Johnson (1984), and peer counseling/listening programs, such as Natural Helpers (C. Hester, personal communication, October 31, 1989), are examples of sensitive programming. These programs could enhance the environment of today's schools that all too often govern all students by a minimal behavioral and performance standard designed for the most problematic student.

Many schools are unusually good at providing diverse curricular and extracurricular programs for an even more diverse population. Schools, often within the same community, differ greatly in performance. And, even in the best of situations, there are changes within our schools that should be occurring more quickly because of our rapidly changing society.

Parents/Families

Empirical research finds that involving parents early in their children's school activities is crucial to keeping students in school (Texas Education Agency, 1989, p. 49). It is also common knowledge that parents' involvement in school decreases every year of the children's school career until in high school it is almost nonexistent (Carnegie Council On Adolescent Development, 1989, p. 66).

It may be the case that parents of adolescents believe that their sons and daughters should become more independent at this stage in their lives, and therefore they determine to be less involved in their children's activities. It could also be the case that parents feel less enfranchised by teachers and students in the secondary schools. Or, perhaps, by this age, because problem behavior or academic deficits have often been recognized and thoroughly documented, parents may perceive that school personnel attribute some of this deficiency to them.

Schools should invite parental participation as a partnership, rather than viewing their participation as just that of another group of persons needing education (Macchiarola & Garner, 1989). Parent training sessions are often helpful, especially if they are initiated by the parents and if these sessions lead to strategic planning with school officials. More important, however, would be the sharing of mutual goals, intervention strategies, and motivational techniques in parent-school collaborative efforts. Escalante (1990), public school teacher extraordinaire, attributes much of his success to his practice of meeting with the parents of his students 2 weeks prior to the beginning of school each year.

According to Berger (1987), parents visit schools primarily to attend specific events (i.e., athletic competitions, PTA meetings, or open house). This formal relationship belies the notion that the schools are an integral component of the family social system. There is some indication, however, that educated parents are involved more fully with the schools, whereas parents who may have experienced difficulty in their own schooling avoid contact with education officials (pp. 101–102). Surely those parents with whom contact is made will have more of an opportunity to assist in meeting the educational goals of their children.

Because of the changing nature of today's families, family roles need to be reassessed. Each major educational report includes statistics pointing to the demise of the American family. Some of the categories that are on the rise are one-parent families, parents who have small children and who work outside the home, more births to single parents, children affected by divorce, transient families, and children in poverty. As discouraging as this all seems, Howard (cited in Berger, 1987) contends that the form of the family may change, but the essence of the family—connectedness and underlying support—remains whether the family consists of one parent, two parents, four parents, or biological or adoptive parents, or there is an extended family (p. 77).

Others, including many teachers, contend, however, that through experience they have come to believe that the family unit has deteriorated to a critical point. Evidence of this phenomenon is revealed by some schools that report too few parents available to even initiate a parent/teacher organization. Both points of view may have some validity. Regardless, the school's role has, indeed, expanded. Where once the home was expected to teach about values, interpersonal relationships, and functional skills required for surviving in our society, schools are now expected to impart these to students.

Parents should become familiar with all aspects of their children's education. They should arrange meetings themselves, rather than wait to be summoned. Collaboration with teachers regarding schedules, assignments, classroom management, motivational techniques, and leadership opportunities, to name a few, should be commonly understood and paralleled or practiced at home as well as in the classroom. Parents and teachers working together for a common goal, in a mutually respectful environment, should provide benefits for the children that have been unobtainable prior to the joint effort.

Business and Industry

It seems too simplistic, but one of the underlying factors of what students declare as "unrealistic and inflexible" curricula in public high schools is that there are too few applications to employment for what they are learning. Decades ago we were not as alarmed at the dropout rate primarily because there were sufficient numbers of jobs for persons without high school diplomas. Although our present economy requires large numbers of people in service occupations and technology has developed equipment that does not require reading or calculation, employers still need persons who have proven that they can complete a goal (e.g., a 12-year sustained educational commitment), have the ability to follow directions, and have the capacity to communicate. It is estimated that unskilled workers will comprise only 5 to 7 percent of America's labor force by the end of the century (Gage, 1989). This statistic is alarmingly low in comparison with the high percentage of students leaving schools unprepared for employment.

Openly stating that we have educational tracks in our public schools is not a popular position; however, one need only to examine individual students' educational schedules to see the patterns emerge: honors, regular academic, vocational, or special education. A continuum of offerings from courses for gifted and talented students to remedial classes exists, but students in all tracks are shunted into extremely rigid programs with little room for electives. If a student is academically gifted, there is likely to be little room in his or her schedule for auto mechanics or construction trades. Certainly we hold this truth to be self-evident that all students should have access to programs that challenge them to reach their highest level of academic potential. However, it is all too obvious that even academically talented students are dropping out of high school unprepared to make decisions that will affect their futures. Surely, all students' interest as well as aptitudes should be taken into account when planning high school curricula.

It is the opinion of many experts that closer ties with the business community will benefit all participants. Not only should we maintain this arrangement through advisory committees, apprenticeships, and cooperative educational experiences commonly used in vocational education, but all facets of education should incorporate the expertise of businessmen and businesswomen to enhance instruction. The benefits of such a venture will enhance all disciplines within the schools.

Businesspersons who understand and use the governmental programs (explained in greater detail under "Governmental Agencies") that encourage the hiring of workers who are disadvantaged or disabled are aiding in this cooperative effort between schools and communities. However, the William T. Grant Foundation (1988) publication reminds us that existing incentives for firms to hire more young people at risk are insufficient. Innovative programs must be developed, such as the Boston Compact, an agreement between schools and employers that, in effect, requires schools to upgrade their educational standards for the promise of 3,000 full-time summer jobs and 1,200 after-school part-time jobs for the students (p. 96). This plan ensures the attainment of skills that comes from staying in school, not the enticement of leaving schools early to obtain employment.

A second example in the William T. Grant Foundation (1988) report describes the California Compact, in which specific goals are determined by businesspersons and schools (i.e., school attendance, grade achievement, and the like). When these personalized district-level goals are achieved by individually targeted students, businesses provide recognition ceremonies or incentives, such as the distribution of "preferred student" membership cards that entitle the bearer to discounts on purchases or improved hiring consideration (p. 101). And, of course, there are many examples of companies that participate in Adopt-a-School programs in which time and resources are shared in a mutually agreed on manner.

As helpful as these arrangements are, they should be made in consultation with school officials to be most effective. According to the national publication

Education Week (September 20, 1989), administrators at a large school district in the southwestern part of the United States were stunned when a prominent businessperson parked a luxury automobile at a high school, left the keys in the ignition, and announced that each week a different student could have the privilege of using the car. The student would be determined by a drawing of students who had "maintained good grades and stayed out of trouble." The businessman also promised cash awards of $1,000 at the end of each grading period and $2,500 at the end of each semester. School board members encouraged this supporter to redirect his offers toward college scholarships. In an effort to focus on all of the students in that (or any) high school, the school board would have been well advised to suggest that other incentives such as jobs, as well as scholarships, be considered.

Businesspersons such as Lester C. Thurow (cited in William T. Grant Foundation, 1988, p. 187) contend that social welfare programs may be a matter of ethics and generosity, but education and training are not. Thurow maintains that he is willing to pay for—indeed insist upon—the education of his neighbors' children not because he is generous but because he cannot afford to live with them uneducated.

Government Agencies

Much good has been accomplished for many by the federally initiated programs delivered by the numerous departments, offices, commissions, agencies, foundations, centers, associations, collaboratives, panels, authorities, boards, and institutes. Without federal legislation and policy, it is quite possible that, left to their own devices, state and local communities might not be as far along in providing assistance to those most in need. It is often the case, however, that although direction comes from the higher level, methods for the actual delivery of services are left to the local citizenry.

In some communities, governmental agencies have secured office space on the public school campuses. This close proximity promotes a better understanding of what services are available and which students are eligible to become recipients of such services. The transition from school to community would be greatly enhanced if students, parents, and advocates had assistance in negotiating the maze associated with adult service providers. Personnel from rehabilitation commissions, employment commissions, Social Security administrations, mental health associations, and housing and transportation authorities, to name only a few, could provide enlightening information for those who may not know these agencies exist, and therefore never apply for needed services.

School counselors should be well informed about beneficial governmental programs such as the Targeted Job Tax Credit (TJTC), which subsidizes the salaries of individuals representing one or more of nine specific groups, including (1) economically disadvantaged youth ages 18 to 24, (2) economically disadvantaged cooperative education students ages 16 to 19, (3) economically disadvantaged summer youth employees aged 16 to 17, and others who would benefit from such assistance in obtaining employment (Gaylord-Ross, 1988, p. 276).

Unfortunately, in a recent United States Department of Health and Human Services study, it was found that three of every four employers interviewed were not interested in hiring TJTC-eligible recipients because they believed them to be unproductive. But those who did hire these employees found them to be as productive as other workers in the same occupation (William T. Grant Foundation, 1988, p. 97).

The decade of the 1980s saw a trend away from federal involvement and an expansion of the state, local, and often private intervention in assisting the unemployed and underemployed. One evidence of this philosophical thought was the passage of the Job Training Partnership Act in 1982. This act created Private Industry Councils (PICs) consisting primarily of local businesspersons familiar with both the local labor market and the needed skills of potential workers. Specific training programs are proposed to the PIC and subsequently funded to meet the needs of both employers and future employees.

It is obvious that there are many people needing social services in our country. What is not so obvious is how to get the services to the people. All governmental agencies have monitoring procedures and evaluation criteria that determine whether they are effective. Unfortunately, most of these procedures deal with finite numbers: How many people did you serve? How many persons are employed using the skills by which they were trained? How many people have maintained continuous employment for 6 months? Certainly these and similar questions are valid objective measures for assessing an agency's performance. However, answers to questions about the quality of services, the recipients' views of training, and others are not available by these easily retrievable methods of documentation. This type of evaluation also contributes to the competitive nature of various agencies and leads to serving those who can succeed most readily, rather than serving those with the greatest needs.

Governmental agencies are a meaningful part of the human service network. Coordination between and among them, however, has been identified as one of the greatest barriers facing persons with special needs in our country today (Hippolitus, Stevens, Meers & Schwartz, 1979). School personnel can assist by accepting the responsibility of becoming the initial "port of entry" for students into the world of adult services. Teams of staff from all agencies can work collaboratively, for the good of the student, in identifying and providing individual services.

Civic Organizations

What would our country be without strong, nonprofit, volunteer organizations? Many dynamic programs result from the work of volunteer advocates and self-advocates. These are successful, to a great extent, because of the close proximity of the workers to the needs of the people to be served. There are literally hundreds of volunteer organizations that exist primarily to serve others. Some that should be familiar to every reader are service clubs, such as Lions, Kiwanis, and Rotary; religious organizations and their youth groups; Scouts of America; Big Brothers/Big Sisters; YMCA/YWCA; and League of Women Voters.

Members of these groups, often aided by professionals in the human resources field, give vitality to communities that are striving to become the best they can be for all of their citizens. Volunteers as role models of social development, occupational achievement, and human caring may have immeasurable effect on the persons with whom they come in contact. It is interesting to note that, by giving of their time, energy, and talents, these participants often declare that they are the beneficiaries of such endeavors.

One example of a mutually beneficial scheme is the enlisting of volunteer retired military personnel by the local school district. Disruptions by children on the daily routed school buses not only were distracting to the bus drivers but also posed a serious safety problem. With the addition of the retired military men or women (or both) on the buses, the situation was corrected. As expected, the students' bus riding behavior improved. That change, however, was secondary to the unsuspected benefit of the information obtained by students about the military as a career and the educational benefits derived from staying in school.

Another example is the use of senior citizens to relate information about education, work experience, and changes in society as they have encountered them. Historical perspectives are always enlightening regarding truths learned in the past, but just as beneficial to discern are mistakes to avoid in the future. Schools and volunteers have much to offer each other, and both have much to gain as well.

Juvenile Justice System

A profile of a predelinquent might show a school-based pattern consisting of truancy, suspension, expulsion, difficulty with authority, and disengagement from positive school activities (Texas Education Agency, 1989, p. 51). In point of fact, our prisons and detention centers are overcrowded with inmates who, without the consistent routine of school and with few or no job-related skills, eventually resorted to committing crimes.

Although juveniles can be incarcerated, the overwhelming majority of youthful offenders receive noninstitutional sentences. The primary alternatives are fines, community service, restitution, and probation. Of these, probation is the most widely assigned disposition of both adult and juvenile cases. More than 70 percent of all adjudicated youth receive probated sentences (Nelson, Rutherford, & Wolford, 1987, p. 41). Whether offenders are detained in prison or released on probation, it is clear that programs to develop work skills, self-esteem, and socially acceptable behaviors must be available.

It is imperative that communities and schools work cooperatively with law enforcement officials to create programs to assist in the prevention of delinquency and in the rehabilitation efforts of those adolescents who have already experienced the juvenile justice system.

In recent years some states have passed laws that hold parents legally responsible for their minors' behavior. For example, parents can be fined, or in some cases jailed, when their children skip school, participate in gangs, harm someone with a weapon, give birth, or use or sell drugs. Some states have begun negating driving privileges for students who drop out of high school (Register & Bradshaw, 1989). Whether these actions will be a deterrent to delinquency and leaving school prematurely is yet to be determined.

For those youth who do find themselves incarcerated, basically two attitudes prevail in a correctional institution: rehabilitation and punishment. Although each attitude can be defended, most emphasis should be placed on rehabilitation through education for juveniles.

Correctional education, as defined by Gehring (cited in Nelson et al., 1987) is

> an organized and individualized self-help strategy to interrupt nonsocial or antisocial behavior through vocational and academic learning activities that foster social attitudes and equip students in contact with the criminal justice system for lives as responsible community members. (p. 57)

One of six goals of correctional education is to reduce recidivism through the provision of academic and vocational skills and work assignments (Wolford, as cited in Nelson et al., 1987). Just as schools are encouraged to make instruction meaningful, so too are prison programs. Relevant vocational training programs, along with social skills development and functional academics, should have been offered in the high schools, but surely they must be included in the curricula for this "last chance" education.

Specific skills training coupled with work assignments is most efficient for both the learner and the facility. Within the bounds imposed by security, inmates should work on real projects, such as food preparation, auto mechanics, and building maintenance, rather than having projects fabricated for practice.

Simulation of work is most regrettable when real work needs to be done and self-esteem could be built by producing a quality, usable product. Apprenticeships and the opportunity to complete high school or a general equivalent diploma (GED) should also be available (Sullivan, 1989).

Taking pride in one's meaningful work might be the first step to a productive life for many of these youth who, prior to this experience, may have exhibited little self-esteem. Just as schools must have significant relationships with other service agencies, so must the juvenile justice system, so that upon release these former inmates might have the expedient assistance they need to enter the mainstream of society through work, family, and friends.

Colleges and Universities

University educators and public school teachers are too often in conflict. University researchers are criticized by public school practitioners for the distance they keep from the issues they study. Likewise, human service providers are sometimes criticized for taking action without reasoned analysis or literature reviews (Schmolling, Youkeles, & Burger, 1989, p. v). University/school collaboratives can work to overcome this negative perception on both sides. These collaboratives should have equal participation from each unit, leadership should be shared, and commonly identified educational issues should be the focus of inquiry and field testing.

Teacher education programs should also be examined to determine whether they are contributing to the problem of many teachers who believe that they are unprepared to teach a diverse group of students, such as those with disabilities or those from ethnic minorities. Teacher education programs that segregate college courses designed for achieving a specific endorsement or certification may falsely portray the role of teachers by not providing a representative picture. Teacher education programs must become mainstream, as have the public schools.

By relating more closely to schools, colleges and universities can benefit in ways that will enhance their instruction; public school personnel can benefit by the empowerment that this association will encourage. Too often, elementary and secondary school teachers have not had a voice in the governance of their profession, often relying on administrative or legislative dictates. In order for education to meet the challenge of inevitable change, those closest to the students—the teachers—must be enfranchised in policymaking. Teacher education programs can instruct pre-service and in-service teachers to be involved in political issues affecting the profession, to be proactive in their involvement, and certainly to maintain a well-informed position through reading contemporary journals and participating in conferences. It is through such activities that teachers will become knowledgeable about community service providers that will benefit the students and the total school system.

SUMMARY

Despite barriers to interagency cooperation, the estrangement of families and school personnel, negative employer attitudes toward persons qualifying for governmental assistance, and so forth, there is reason to be optimistic. It is often the case that situations reach epidemic proportions before they are recognized and treated. Certainly it is time that all of the entities listed in this chapter begin to work cooperatively to solve the problem of a predicted unprepared society. Through the efforts of all of these entities it is becoming increasingly evident that the necessary components exist to ensure success in this effort. To accomplish this important goal there is a need to re-examine roles, eliminate duplication of effort, and communicate openly and regularly for the good of the students.

Schools are the key to the success of this venture. They need to become communities within themselves, providing a continuum of options for all students. Schools should be places where success is not only encouraged but virtually guaranteed (Macchiarola and Garner, 1989, p. 174).

Schools must also provide the bridge of transition to adult life by working closely with all elements of the system that traditionally follows the school experience, whether it is higher education, employment, social service recipience, or the criminal justice system. Existing roles must be changed, resources must be allocated, and—most important—partnerships must be formed.

It is no wonder that a tremendously popular television program for youth and adults has as its theme song words that express people's need to be accepted. The lyrics are: "Sometimes you just want to go where everybody knows your name and they're always glad you came" (Theme song for *Cheers*, 1982). Schools need to be places where every student is valued, and their ability to excel in some dimension of that environment has been discovered and nurtured. It is a difficult task, but a noble one that we cannot afford to neglect.

REFERENCES

Berger, E.H. (1987). *Parents as partners in education: The school and home working together.* Columbus, OH: Merrill.
Buccino, A. (1988). Redefining competitiveness and national well-being. In D.C. Corrigin (Ed.), *The purpose of American education* (pp. 21–32). College Station, TX: Association of Colleges and Schools of Education in State Universities and Land Grant Colleges and Affiliated Private Universities.

California Advisory Council of Vocational Education. (1977). *Barriers and bridges: An overview of vocational services available for handicapped Californians.* Sacramento, CA: Author.

Carnegie Council on Adolescent Development. (1989, June). *Turning points: Preparing American youth for the 21st century.* New York: Carnegie Corporation of New York. (Report prepared by the Carnegie Council on Adolescent Development's Task Force on Education of Young Adolescents.)

Corrigan, D.C. (Ed.). (1988). *The purposes of American education.* College Station, TX: Association of Colleges and Schools of Education in State Universities and Land Grant Colleges and Affiliated Private Universities.

Escalante, J. (1990, September 22). *Stand and deliver.* Distinguished Lecture at the Joint Conference for Texas Association of School Boards and School Administrators, Houston.

Gage, D. (1989, November 17). *Dropout data from our nation's schools.* Paper presented at the meeting of the President's Committee on Education, College Station, TX.

Gaylord-Ross, R. (1988). *Vocational education for persons with handicaps.* Mountain View, CA: Mayfield.

Gruskin, S.J., Campbell, M.A., & Paulu, N. (1987). *Dealing with dropouts: The urban superintendent's call to action.* Washington, DC: Office of Educational Research and Improvement. (ERIC Document Reproduction Service No. ED 286 992).

Hippolitus, P., Stevens, M., Meers, G., & Schwartz, S. (1979). *A blueprint for action.* Washington DC: President's Committee on Employment of the Handicapped.

Johnson, D.W., Johnson, R.T., Holeuvez, E., & Johnson, R.P. (1984). *Circles of learning.* Alexandria, VA: Association of Supervision and Curriculum Development.

Johnson, H.W., McLaughlin, J.A., & Christensen, M. (1982). Interagency collaboration: Driving and restraining forces. *Exceptional Children, 48,* 395–399.

Macchiarola, F.J., & Garner, A. (1989). *Caring for America's children.* New York: Academy of Political Science.

National Commission on Excellence in Education. (1983). *A nation at risk: The imperative for educational reform.* Washington, DC: U.S. Government Printing Office.

Nelson, C.M., Rutherford, R.B., & Wolford, B.I. (1987). *Special education in the criminal justice system.* Columbus, OH: Merrill.

Register, H., & Bradshaw, K. (1989, December). Should parents pay for their children's sins? *NEA Today, 8*(5).

Schmolling, P.F., Youkeles, M., & Burger, W.R. (1989). *Human services in contemporary America.* Pacific Grove, CA: Brooks/Cole.

Staff. (1989, September 20). *Education Week, 9*(2).

Sullivan, T.D. (1989, Winter). Out of the ashes: A better prisoner training program. *Training Trends Newsletter,* p. 1.

Texas Education Agency. (1989). *Characteristics of at-risk youth* (Practioner's Guide Series Number One). Austin, TX: Author.

Theme song for *Cheers.* (1982). New York: National Broadcasting Company.

William T. Grant Foundation. (1988). Commission on Work, Family, and Citizenship. The forgotten half: Pathways to success for America's youth and young families. Washington DC: Author.

Wehlage, G.G., Rutter, R.A., Smith, G.A., Lesko, N., & Fernandez, R.R. (1989). *Reducing the risk: Schools as communities of support.* Philadelphia: Falmer Press.

chapter 10

Evaluating Dropout Prevention Programs

Jay Smink

One of the most serious issues facing school administrators is the high rate of school dropouts. Community, civic, and business leaders are concerned about the high percentage of students leaving school before graduation, without the basic academic and occupational skills needed to participate in the workforce. State and federal legislators responsible for educational processes are willing to provide resources for dropout prevention programs. However, when policy, funding, and administrative decisions are made regarding dropout prevention programs, these decisions are frequently based on emotions, on the influences of special interest groups, or in reaction to the pressure of powerful advocates of other existing projects operating in the state or community.

It is critical to the future of dropout prevention programs that policymaking and funding agencies receive information about the effectiveness of various strategies in reducing the student dropout rate. Armed with this information, these agencies will be able to make informed decisions for program funding and continuations that are based on comparisons of the success of specific program approaches and the cost/benefit analyses of continuing their operation. The data needed for this kind of informed decision making would be available if all dropout prevention programs included an evaluation process in their program planning.

Sponsoring agencies and institutions must know which dropout prevention programs are effective. Community leaders, school administrators, teachers, and parents must know whether these programs are indeed having an impact on the school attendance rates of high-risk students and on the overall school dropout rate. The business community needs to know whether the cooperative vocational training provided for students through business-education partnerships is successful in helping students attain marketable skills. A state agency funding a substance abuse activity as part of the comprehensive dropout prevention program must know the results of that component. These issues can be answered by a well-planned dropout prevention program evaluation process.

233

An evaluation process documents the success of a dropout prevention program through the systematic collection of data, data analyses and interpretation, and data reporting to describe the degree to which the program has achieved its goals and objectives. This chapter presents a brief overview of evaluation and then describes an eight-step process that can be used to produce an evaluation procedure for a dropout prevention program.

WHY EVALUATE DROPOUT PREVENTION PROGRAMS?

The important reasons for having well-planned and well-executed evaluation processes are to

- determine the value of a dropout prevention program relative to costs or to improved academic and occupational skills of students
- decide the effectiveness of a program relative to established standards or program objectives
- provide information for decision making regarding program continuation, modification, or termination
- provide valuable accountability information to program sponsors
- provide instructional improvement information for program planners
- design professional staff development activities

Peck (1988) suggests three reasons for evaluation falling into the categories of financial, political, and programming (p. 7). Whatever the need or the reasons for evaluation, it is a valued mechanism used for decision making. The published evaluation report can provide information about successful dropout prevention programs and practices, and it can be used as the foundation of a public relations program. A comprehensive evaluation of dropout prevention programs can provide reports that will clarify school policies and standards, justify increased direct support of dropout prevention programs by the private sector, improve and increase communication and cooperation among school administrators and legislators, and promote a better understanding of dropout prevention programs and issues by school board members. The information generated by an evaluation can promote the exchange of ideas between various school- and community-based organizations serving at-risk youth. Increased support, both financial and administrative, for dropout prevention programs can result from the publication of program evaluation results.

Evaluation findings will answer three major questions about a specific program:

1. What changes in students (e.g., occupational skills, communication skills, or work ethic) have occurred as a result of the new program?
2. What observable student behaviors have changed as a result of the new program (e.g., increase in self-esteem, decrease in substance abuse)?
3. How do we know that these changes occurred in students because of the program?

WHO IS RESPONSIBLE FOR EVALUATION?

The dropout prevention program director or project manager has the primary responsibility for administration of the program implementation and the evaluation process. Evaluation is an integral part of implementation activities.

Consider the following scenario: A local school district received a grant from the state department of education for a dropout prevention program. The district received the award because the proposal submitted contained excellent data supporting the need for a dropout prevention program, and the proposed intervention strategies appeared to be closely aligned with the needs of the students and staff in the participating schools. Furthermore, several community agencies and local business leaders endorsed the proposal and agreed to support part of the program's costs. The newly assigned program director was disturbed by the proposed evaluation activities. There appeared to be very little thought given to this section of the original proposal, except that the program director would be responsible for designing and managing the evaluation process, including the preparation and dissemination of the final reports.

The scenario suggested is not the exception. Today, the lack of attention to evaluation in proposed dropout prevention programs is common; almost as an afterthought, the program director must find an evaluation person or team to design and carry out all of the evaluation procedures. Often the evaluation person will be an internal staff member with or without expertise in this area who will perform an internal evaluation. Frequently an external evaluation team is hired to do the evaluation; sometimes both internal and external evaluators are used.

The self-evaluation approach does not rule out external assistance to develop the evaluation design, to collect data, to analyze data, or to report results. Self-evaluation, perhaps with no external assistance, does, however, require the project director to manage the evaluation process, make self-improvement decisions, and provide tangible results at selected points during the project or program. The program director and program implementation staff have a better understanding of the program and tend to have a positive, proactive attitude toward the evaluation activities when they are directly responsible for them. They will be more likely to identify the most positive aspects of the program and to feel at ease in reporting the components that may need to be modified. They will also be comfortable in discussing strategies that were not effective and will be capable of documenting why these strategies did not work.

TYPES OF EVALUATION

Two types of evaluation are needed to document the success of a dropout prevention program, formative evaluation and summative evaluation.

Formative Evaluation

Formative evaluation is often called *process evaluation* because it looks at the day-to-day overall program operation in an educational institution. Before a dropout prevention program is initiated in a school or a community, a delivery system with defined procedures, specified schedules of events, and required staff-student involvement is carefully developed. The delivery system will vary depending on the complexity of the program design. However, when the delivery system begins to function in the school or community, its ongoing operation must be evaluated to determine whether or not the program components are in place and whether they are functioning as specified in the program plan. The formative evaluation procedures answer the question, Are we doing what we said we were going to do in the way we expected to do it?

Formative evaluation provides information on a continuous basis to the program director while the program activities are in progress. If discrepancies are found between the program design and actual practices, the director will modify either the program operation or the program design and document the reasons for the changes.

Formative evaluation can provide program directors with information that supports the redesigning of the program activities to increase the impact of the program on student outcomes. A wide range of data sources, including questionnaires, checklists, input from staff, client interviews, school records, and referrals from files maintained by related community agencies, are used in formative evaluation.

Summative Evaluation

Summative evaluation is sometimes called *product* or *outcome evaluation* because it documents student outcomes of the program. The basic question answered by summative evaluation is, How much have students changed or improved as a result of the program?

Data are obtained from sources such as school records, employer interviews, teacher and counselor interviews, community surveys, student observations, and pretest and posttest scores. The data are analyzed against specific agreed on standards and are compared with program baseline data. The data analyses produce evidence of program effectiveness—the bottom-line statement of the impact of the program on students.

Both formative and summative evaluations are vital in documenting the ultimate success of a dropout prevention program. The data collected may be used to focus on the dropout program process or on the final result or effectiveness of the dropout prevention strategy. Regardless of the data collected, the analyses used, the results reported, or the format used to tell the story—program evaluation is a critical part of any dropout prevention program.

STEPS IN CONDUCTING A PROGRAM EVALUATION

The processes or sets of activities used to conduct program evaluations are somewhat standard. The following eight steps, based on a similar process developed by Halasz & Behm (1982) to evaluate vocational education programs in correctional institutions, will help persons to plan an evaluation process. These steps are presented as a planning tool for a program director responsible for managing and evaluating a dropout prevention program. Researchers and evaluators consistently caution the evaluation planner or program director that program evaluations must be developed and tailored to the unique characteristics of the program under scrutiny (Moberg, 1984, p. 7).

The need to plan and conduct an evaluation of a dropout prevention program is often very pressing and sometimes frightening to those unacquainted with the process. These eight steps are intended to serve as an overview for planning, organizing, and carrying out a program evaluation.

The eight steps for planning and conducting a program are as follows:

1. Determine the purpose of evaluation.
2. Establish expectations.
3. Identify evaluation questions.
4. Establish standards of comparison.
5. Design and select data collection and analysis methods.
6. Collect data.
7. Analyze data.
8. Prepare an evaluation report.

During the initial planning for program evaluation, detailed information about the dropout prevention program is needed. A detailed description of the dropout prevention program must be available. In the early stages of planning an evaluation, these three questions must be answered: (1) What is the primary purpose for evaluating the program? (2) Who are the primary clients expected to use the evaluation results? (3) What staff and other resources are available for organizing and conducting the evaluation?

Information about the dropout prevention program to be evaluated is usually found in the program proposal. Commercial program descriptions and school documents used to develop curriculum guides may be helpful. A thorough understanding of the personnel requirements, the program components, and the time frame for activities is essential when planning evaluation procedures. In addition, a clear definition of how each program component will be used with students should be available to evaluation planners. The program director must be knowledgeable about the characteristics and the official status of the clients who will use for decision making the evaluation information about the ongoing operation of the program and its impact on students. It is not necessary to know the identity of the users and the decision makers, but it is critical to know what agencies and institutions are represented and how the evaluation results will be used for policy changes within their respective power structures.

Key program staff should always participate in the development of the evaluation plan. The program director will have major responsibility for project administration and must have access to staff, inside or outside the organization, with expertise in evaluation. Program evaluation plans will vary, and large districts, communities, or institutions may have sufficient staff and an organizational structure that will allow for an evaluation team completely independent of the program management team.

Determine the Purpose of Evaluation

The first and foremost purpose for evaluating a dropout prevention program is to assess its effect on the participating high-risk students. However, there are other reasons to evaluate programs. When planning an evaluation it is crucial that both primary and secondary reasons for evaluation be identified and clarified and then ranked in terms of priority. Exhibit 10-1 may be used as a checklist for these processes.

Establish Expectations

After the purpose of the evaluation has been determined, the program director must clarify what the dropout prevention program is attempting to accomplish.

Exhibit 10-1 Evaluation Purposes Checklist

Will the evaluation results be used for:	*Yes*	*No*
1. Program Planning? Information such as the adequacy of the facility and the equipment in an alternative school, the qualifications of the staff, the numbers of at-risk students is useful in planning the types of intervention and occupational programs that can be offered.	——	——
2. Decision Making? Decisions must be based on a certain amount of information. Decisions about assignment of "caring" staff to programs, and the selection of students for participation may all require some justification. One way to make defensible decisions is to gather objective evidence to support the decisions.	——	——
3. Professional Development? Evaluation can benefit teachers, administrators, and support staff. An evaluation system that identifies deficiencies and strengths in staff performance will help promote desirable changes.	——	——
4. Program Improvement? Improving the intervention program is an important reason for evaluation. Evaluation activities should identify the actions, components, or characteristics that promote desired or undesired outcomes. Once program deficiencies have been identified through evaluation, action may be recommended to correct them.	——	——
5. Accountability? Accountability requires a presentation of program results (such as attendance increases, reduced disciplinary problems, increased occupational competencies, decrease in substance abuse, and increased achievement scores) in relation to incurred costs and established desirable outcomes. Internally and externally these accountability measures can help at-risk administrators justify the resources spent for programs.	——	——
6. Accreditation? Evaluation of modified academic and occupational programs for at-risk students is often done to determine compliance with the requirements of accrediting agencies.	——	——

Source: Adapted from Wentling, 1982.

Additional information about the desired outcomes of the program must be identified. These data can be abstracted from the mission statement of the dropout prevention program. Detailed statements of desired outcomes and expectations are easily formulated from well-thought-out explicit goals and objectives. Goals are broad general statements and are not directly measurable, but objectives have a central focus with specific statements that are measurable. The development of a measurable outcome objective is presented in Exhibit 10-2.

Exhibit 10-2 Steps To Develop Outcome Objectives

---

1. Write Down General Goals

Goals are broad statements of program purpose, such as "keeping pregnant teens in school," "improvements in job-related academic skills," or "to improve future occupational choices of participants." Given that goals are broad statements of purpose, most programs will have only one or two goals.

2. List Possible Indicators of Goal Achievement

Indicators are specific and observable changes in attitudes, knowledge, or behavior linked to goal achievement. At this step, a large and exhaustive number of indicators of goals achievement should be generated. Examples of indicators include "greater number of job placements" or "fewer pregnant teenagers dropping out of school."

3. Select the Best Indicators

Choose the best indicator(s) from the list you generated, based on their significance and relevance to your target population, their importance to decision makers, the ease with which they can be measured, and your program's ability to have an impact on them.

4. Translate the Indicators into Measurable Objectives

Measurable objectives should contain a statement of the indicators and target population, a time frame, and either a statement of the proportion of the target population expected to show change or the amount of change expected on the indicator. Alternative formats are:

A. _____,_____ of _____ will _____.
   By When?   % or   Who?   Indicator
            % Change

B. _____,_____ will _____ of _____.
   When?   Who?   % Change   Indicator

Source: Adapted from Cantor, Kaufman, & Klitzner, 1982.

Two examples derived from the recommended steps are as follows: (1) "By the end of the school year, 90 percent of the identified at-risk students will still be enrolled in school." (2) "Within the initial 6 months of the project, 10 or more business partnerships will be started with a signed agreement identifying activities to be completed." A clear mission statement with goals and measurable objectives will set the stage to identify the relevant evaluation questions.

Identify Evaluation Questions

The third step in evaluation planning is identifying the evaluation questions. Questions to guide the depth and breadth of the evaluation must be generated, such as: (1) Which components of the dropout prevention program should be examined and to what degree? (2) Should the evaluation concentrate on student outcomes, staff outcomes, or both? (3) Should the evaluation focus on process activities or outcomes? Questions should also be developed for both formative and summative evaluations.

There are different ways to ask evaluation questions about a prevention program. Most program evaluations concentrate on looking at the program results or the final outcomes. Although important decisions are made on the basis of this outcome information, these final outcomes can be modified greatly if the program director observes the progress during the implementation stages and makes adjustments as necessary. Hawkins and Nederhood (1987) suggest that questions should be grouped into three categories that show the relationship of effort, effectiveness, and efficiency to the program (pp. 12–17).

Effort questions are formative or process evaluation questions. Examples of effort questions are:

- Is the project doing what was planned?
- How many students were assigned mentors and completed a job shadowing experience?
- How much time is spent in vocational counseling?

Other typical formative questions relevant to implementation activities may include:

- How well was the program managed?
- How many of the potential at-risk students had a chance to participate in the program? How many students had a chance to participate in the cooperative education component?
- Was the staff provided adequate in-service training to conduct the required occupational and substance abuse counseling?
- Was the field visitation scheduled at the correct time in the program sequence?
- Were the material resources sufficient to conduct the workshops for the teachers?

Effectiveness questions are most important and usually ask: "Did it work?" Effectiveness questions are used to focus summative or outcome evaluation. Questions that address the effectiveness of a dropout prevention program are:

- How does the tutoring program contribute to the completion of homework assignments on time?
- Do students who receive weekly independent counseling sessions have a lower dropout rate than students without this counseling?

- Do students increase their self-image as a result of the tutoring program and the independent counseling sessions?
- Did more staff volunteer for mentoring at-risk students after implementation of the new incentive program for staff development?

Questions related to the costs associated with achieving the program objectives fall into the efficiency category. The program outcomes may be measurable in terms of dollars, time, and material. Efficiency questions include:

- Which business awareness strategy (invitational letter or television advertisements) is the most efficient way to secure business-education partnerships?
- Do mentoring activities conducted by school staff or by community volunteers result in fewer dropout students?
- Are the drug abuse activities conducted in the school environment less costly than similar activities conducted in a community setting?
- Is it more efficient to hire a social caseworker to provide parenting skills to teenage parents in the home environment, or to work in small groups in a school environment where day care service needs to be a part of the program?

One way to identify the evaluation questions is to list the desired outcomes or measurable objectives in one column and prepare a list of the possible evaluation questions for each outcome or objective. The program director or the evaluation planning team should prepare multiple questions for each objective as illustrated in Exhibit 10-3.

Exhibit 10-3 Measurable Objective and Related Evaluation Questions

Measurable Objective	Evaluation Questions
• By the end of the school year, more than 50 percent of the 11th- and 12th-grade high-risk students will remain in school.	• Did the students in the dropout prevention program report more days absent? • What caused the students to stay in school? • Did the cooperative education component contribute to the decision to stay in school? • What reasons were provided by those students who dropped out? • Did the students in the program participate more often in the tutoring program?

Most program evaluations concentrate on looking at the program results or the final outcomes. Although important decisions are made on the basis of this outcome information, these final outcomes can be modified greatly when the program director observes the progress during the implementing stages. Therefore, a set of formative evaluation questions should be prepared to address program implementation issues. Typical questions relevant to implementation activities may include:

- How well was the program managed?
- How many of the potential at-risk students had a chance to participate in the program? How many students had a chance to participate in the cooperative education component?
- Was the staff provided adequate in-service training to conduct the required occupational counseling?
- Was the field visitation scheduled at the correct time in the program sequence?
- Were the material resources sufficient to conduct the workshops for the teachers?

Regardless of how the evaluation questions are generated, consensus among the program director and staff on the most critical questions is important. The questions should be thoroughly discussed and then prioritized to set the relative importance of each. The questions finally selected will guide the total evaluation process.

Establish Standards of Comparison

The standards may be formatted as changes in time, as specific levels or grades of success, or by comparison of groups. However, they should be determined before the evaluation design is final and data collection begins. This will avoid any question regarding objectivity or usefulness of the final results. Exhibit 10-4 illustrates examples of standards.

Design and Select Data Collection and Analysis Methods

Once the purpose of the intervention dropout prevention program evaluation has been determined, goals and objectives have been clearly stated with measurable questions to be asked, and standards have been established, it would appear that the next step is easy. The selection of data collection techniques and

Exhibit 10-4 Standards for the Community Tutor Program

Question: Does the 2-day training activity provide volunteers with the skills and knowledge to assist at-risk students in developing a positive attitude toward school?

Standard: Based on changes over time, example standards are illustrated below.

At the end of the training program:

- Volunteers will answer 80 percent of the student's questions about job interviewing skills.
- No more than 10 percent of the students will be dissatisfied with the assistance from a volunteer.
- At least 75 percent of the volunteers will accept a mentoring assignment for the second semester.
- At least 75 percent of students will show an increase in positive attitude toward school as measured by semantic differential.
- At least 90 percent of students will show a positive attitude about themselves as measured by a locally developed survey.

related analysis methods is extremely important and needs considerable attention because there is no one evaluation method or design that is best. A wide variety of evaluation techniques and approaches is now available to project managers. An authoritative resource for evaluation designs is Quasi-Experimentation Design and Analysis Issues for Field Settings (Cook & Campbell, 1979). Another valuable source for evaluation designs pertinent to drug prevention programs and easily adapted to dropout prevention programs is the Handbook for Evaluating Drug and Alcohol Prevention Programs (Hawkins & Nederhood, 1987).

One other source that suggests six evaluation designs (e.g., one group pretest minus posttest, nonequivalent control group) appropriate for dropout prevention programs is the Handbook for Evaluating Dropout Prevention Programs (Smink & Stank, in press). No attempt is made here to describe in detail the many design possibilities suitable for each evaluation question. The sources noted earlier or advice from evaluation specialists is recommended. In general, there are two basic evaluation approaches, categorized as either quantitative or qualitative.

Quantitative approaches rely on the collection of data that can be quantified and subjected to various data analysis techniques. This includes such information as enrollment and attendance figures, graduation rates, discipline incidents, academic grade levels, and family-related data. These data are usually collected by questionnaires or checklists or by reviewing school records, test scores, and demographic information.

In qualitative evaluation the information collected includes descriptions of facilities, characteristics of staff or students, student attitudes and behavior patterns, perceptions of efficiency, and opinions of community and business leaders. Data may be collected through observations, questionnaires, individual interviews, and structured group interviews.

Most evaluations use both quantitative and qualitative approaches. Evaluation questions identified earlier can be answered by using all of these data collection methods.

Collect Data

The collection of data is vital to the evaluation design and to the ultimate results. The data collection techniques must provide consistent and accurate information. Management of the collection process is extremely important so that the scheduled data collection activities will use people's time and talents productively.

Management of the data collection process includes deciding who will be responsible for collecting the information. This decision is as important as selection of the instruments and how and when to use them in the project setting. Arguments can be made for project staff, if available, to complete this assignment because they understand the purpose of the project and would likely obtain more accurate data. On the other hand, outside evaluators can provide a more objective point of view in obtaining data. The notions of consistency, reliability, accuracy, and costs are parts of the formula that each program director will consider when making this decision. The actual data collection must be as unobtrusive as possible when it occurs with a student or program staff.

Data collection instruments should be designed to secure the information that relates directly to the evaluation questions. If possible, use standardized instruments that are reliable and valid. If new instruments need to be created, they should be pilot-tested and validated. This alone is a very complex task involving substantial time and cost. Several key items are offered as a guide to follow in selecting or constructing data collection instruments: (1) determine from whom you will need data to answer each evaluation question (e.g., students, staff, business leaders); (2) list the data categories (e.g., hours of work experience, attendance records); (3) identify and secure available instruments; (4) identify need and develop format and items for new instruments; (5) construct instruments through field tests and revisions; and (6) produce and use instruments as designed. Nevertheless, collect only the information needed to answer the questions; additional information is costly and many times obscures the real questions to be answered.

The collection of information is always a challenge. Additional precautions to a program director would be to (1) use more than one method of collecting information for the most important questions; (2) use professionally developed instruments to assess interests, values, and attitudes; and (3) use an evaluation specialist to review and confirm the uses of instruments selected and the collection procedures.

Analyze Data

The data collected through various methods (including questionnaires, observations, interviews, and the like) must be recorded and analyzed using technically sound processes. The plan for analyzing the data is determined when the evaluation design and data collection instruments are selected. Two kinds of statistics may be used to analyze and report data: descriptive statistics and inferential statistics.

Descriptive statistics answer questions that are quantitative in nature and use numeric summaries, including averages, standard deviations, proportions, percentages, frequency distributions, and percentiles. Evaluation questions are questions such as: What was the average number of student absentee days during the program? Was this average higher or lower than it was before the program? What was the dropout rate before and after the program? Were fewer students involved in substance abuse at the end of the program or school year? Was there a change in the percentile distribution of academic test scores?

Inferential statistics generate data that show relationships among the variables or components being evaluated using inferential statistics such as correlations, chi square, analysis of variance, analysis of covariance, and multiple regression. The relationship between program components and program impact on students can be examined and causal effects of the program can sometimes be identified. Tests of statistical significance can be completed on the results of these statistical analyses to find out if the changes in students happened by chance or because of the program. These inferential statistics can also be used to compare one program with another or to compare a program with a control group.

The questions answered by inferential statistical analyses are: Is there a difference between the students in the dropout program and similar students who were not in the program? Is the difference between these groups of students statistically significant? Is the difference educationally significant for practical purposes?

A wide variety of data analyses and statistical techniques is available. If the data analysis and statistical techniques were not included in the evaluation design, the program director should consult an evaluation specialist to select the most appropriate statistical tools for use in data analyses.

A recommended source providing a discussion on data analyses and statistical procedures that would be helpful to evaluators and program managers is Research in Education (Best & Kahn, 1989).

Prepare Evaluation Report

The final report must be prepared with final interpretations based on the analyses completed and a thorough review of the statistical significance shown for each intervention strategy. The results, both negative and positive, represent a tremendous investment of program and evaluation effort and should be given considerable thought before final reports are prepared. For example, various audiences may require a different type of report or presentation format. A different emphasis may need to be placed on selected questions or different aspects of the intervention project for different audiences. Franchak (1981) has listed 17 factors to consider in preparing an evaluation report (p. 53). These factors are offered in the form of suggestions, and they serve as an excellent review for the individual preparing the report.

Generally, a final report should be prepared to address the audiences who will make decisions about the programs under review. Alternative final reports may need to be tailored for different audiences. Nevertheless, the general outline in Exhibit 10-5 is the recommended content for a final evaluation report.

Regardless of the report format, the findings should not be presented in broad, sweeping, global statements that condone or support an intervention strategy. For example, statistical presentations will provide only the bases upon which evaluators and decision makers make inferences and may be intimidating interpretations. The program director has a significant task to manage the preparation of this report in a manner that fairly represents all aspects of the program. The final evaluation report is the official record for the public or sponsor. The report must be meaningful to both the layman and the professional. The final report should offer recommendations only for those aspects of the program the evaluation was designed to study—no more, no less, but accurately.

Exhibit 10-5 Contents of Final Evaluation Report

- Executive summary
- Program description
- Evaluation objectives and questions
- Description of research design and methodology (including instruments and data collection and analysis procedures)
- Description of findings (including various presentations of information)
- Interpretations of findings (including program strengths and weaknesses, implications, conclusions, and recommendations for actions)

DISSEMINATION AND UTILIZATION OF EVALUATION REPORTS

The evaluation report, and alternative reports for selected audiences, must be presented in a timely and understandable fashion. The report must clearly communicate the evaluation results to each of the audience groups or stakeholders interested in the results.

Targeted Groups

Rossi and Freeman (1982) suggest that there are nine primary stakeholder groups involved in the "politics of evaluation," who participate in one way or another in the conduct and outcome of an evaluation (p. 310). Among this group, the program sponsor and policymakers who make decisions about whether a program is to be instituted, continued, discontinued, expanded, or terminated appear to be the most influential. Policymakers and decision makers could represent a vast target group. Nevertheless, this group is the target audience for most final reports.

While most evaluation efforts conclude with a final written report, other formats may be used. A videotape presenting intervention strategies from the dropout prevention program, along with well-documented participant interviews and supporting evaluation results, can make an impressive final report to decision makers. Other useful reporting formats include audio and/or verbal reports with supporting visual aids. Evaluation results excerpted and prepared for radio and television are excellent dissemination approaches. News releases and articles written for professional audiences and publications are always acceptable and encouraged.

Utilization of Results

The utilization of evaluation results is the final test of the quality of the evaluation and the bottom line for the dropout prevention program described by the evaluation. The degree of utilization of evaluation results is directly related to the credibility of the evaluation design and the relevance of the data to the major issues in dropout prevention.

Evaluation results are used by decision makers if they pass the "truth test" (Rossi & Freeman, 1982, p. 325). This test includes questions such as:

- Is the evaluation trustworthy?
- Will it hold up under challenges?

- Does it provide direction for policy changes?
- Does it provide a basis for immediate action?
- Can it be used as a basis for considering alternative approaches?

Evaluation results are used by many stakeholders and decision makers. Hopefully they will make informed judgments about the dropout prevention programs in the nation's schools and communities that will benefit the true stakeholders of these programs—the high-risk student, a potential dropout.

REFERENCES

Best, J.W., & Kahn, J.V. (1989). *Research in education* (6th ed.). Englewood Cliffs, NJ: Prentice-Hall.

Cantor, J., Kaufman, N., & Klitzner, M. (1982). *Four steps to better objectives.* Madison: WI: Wisconsin Clearinghouse.

Cook, T.D., & Campbell, D.T. (1979). *Quasi-experimentation design and analysis issues for field settings.* Chicago: Rand McNally.

Franchak, S. (1981). *Using evaluation results.* Columbus, OH: Center for Research in Vocational Education, Ohio State University.

Halasz, I., & Behm, K. (1982). *Evaluating vocational education programs in correctional institutions.* Columbus, OH: Center for Research in Vocational Education, Ohio State University.

Hawkins, J.D., & Nederhood, B. (1987). *Handbook for evaluating drug and alcohol prevention programs.* Washington, DC: U.S. Department of Health and Human Services. (Available from U.S. Government Printing Office)

Moberg, D.P. (1984). *Evaluation of prevention programs: A basic guide for practitioners.* Madison, WI: Wisconsin Clearinghouse.

Peck, N.L. (1988). *What works and why: A guide to evaluating teen pregnancy/parenting program.* Coral Gables, FL: Center for Dropout Prevention, University of Miami.

Rossi, P.H., & Freeman, H.E. (1982). Evaluation: A systematic approach (2nd ed.). Beverly Hills, CA: Sage Publications.

Smink, J., & Stank, P. (in press). *Handbook for evaluating dropout prevention programs.* Clemson, SC: National Dropout Prevention Center, Clemson University.

Wentling, T.L. (1982). *Locally-directed evaluators handbook* (2nd ed.). Springfield, IL: Illinois State Board of Education.

chapter 11

Dropout Prevention and At-Risk College Students

James Lewis Ratcliff

Preventing dropouts and assisting at-risk students have been major objectives for postsecondary education. For a variety of reasons, colleges and universities have increased the number and proportion of students who are disabled, educationally disadvantaged, culturally diverse, and from nontraditional age groups. From the most prestigious research universities and liberal arts colleges to the local community college and regional state university, these institutions have implemented programs and services to prevent at-risk students from dropping out. Many of these programs have been reported in journals and books. Most claim success. Yet, some programs designed to assist at-risk students may inadvertently build dependencies that preclude them from succeeding in the regular college classroom (Richardson, Fisk, & Okun, 1983). What programs and services really work? Can successful programs at one college be adapted readily to the different organization, staff, students, and climate of another institution? How generalizable are the substance and procedures of a program developed in one college environment to another? To address these questions, we examine the research on dropout prevention and student retention in higher education. In doing so, we assess the extent to which these programs actually assist in the progress, performance, persistence and degree completion of at-risk students in postsecondary education.

An important lesson from the research literature is that designing truly beneficial programs and services is unfortunately a complex task, rather than a simple one. One issue is how to define persistence. Community college leaders argue, for example, that the dropout rate at their institutions is often exaggerated in the statistics because students who did not have the goal of obtaining a bachelor's degree are counted in many college transfer and persistence studies (Eaton, 1988). Dropout rates are influenced by the social, economic, and academic background of the student as well as the faculty, curriculum, out-of-class learning environment, and organizational policies and procedures of the college or university. The mix of students, faculty, resources, curriculum, and organizational climate changes somewhat each year, bringing new, unique, and special problems for assisting students at risk. A distinction can be made between two types of formal programs to assist at-risk students. *Transition programs* assist students in making the passage from high school to college, from work to college, or from homemaking to college. *Developmental programs*, in contrast, provide counseling, tutoring, and study-skills to help at-risk students already enrolled in college. Within each of these two categories are found programs and services targeted at different student groups and providing different mixes of programs and services. That these programs have such diverse purposes, procedures, and practices underscores the fact that it is the interaction between student characteristics and college characteristics that produces the environment wherein at-risk students succeed or fail. There is no generically superior program for at-risk students. The first step in program planning is to understand the salient characteristics of students that may impede or promote their success in college.

STUDENT CHARACTERISTICS AND COLLEGE CHARACTERISTICS

Various student characteristics influence academic success. The most important factor in determining student success in college is prior academic achievement (Dellow, Douzenis, & Ross, 1988; Donovan, 1983; Fox, 1987; Morrisey, 1971). One ingredient of that prior achievement is native intelligence. Another part is prior success in school. Students' study skills also have a bearing on their achievement (Christoffel, 1986; Donovan, 1983; Kember & Harper, 1987; Spady, 1970). Study skills are part of the adaptive ability of students. They affect the extent to which at-risk students are able to apply the rigors and routines learned from one subject to those of another. Thus, achievement is both adaptive and academic (Tinto, 1975).

Affective characteristics also influence student success. The values, attitudes, and aspirations of students have direct bearing on their success in college. Jencks and Riesman (1969) suggested that conflicting values among students and their parents from lower socioeconomic groups made them less likely to complete college. Jencks and Riesman found that the parents of these students wanted their sons and daughters to complete college as much as or more than did the parents of students of middle-class backgrounds. Middle-class parents were more likely to assume that their children would get a college education. Still, students from lower socioeconomic groups tend to consider their parents successful role models. They know that their parents survived successfully without a college education. In contrast, the middle-class students—particularly those whose parents both had a college education—only see failure and disgrace if they do not complete their college education. Jencks and Riesman attributed the lower success rate of students from lower socioeconomic groups to the difference in values and attitudes toward higher education.

Similar value conflicts exist for the working student and the part-time student. These individuals are deprived of the regular, reinforcing interaction with other students and with faculty outside of class. In their place, these students interact with workers and other nonstudents who may not value and encourage the college-going behaviors of the part-time student (Kember, 1989). Also, disabled students may attend college in an environment of lowered expectation of success. Kay (1982) reported that institutions, individuals, and society at large often did not expect disabled adults to pursue a college education.

Student values and attitudes influence directly and indirectly their probability of dropping out. Student attitudes toward going to college and their sense of themselves as independent learners, for example, have direct bearing on their academic achievement but not on their persistence in college (Morrisey, 1971). However, since academic achievement is the strongest predictor of student persistence, student attitudes and independence have an indirect effect on the likelihood of dropping out. The college or university environment mediates student attitudes and values (Pascarella, 1985a, 1985c; Tinto, 1987, 1988). Such mediation includes both formal classroom experiences and out-of-class interactions with students and faculty. The majority of time, even for full-time students, is spent out of the classroom. The institutional mediation of student attitudes and values occurs within the context of the total waking hours of the student, not just their classroom experiences.

While attitudes, values, and beliefs affect students' decisions to drop out, there is no consistent personality profile for dropouts in college. Students' social maturity aids in degree attainment. Likewise, their achievement according to traditional academic standards as well as their own expectations are characteristics of those who do not drop out. Persisters are independent self-starters with a realistic assessment of what they can and cannot accomplish (Cope & Hannah, 1975; Pascarella, 1983a; Spady, 1970, 1971; Tinto, 1987).

Family background influences students' decisions to attend college and their choice of a college. Again, its effect on students' proclivity to drop out may be indirect. Students from average or above-average income families are more likely to complete their education. Those with a more cosmopolitan outlook and with parents who have been to college are more likely to finish. Families that are rigid in their interactions and that have an authoritarian framework are those that spawn dropouts. Persisters tend to be more amenable to conforming to the environment in which they find themselves and to abiding by parental requests and norms (Spady, 1970; Tinto, 1975).

Other background characteristics can be used to identify potential dropouts. Students from small towns and rural environments are more likely to drop out of college (Christoffel, 1986; Dellow et al., 1988; Ramist, 1981; Summerskill, 1968). Students' religions affect their likelihood of completing college. Certain religions value higher education more (Judaism, for example). Evangelical religions place more value on experience than on education and therefore have supported higher education less enthusiastically (Rudoph, 1962; Ramist, 1981).

Women and men are equally as likely to be dropouts, but for different reasons. Men who leave college usually cite academic difficulties. Women give personal and intellectual reasons for leaving college (Summerskill, 1968; Tinto, 1975). Age, too, has an indirect effect on persistence. Adult students may enroll with a great sense of self-motivation and purpose. Yet, their goals may conflict with the faculty member's purpose for the course. The once-enthusiastic adult is now at risk, discouraged, and frustrated. If the goal conflict is not mediated satisfactorily, the student will drop out (Kember, 1989). Such mediation may range from course redesign to a simple conference with the at-risk student to help the individual understand better why the course takes the direction it does.

The most significant determinant of college success is prior academic achievement. This includes prior learned abilities as well as native intelligence. The students' values, attitudes, sense of purpose and independence, family background, age, and gender also help predict the likelihood of success. However, there is no one "dropout personality" or profile. Rather, it is the interaction of the specific student with the college climate and environment that leads to persistence or attrition.

Also of importance to at-risk students' persistence is the institutional environment in which they receive their college education. There are institutional environments in which students are more likely to complete their college education. Students who first enter a community college are less likely to earn a bachelor's degree than are those who choose a baccalaureate institution (Adelman, 1989; Anderson, 1984b; Christoffel, 1986; Ramist, 1981). Those who attend a small, private, selective liberal arts college are more likely to persist to the bachelor's degree than are students who attend large, open-admissions, public institutions. Predominantly black colleges and universities may have lower retention rates as well (Astin, 1985; Ramist, 1981). However, these statistics do not mean that these institutions are less effective in assisting at-risk students.

Caution is needed when examining the relationship between college characteristics and dropout rates. The student population of a college is a self-selected group; that is, the students chose to attend the college over other institutions and over nonattendance. The effect of the self-selected nature of the student body is most evident in the finding that the students of small, private, selective liberal arts colleges are most likely to persist in college. These colleges in fact attract students with the highest academic ability, achievement, and socioeconomic status. In short, students who attend these institutions already possess the highest concentration of characteristics associated with persistence, progress, performance and degree completion. In contrast, it is at the community college, at the urban commuter university and at the institutions serving the needs of the African Americans, American Indians, and the disabled that the at-risk students are most likely to enroll (Astin, 1984). To find strong correlations between such institutional characteristics and the rate of student dropout is only to identify the problem; it does little to suggest a solution to combat dropping out.

BEYOND CHARACTERISTICS: STUDENT INVOLVEMENT THEORY

Students' prior academic achievements, social and economic backgrounds, and attitudes and values are predictors of their likelihood to complete or drop out of college. Likewise, certain characteristics of the colleges students choose are related to those students' persistence. Characteristics alone, however, do not provide a clear basis for the design and development of programs and services to assist at-risk students. The actions and events that lead to at-risk students' decisions to leave college must also be understood before a college can intervene effectively.

Theories explain actions and events. Theories about why students drop out of college can help institutions plan interventions to help at-risk students. The student involvement theory provides a useful explanation of how students come to persist or drop out of college. The theory postulates that the more students are involved in the activities of the campus environment, the more likely they are to complete the bachelor's degree. Involvement means student integration into both the academic and social spheres of college life. Involvement implies a fit between the person and the environment (Astin, 1985; Pascarella, 1985a; Spady, 1970, 1971; Tinto, 1975, 1987). Student involvement results from the time and the physical and psychological energy students invest in their college education.

Defining student involvement in this manner is not without problems. How do students come to devote time and energy to a college education without involvement? How do the uninvolved become the uninvolved? The definition has a circular nature to it. Still, the student involvement theory presents a challenge to the institution committed to reducing its dropout rates and assisting its at-risk students. From the vantage of the student involvement theory, persistence is an ongoing process. At many different points in their educational careers students reassess and reaffirm their decision to complete their educational goals (Tinto, 1988). Colleges and universities can achieve educational excellence through their efforts to challenge the intellectual and personal development of their students (Astin, 1985).

Academic and Social Integration

The value of the student involvement theory rests on the extent to which it explains that which it describes. Research shows that the academic and social involvement of students directly affects their persistence. In contrast, student background characteristics have only indirect effects (Pascarella, 1986). Understanding the concepts of academic integration and social integration can assist in the design and development of institutional interventions for college students at risk.

Academic Integration

Academic integration involves both student performance and conformance. By conformity, we mean the extent to which students adapt and operate within the norms and values of campus life. Student performance on standardized tests, such as the ACT COMP, the ETS Academic Profile or the Graduate Record Examination, measure general academic abilities or achievement relative to national norms. Low scores on standardized tests alone do not indicate that students are at risk. Low scores relative to the at-risk students' peers at the college of attendance do indicate the probability of nonpersistence. Such students are at risk because they are at a significant academic disadvantage relative to the other students.

Grades also indicate students' performance relative to their peers at the same college or university. Grades measure the degree of the students' adaptation to the academic setting relative to these peers, as well as the students' academic achievement in the class. Disengagement from class activities is a clear predictor of dropout behavior (Brown & Robinson, 1988; Fox, 1987; Stage & Richardson, 1988). Yet again, the observation is circular in nature. Students who do not engage in class activities or even "cut" class are more likely to drop out. The concept of academic integration does explain students' probability for dropping out. Alone, its explanatory power does not take us much beyond commonsense understanding. To enhance its power, we must also attend to students' social integration into college life as well.

Social Integration

Social integration encompasses the informal friendships, support groups, and networks that students may form during their college experience. These relationships and friendships may help students identify with the college or university they are attending. As one might imagine, the nature of the friendships and the strength of the support groups and networks vary according to the type of institutional environment. Commuting students spend less time in building such relationships, for example. The more integrated a student is in the social activities of a campus environment, the more likely the student is to persist in college. Dropouts have low degrees of identification with college social norms and have limited support from friends and informal networks (Brown & Robinson, 1988; Spady, 1970; 1971).

Certain at-risk student groups are more likely to have weak social integration. Students who commute to attend a community college or state college may be less likely to develop strong ties to fellow students or to campus activities. Research in such settings consistently finds that students' precollege characteristics are stronger predictors of their performance, persistence, progress, and degree attainment (Pascarella, 1983a, 1983b; Webb, 1988). But these findings only underscore the weakness of the social and academic integration of these students. Coping with the college environment can be a major task for students from culturally diverse backgrounds. For example, Hispanic students in a large state university setting found coping and adjusting to college life, norms, and behaviors to be their most consuming activity (Attinasi, 1989). Programs and services designed to assist the physically disabled have traditionally focused on the students' physical access to campus and on their academic integration. Ramp and elevator access for the physically disabled, interpreters for the hearing impaired, and texts in braille for the visually handicapped are common services to promote access and academic success in college (Bieber, Kay, Kerkstra, Ratcliff, & Prihoda, 1987; Kay, 1982). Yet such programs do not address any social alienation that disabled students may sense from campus activities and college life. Each at-risk student group presents a different set of needs to promote their social integration. Promoting both the academic and social integration of at-risk students is key to their success.

Goal Commitment and Institutional Loyalty

Two factors found to influence persistence among college students are the students' commitment to their educational goal(s) and the students' commitment to the postsecondary institution they are attending. Students with weak or unclear goals are at risk. Many students coming to college for the first time do not know what they want to do with their lives or what they want to study. This time of exploration is also a time of risk, particularly among students with backgrounds strongly associated with high dropout rates (Brown & Robinson, 1988).

Institutional loyalty and commitment prove to be important factors in persistence. Students at commuter institutions have lower levels of identification with the institutions they are attending. Student participation in college life strengthens institutional commitment. For this reason, residential colleges have lower dropout rates among their students.

When students develop a sense that they are making progress toward attaining their educational goals, they are less likely to drop out. Students who report progress in gaining a broad general education are more likely to succeed in college (Brown & Robinson, 1988; Hanson, 1988). Such general education includes enhancing their ability to analyze ideas, write clearly and effectively, and become actively involved in campus life.

Students attend college for different reasons. Knowing why students have chosen to attend college may help in understanding and strengthening their goal commitment. Many students are vocationally or career oriented. They seek to earn a degree to enhance their ability to get a job. Academic integration and commitment to the institution are strong predictors of student success among career-oriented students. Other students go to college for purely academic reasons. In essence, they are learning for the sake of learning. Certain adult students, for example, may not be motivated to attain a degree or to prepare for a career; for them, a college education is a means to satisfy a lifelong thirst for inquiry. For academically oriented students, regardless of age, academic integration and commitment to the institution are important indicators of progress, persistence, performance, and degree completion. A third group of students attends college to prepare for community service. Service-oriented students seek to better humanity, or at least their own community. For this service-oriented group, social and academic integration are only indirectly related to persistence. Students' commitments to their educational goals and to their institution are directly related to their persistence (Brown & Robinson, 1988; Stage & Richardson, 1988). Different students have different goal orientations. Some are there because of the love of learning; some to get or enhance job skills. Each produces a different motivation to college success (Kember, 1989).

Informal Interaction between Students and Faculty

One of the strongest organizational impacts on student persistence is the informal interaction that faculty may have with students (Pascarella, 1980, 1985a). It is also one of the easiest dropout prevention measures to encourage, implement, and adopt; it requires little structural change in most colleges and universities. It simply involves encouraging faculty to be proactive in their interactions with students outside the classroom. Such interaction often transmits the social norms and values of the college environment as well as assists in the academic integration of the student. In short, such interactions can heighten students' involvement in their learning.

Student interactions with faculty are particularly influential on students' progress and success in their field of study (Brown & Robinson, 1988;

Pascarella, 1980; Terenzini & Pascarella, 1980; Tinto, 1975). Such interactions may be extensive and may constitute mentoring (Lewis, 1986), or they may be incidental and informal. Nevertheless, these informal interactions clearly help students develop stronger educational and personal goals and help them make lucid, practical career choices.

Informal faculty interactions with students and mentoring promote the intellectual and personal development of at-risk students. The more frequently students have contact with faculty outside the classroom, the greater their academic, intellectual, and personal growth regardless of the institutional setting. The quality of these interactions also is related to the students' development. Thus, both the quality and the quantity of faculty-student interaction promote student progress, performance, persistence, and degree attainment.

These informal contacts strengthen students' commitment to the college or university attended and increases their persistence. Faculty interaction with students may have the greatest effect during the first 2 years of college (Pascarella, 1980); yet it is during these years that students are least likely to have informal contacts with faculty, particularly at large research universities and at urban and commuter colleges.

Reasons Students Give for Dropping Out

Students give a wide variety of reasons for dropping out. These self-reported explanations should be read with some caution in mind. How questions are posed in exit interviews influences the reasons students give for leaving. Similarly, the responses of those willing to provide information on an exit interview may be different from the responses of those who were unwilling to communicate their reasons for leaving.

Often, the most frequently cited reasons for students' leaving college are not directly within the college's control or sphere of influence. At a suburban community college, students completing an exit interview reported a conflict between their jobs and their education as the most important reason for dropping out of college. Other important reasons were the need for a break from school, achievement of their educational goals, and uncertainty about their educational goals. Factors directly under the control of the institution were the dropouts' dissatisfaction with grades, course scheduling, teaching quality, and personal uncertainty about doing well in college studies (Calhoun & Brown, 1988). However, how important were these factors according to the student involvement theory?

Braxton, Brier, and Hossler (1988) studied the value of exit interview information in learning why students drop out. They examined the six most frequently cited reasons for students' withdrawal from college programs: (1) the ability to enroll in desired courses, (2) the ability to enroll at convenient times, (3) the ability to succeed in desired courses, (4) the ability to balance time requirements of college and job, (5) the ability to cope with personal problems, and (6) financial problems. Once the effect of student background characteristics, initial commitment to their college education, academic and social integration, and subsequent commitment to educational programs were held constant statistically, none of the six most cited reasons for dropping out proved to be significant. The study by Braxton et al. showed that a strong student commitment to a college education outweighed logistical problems regarding course scheduling, course difficulty, financial problems, or balancing college and work. Colleges need effective strategies for enhancing the value and involvement students give to their education.

The student involvement theory provides a means of understanding how students decide to continue or leave college. That decision occurs on an ongoing basis throughout the students' undergraduate education. For at-risk students to succeed in college, they must become socially and academically integrated into the college environment. Dropout prevention programs need to intervene on both fronts. Providing access to higher education or working toward the development of students' cognitive skills is not enough to ensure student success. Students need help in making the transition from the norms, values, and attitudes of their peers prior to college attendance. They need encouragement in trying out the new life styles and outlooks they may encounter in the college environment. The social and academic integration of students can be facilitated when their goals in attending college are clarified, enhanced, and met. Similarly, as students become socially integrated into the college environment, their institutional loyalty grows. This in turn increases their likelihood to persist. One of the simplest and most powerful tools in promoting goal clarity, institutional commitment, and the social and academic integration of at-risk students is their informal interaction with faculty. Programs and services that promote students' involvement in their own learning prove to be more effective than those aimed solely at the reasons students give for leaving college. To prevent dropouts, colleges and universities must build on the reasons students stay in college, not merely respond to the reasons students give for leaving.

TARGETING THE DROPOUT: PREVENTION INTERVENTION

While some colleges set goals to reduce their overall dropout rate, programs that target specific student populations are most likely to be effective (Shanley,

1987; Tinto, 1987). The democratic impetus behind efforts to assist at-risk students is not new to higher education. The first land-grant colleges initially had very few college-level students. The sons and daughters of farmers and ranchers came for the first time to college with little secondary education or college preparation. In many of the land-grant colleges and universities, developmental and college preparatory courses constituted more than half of the institutions' initial enrollments. Similarly, some of the first 2-year colleges—those established during the first decades of the 20th century—served specific immigrant populations. Although the idea of targeting assistance to those with specific needs is not new, it has become an involved activity of assessment and academic guidance within the complexities of large, multipurpose colleges and universities. With baseline assessment information, dropout prevention programs can be planned for specific at-risk student populations.

Dropout Prevention for Students with Disabilities

Within the past decade, increasing numbers of individuals with disabilities have enrolled in higher education. Historically, many of these students would not have been able or allowed to attend a postsecondary institution because of specified or unspecified limitations. While many physically disabled persons were not specifically excluded from higher education, the lack of physical access to facilities and support services needed to carry out an effective program of study precluded individual participation. Similarly, preconceptions about what disabled students could or could not do caused the establishment, in certain instances, of regulations that specifically excluded them from educational programs. Many of the limitations of disabled student groups are similar to those of other at-risk populations: prior educational preparation, academic achievement, socioeconomic status, gender, age, and ethnicity; other very significant limitations are directly attributed to their specific disabling conditions.

To accommodate the diversity of students with disabilities, public and private colleges and universities implemented special and supportive programs to help these at-risk students succeed (Hippolitus, 1987). The development and expansion of postsecondary programs for disabled students were stimulated through federal legislation: the Education of the Handicapped Act and Amendments (particularly P.L. No. 94-142), the Vocational Education Amendments of 1976 (P.L. No. 94-482) and subsequent amendments, and Section 504 of the Rehabilitation Act of 1973. Certain states, such as California and Iowa, charged community, junior, and technical colleges with the responsibility of providing relevant postsecondary educational programs and services for disabled students (Bieber et al., 1987). Other states have not supported the education of disabled students beyond high school.

In 1977 the President's Committee on Employment of the Handicapped reported programs and services available to disabled students at 500 2- and 4-year colleges. Ten years later, a subsequent survey identified services provided by more than 2,300 colleges and universities (Jarrow, 1987; Thomas & Thomas, 1986). Although such programs and services exist at all levels of higher education, the majority of such dropout prevention and support efforts occur in public community colleges.

Programs and services available to disabled students are quite wide-ranging. These are often essential to the students' access and success in college. They may include academic and career counseling, diagnostic testing, vocational planning, accessible facilities and technology to assist in learning, adapted educational materials, learning support centers, transportation assistance, aides and attendants, support groups, and equipment loan and repair (Bevilacqua & Osterlink, 1979; Bryan & Becker, 1980; Caparosa, 1985; Harkins, 1978; McElroy & Rupp, 1979; Moss, 1984).

Students with disabilities do not come to college with only educational deficits. Many possess strengths that nondisabled students do not have. Nevertheless, their disabilities and their special needs put them at risk in the college environment. They may, in fact, face substantial barriers to their progress, performance, persistence, and degree completion.

Kay (1982) examined factors associated with disabled students' success at three Missouri community colleges. In each college the number of disabled students was low relative to the population of disabled persons in the district. Students were committed to and satisfied with their campus environment, but they did express dissatisfaction with their access to social and cultural activities. The isolation that other at-risk groups experience was also felt by these disabled students. Persistence in the educational programs was related to utility of the course content and its relevance to career goals. Those disabled students who were pleased with the friendliness and social interaction on campus and with the cultural and social opportunities available to them had higher grades. Student satisfaction with specific program inventions (e.g., note takers, tutors, and interpreters) was tied to social and academic integration into the campus environment. Student persistence, in turn, was related to their satisfaction with college programs, services, and environment. While the majority of interventions were academically oriented (that is, they were designed to assist students in coursework), the majority of student satisfaction criteria were related to social integration into campus life.

Goal commitment, career planning, and task and time management skills have been tagged to student persistence and success in college. Burkhead (1980) found that the extent to which physically disabled students were aware of the developmental tasks before them, were familiar with situational and personal resources available to them to cope with these tasks, were oriented toward seeking options and choices in their lives, and were cognizant of relevant information was superior to the extent of those skills in non-physically disabled students. Thus, disabled students bring a unique set of assets and liabilities that influence their special needs relative to college success.

Dropout Prevention for Minority Students

At-risk students frequently come from large urban schools rife with social and educational problems (College Entrance Examination Board, 1985). Such students come to college without a strong, positive experience with an educational system. While not all minority students are at risk or come from large urban schools, higher proportions of minority students do. Research on dropout prevention, attrition, and retention in higher education is far more pervasive for the student body as a whole. Although there is important information available on what factors assist minority students at risk, there is ample room for further investigation.

No clear relationship has been shown between race and dropping out. The majority of at-risk students are white lower- and middle-class students. The proportion of at-risk students is greater among several minority groups, but since there are fewer minority students (hence, the use of the term minority), the actual number of at-risk students is greater among whites (Cross, 1974, 1976; McCauley, 1988).

Traditional measures of academic success relate to persistence, not race. For example, low grade-point-averages among African Americans may predict whether individual students will drop out, as is the case for all students (Suen, 1983). However, certain studies have failed to find relationships between high school rank or Scholastic Aptitude Test scores and African American persistence rates (McCauley, 1988). While initial relationships can be established between race or ethnicity and dropout rates, once the effect of lower socioeconomic status is controlled among student groups, performance, progress, persistence, and degree attainment prove to be unrelated to race or ethnicity (Grossman, Dandridge, Nettles, & Theoney, 1982; Ramist, 1981).

African Americans on predominantly white campuses often feel alienated and deprived of a group with which to socialize and identify. Dropout rates among African Americans on predominantly white campuses tend to be greater than the norm (McCauley, 1988; Suen, 1983). The social integration of African Americans on predominantly white campuses is critical to dropout prevention. Factors that promote persistence and success among African American students are a high level of self-esteem, a realistic view of one's own abilities, and clear long-term academic and career goals.

Successful African American students have a strong sense of control over their lives and hold high aspirations for themselves. In the first 2 years of college, African American students whose college plans were supported by peers, friends, and family and who had clear long-range goals were more prone to success. In the later college years, African American students who showed an understanding of the nature of racism and who participated in various forms of community service were prone to persist and to perform well in college (Epps, Gurin, Lao, & Beattie, 1969; Pfeifer & Sedlacek, 1970; Ramist, 1981; Steward & Jackson, 1988). Successful dropout prevention programs for African Americans focused on their social integration during the first 2 years of college and provided for community service and campus involvement in the junior and senior years.

African American students who chose predominantly black institutions of higher education received higher grades and were less likely to drop out than were their counterparts who attended predominantly white institutions. However, when there is a sufficiently large population of African Americans in a predominantly white institution, African American students are able to locate friends, supporters, and role models with whom they can identify; in such environments, little difference is discernible between the persistence of African American and non-black students (Anderson, 1984a, 1984b; Grossman et al., 1982; Robinson, 1988; Shanley, 1987). Although this research makes a strong argument for developing and maintaining critical masses of minority students on predominantly white campuses, there is no clear indication of what constitutes a critical mass.

The research of persistence of at-risk minority students has been confined largely to predominantly African American and predominantly white institutions. Studies on dropout rates and factors contributing to the success of other specific minority groups and persistence in culturally diverse institutional environments are needed. Multicultural institutions—those with nearly 30 percent minority enrollment—have been noted for their genuine commitment to the success of at-risk minority students and have been characterized by diverse, interactive student cultures. These institutions tend to provide integrated programs and services for at-risk students, rather than establishing specific programs for minority students experiencing difficulty with academics or college life (Crosson, 1987). The milieu of cultural diversity and the difference between the organization of programs and services for at-risk students at these institutions and that at predominantly white or African American colleges and universities argue for further investigation of their unique qualities and the effectiveness of their programs.

Factors cited as influential in dropout studies of whole college populations frequently do not prove significant in identifying potential dropouts among minority students. Traditional measures of precollege ability, such as the

Scholastic Aptitude Test and high school grades, may be poor predictors of college success for minority students (McCauley, 1988; Robinson, 1988).

African American students at predominantly white institutions may come to feel less able to succeed in such environments. Steward and Jackson (1988) compared African American persisters and dropouts at a predominantly white university. African American persisters felt more competent in adapting to different academic settings, in planning, in exercising self-control, in coping with failure, in managing anxiety, and in differentiating their feelings than did African American dropouts. Academic integration is a doubly important predictor of success among minority students (Whitaker, 1987).

Peer counseling assists at-risk students from minority groups. Regular assistance from talented upper-class minority students in academic tutoring, social support, and positive role modeling enhances minority freshmen's probability of succeeding in college (Carroll, 1988; Guon, 1988). These and other interventions that promote academic and social integration of minority at-risk students may be effective tools in dropout prevention.

Colleges and universities can take some clear actions now to lower the dropout rate among at-risk minority students. A variety of programs are designed to assist the minority first-year college student at risk. The links between student plans and persistence are strong, and there are programs that assist students with their initial academic, financial, personal, social, and career planning. Such programs rely on research on the specific needs of the mixtures of races, peoples, and cultures now found in the United States (Astin, 1984). Other intervention programs assist with the transition of minority students to college. The relationships among social integration, role models and support groups, and persistence are robust. Successful programs providing peer counseling, faculty mentoring, social events, and high school-to-college transition work to strengthen the social integration of the student with the college environment (Astin, 1984; Carroll, 1988; Corbie, 1983; Crosson, 1987; Lewis, 1986). Targeting the dropout prevention program to the specific needs of minority students involves the use of the student involvement theory and the application of knowledge about the social, cultural, and economic backgrounds of the students.

Dropout Prevention for Commuter Students

Commuter institutions—community colleges, urban universities, and many urban liberal arts colleges—attract students who are at risk. Part-time students, returning adults, students from culturally diverse backgrounds, students from lower socioeconomic groups, and disabled students all have lower rates of persistence in postsecondary education. These student groups predominate in commuter institutions.

What differentiates students who succeed from those who drop out at commuter institutions? Rotter (1988) studied a cohort of freshmen at an urban technical university. She found that students who spent more academic hours per week at school, who spent more time studying at home, and who spent less time visiting in the student cafeteria were less likely to miss classes, were more likely to get class notes and makeup assignments when they were absent, were more likely to participate actively in class, were more likely to ask an instructor for help, and were more likely to get good grades. In short, increasing time on the academic tasks of coursework reduced the likelihood of dropping out. Students who dropped out had less favorable attitudes toward their instructors, were less likely to engage faculty in conversation outside of class, and were less committed to earning a college degree.

The extent to which community college students are academically and socially integrated and the extent to which they hold strong goal and institutional commitments appear to be less strongly related to persistence than for 4-year college students. Focus of control and self-esteem are important factors affecting the progress, performance, persistence, and degree completion of community college students (Williamson & Creamer, 1988).

Studies of commuter institutions indicate that students typically spend a smaller proportion of time on campus. While social integration is found to be important to dropout prevention, academic integration is a far stronger predictor of student progress and success (Fox, 1987). Still, the commuter students have a similar need to develop an intellectual and a personal sense of themselves. The weaker predictive strength of social integration is not due to any diminished value of the concept of student retention. Rather, it is an artifact of research at commuter institutions, where the environment is less conducive to involvement in college activities. Positive actions on the part of the institution and the student can promote academic and social integration, which in turn, mediates the effect of attending a commuter institution (Pascarella, 1985b, 1985c). Support systems can be developed to overcome and compensate for the diminished involvement found among commuter students.

Commuter colleges and universities have higher dropout rates than do residential colleges. Commuter schools attract students who are more prone to noncompletion, sometimes for very legitimate reasons. Nevertheless, the extent of attrition has led several researchers to examine the problems of the institutions, rather than the deficiencies of the students who enroll in them (Adelman, 1989; Avakian, MacKinney, & Allen, 1982; Creamer, 1982; Lee, 1988; Zwerling, 1974). Successful dropout prevention needs to focus on the specific needs of at-risk students and the ways in which colleges and universities can mediate those needs.

Dropout Prevention for Students in Distance Education

Increasingly, part-time and adult students are pursuing their education at a distance through college courses offered via television and computer technology. The knowledge, skills, and abilities of the workforce are being renewed and refreshed through professional development, continuing education, and college degree programs taken at a distance. These learning environments produce their own set of unique problems relative to dropouts. Students who have allowed several years to lapse since their last encounter with an educational program are more likely to be at risk. Students who just as easily could have attended campus-based programs are less likely to complete the distance education program. Older, more mature students who live at a distance from campus, and students who continue their education from high school to college or from undergraduate to graduate degree are more likely to succeed in distance education programs (Langenbach & Korhonen, 1988).

Until recently, research on college dropouts has focused on traditional and nontraditional student populations. Students enrolled in distance education programs differ from common notions of nontraditional students. For example, nontraditional students live off-campus and commute to classes (Bean & Metzner, 1985). Students in distance education may never encounter traditional classrooms, as they use correspondence study and various means of telecommunication and computer technology to receive courses, programs, and degrees. Students are usually taught individually, not in groups, with the exception of occasional meetings for social and pedagogical reasons.

Under such circumstances, students in distance learning situations are more significantly affected by family, work, and social life. The students' individual situations and home environments have a profound effect on their dropout or persistence rates in postsecondary education. There is virtually no separation from previous social and educational environments, and there are no traditional opportunities for social integration (Kember, 1989). For these reasons alone, students involved in distance education may have greater proclivity for dropping out.

Earlier research on the characteristics of students in distance education found age, gender, prior education, and occupation to be significant factors in predicting persistence. One research study reached the discouraging conclusion that the dropout process in distance education is not controllable by the institution (Kennedy & Powell, 1976). Although background characteristics are strong determinants of persistence, traditional grades explain only a small proportion of the probability of students in distance education to drop out.

The clarity and commitment of students to their goals are important generally in dropout prevention. The take on additional new meanings for students in distance learning environments. The reason the student is enrolled is more likely to be in conflict with the traditional notions of pedagogy, wherein the instructor decides for the student what is important to learn. The unemployed worker may enroll as part of a general career change. The employed worker may enroll to gain specific work role skills. The displaced homemaker may seek to renew her education before re-entering the workforce. These are among a few of the multitude of extrinsic motivations of students in distance education. Extrinsic motivation is far more subject to the student's situation. Workers and employers can be supportive of distance learners' efforts to enhance skills, earn a degree, or improve their abilities. They can also be jealous and resentful and attempt to sabotage the students' plans for an educational program. In a similar manner, family can have far more direct bearing on the students' extrinsic motivation to achieve an educational goal (Kember, 1989).

As noted previously, central to dropout prevention research at the college level are the twin concepts of academic and social integration. The effects of academic integration, as exemplified by a wide range of materials, processes, and procedures used in distance education, have been found to be related to students' decisions to drop out or persist. Rekkedal (1973) found that a greater frequency of contact between instructor and student by telephone and the turnaround time in which instructors provided assessments of the student's work were related to persistence. Kember and Harper (1987) found that the more the students in distance education relied on rote learning, the more likely they were to drop out. Instructors of distance education courses often expected and demanded in-depth, analytical skills of their students. Dissonance between the learning style of the students and that required by the course contributed to dropout rates.

Prior academic achievement, although not directly predictive of attrition among students in distance education, has an indirect bearing. Students with less formal education and no recent history of study face a more severe transition in academic integration. Similarly, students without a significant preparatory educational background may not have developed the independent study habits prerequisite to success in distance learning.

While the standard concept of social integration may not apply to the student in distance education, there are parallel notions that may be appropriate. The extent to which the student is able to harmonize the demands of part-time study with family, work, and social demands may well be an important factor in student success. Distance education programs that are sponsored or endorsed by employers may have lower dropout rates because of the integration of work and schooling (Kember, 1989).

Students enrolling in distance education programs are often at-risk students. Many of the normal forces contributing to persistence, progress, performance, and degree completion are not present or are weak indicators. The college's manipulation of academic integration forces and factors, through cooperative arrangements with sponsoring employers; through frequent, intentional interaction between faculty and student; and through the appropriate match of learning materials and the students' intrinsic and extrinsic goals, can foster lower dropout rates among this student population.

DROPOUT PROGRAMS THAT WORK

Many dropout prevention programs claim success; few can document it. Then too, there is little evidence that a successful program at one college can be directly implemented in another environment. For these reasons, college leaders who wish to design and develop dropout prevention programs should plan for the regular assessment of the programs' effectiveness. In this section, we provide examples of three kinds of programs that work: programs that facilitate the transition of at-risk students from high school to college, multicultural education centers on university campuses, and community college developmental programs. Each set of examples finds a different set of student and college characteristics. The unifying factor in these programs is the quest to promote student involvement.

High School-to-College Transition Programs

The transition of an individual from one group to another produces stress as the person attempts to cope with the change. Such transitions in a social context are accompanied by rites of passage. Making the transition from high school to college is accompanied by various rites of passage that confer recognition and responsibility on the student. Thus, the first-year college student initially experiences separation from his or her old group. This is best characterized by high school graduation ceremonies and "going away" parties for students attending residential colleges. Next, the student tries different roles and behaviors as he or she attempts to cope with the college environment. Finally, the student hopefully establishes stable and enduring forms of interaction with other students and faculty that reflect his or her incorporation into the role of college student. This transition from separation to incorporation subjects the student to uncertainty, isolation, and vulnerability (Attinasi, 1989; Tinto, 1988). Formal rites serve to announce new membership and provide a structure that allows the student to integrate into the college environment (Van Gennep,

1960). A more pronounced and extreme portrayal of the transition process is represented in the sorority and fraternity rush and pledge processes for first-year students.

The separation, transition, and incorporation stages involve distinct actors, locations and norms. The separation stage relies heavily on the student's peers and parents. Do either of the parents have some college education? How is college attendance viewed in the high school from which the student graduated? What is the quality of the academic and social preparation the student received during his or her secondary education? Answers to these questions reveal the primary indicators of student success during the separation stage.

Separation may be less definitive for the commuter student. Initially this may be helpful because it reduces the stress of loss of friends and familiar surroundings. But later, commuter students may experience more difficulty in adapting to and adopting the new behavioral norms of the college environment. Old friends may not support good study habits and may attempt to undermine the student's commitment to college. Time constraints and conflicts with work and family roles may also interfere with the development of support groups, networks, informal contact with faculty, and other factors that contribute to the social and academic integration of students.

The transition from high school to college is a significant dropout point for at-risk students. Some students withdraw from college because they cannot adjust to the new behaviors; others quit because they simply cannot handle the stress. Colleges and universities can and do intervene effectively in the high school-to-college transition. The effective intervention is based on the notion that there is a gap between the attitudes and norms of the high school and those of the college environments (Tinto, 1988).

Summer transition programs represent one form of high school-to-college transition endeavor for which there are more than 10 years of experience and evaluation. They most frequently involve 4 to 6 weeks of orientation to campus life; study skills workshops; and remedial courses in English reading and writing, precollege math and calculus, and coursework in introductory science or social sciences (Aschuler & Wallace, 1983; Buck, 1982; Crosson, 1987; Minnesota University General College, 1982; Welsh, Conway, & West, 1987). The focus of the programs is most frequently on academic skills. The programs seek to identify the gap between high school and college environments for at-risk students in terms of educational disadvantage. They are founded on the premise that an early start on coursework and study skills will influence academic preparedness and integration of at-risk students. Indirect consequences of these programs are that students are able to develop familiarity with the campus environment without the full press of students encountered during the onset of the regular academic year. There is also a greater opportunity to have informal contact and conversation with faculty and other students.

Many of these programs provide student counseling on such subjects as study habits, time management, and coping with the loss of old friends and with the changes implicit in the new environment. Tutoring is provided to students with clearly identified special needs, and financial aid counseling is also frequently provided. High school-to-college transition programs should help promote social and academic integration of at-risk students. Unfortunately, there is scant confirmatory research on the effectiveness of high school-to-college transition programs.

Multicultural Education Centers

Multicultural education centers have been created at predominantly white institutions, often at the request or demand of minority student groups. They often were established in response to renewed racial attacks and harassment on campus. Such centers act as a cultural refuge for the able and the at-risk students of color. Many multicultural education centers were established during the Civil Rights movement of the 1960s. By the late 1970s and early 1980s, these centers had all but disappeared. While the multicultural centers helped minority students feel less isolated from the mainstream, the centers became isolated from the rest of campus life and thus became of less relevance and interest to students (Seelye & Wasilewski, 1981). With the recurrence of blatant incidents of racism in the late 1980s, multicultural education centers are re-emerging as a dropout prevention tool on predominantly white campuses (Terrell & Wright, 1988).

Coping with social isolation may be part of the initial challenges facing minority students (Attinasi, 1989). African American students in predominantly white institutions, for example, may feel in the college environment, but not of the college environment. The isolation that first-year minority students may feel is in sharp contrast to the familiarity of their home and high school environments. They are at risk because the challenges this transition presents are more extreme and more pronounced than those for students of the majority. Problems of isolation and alienation may be heightened by faculty and student stereotyping of all minorities as underprepared and below average students (Reed, 1979). Without support and reaffirmation, the commitment these students have for the institution and their personal and career goals weakens and they drop out (Fleming, 1984).

Increasing minority enrollment increases the demand for ethnic-specific activities and services. Multicultural education centers provide a location on campus where minority students and faculty can meet informally, where social and cultural events can be planned, and where support networks can form. American Indian, Hispanic and black students value these centers and seek ethnic-specific programming to augment their college environment (Davis, 1977; Wright, 1985). A multicultural education center on campus needs to be more than a building or a physical location. To be an effective dropout prevention entity, a multicultural education center needs to be effectively organized, with a staff knowledgeable and experienced in issues of cultural diversity and capable of strong and innovative leadership.

One of the older centers is the Multicultural Education Center (MEC) at the University of Wisconsin-Oshkosh, as profiled by Terrell and Wright (1988). It developed in the late 1960s from the Afro-American center on campus, advocating a philosophy of cultural pluralism. During the most recent decade, four-fifths of its programs and services have been targeted specifically to black, American Indian, Hispanic, and Asian peoples and cultures. A remaining one-fifth of MEC activities have been devoted to women and to the European ethnicities that populate Wisconsin and the upper Midwest.

In 1978 the MEC focus expanded again, from cultural and social activities to academic and student services. This was accomplished through the affiliation of the MEC with the college of education. Upon becoming an organizational unit of the college, it diversified its programs and was restructured to provide support services to academic departments, student services divisions, and community agencies. The courses MEC offered added to its academic credibility. The MEC became a practice teaching site for the teacher corp project housed at the university. MEC developed a children's program for area schools and social service agencies and involved minority students. It cosponsored an ethnic heritage staff development program for the university and provided guest lectures to the various colleges. The 1980s had transformed the MEC from a center for social and cultural activities to one with significant interdepartmental and interdisciplinary teaching and service functions.

Courses that helped students understand the ethnic experience were developed in cooperation with nearly 20 departments, from anthropology to journalism to special education. Similarly, cooperative programs in student services were developed in admissions, housing, alumni relations, financial aid, student publications, the office of the dean of students, and the writing center. Funding for programs came from the dean of students and from the college of education. Through this broad collaboration and involvement with academic departments and student services divisions, minority students became increasingly involved in the mainstream of campus life.

Although no comprehensive evaluation of multicultural education centers has been identified in the literature, one may extrapolate that an effective center must establish a cultural refuge for minority students. But it also must be much more. It must go beyond being an enclave for minorities to a vehicle for the social and academic integration of students into the college environment. Organizers of such centers should conceptualize the center in the context of other college or university groups "that foster music, religion, gender, recreation or group membership for like-minded groups of university constituencies" (Terrell & Wright, 1988, p. 93). Doing so promotes the social and academic integration of minority students, reaffirms their commitment to the institution, allows for informal interaction between faculty and students, fosters support groups and networks, and assists in the prevention of dropouts among the minority student population.

Programs at Community Colleges

A wide variety of programs exists to promote and retain at-risk students in community colleges. Dropout prevention typically includes student assessment, student advisement, student personal development, social integration programs, the organization of student services for at-risk students, financial aid programs, and developmental and remedial skills programs. Lee (1988) catalogued seven basic types of dropout prevention initiatives. In developing the catalog, Lee reviewed studies that examined what community colleges did that effectively held at-risk students in educational programs (Gardiner & Nazari-Robati, 1983), rather than studies of what causes students to leave community colleges in larger numbers than leave other institutions of higher education. Lee queried 93 community colleges on their practices, their programs, and their services for at-risk students.

Colleges with less than 1,700 full-time equivalent enrollments (FTE) were categorized as small; those above 1,700 FTE, as large. Colleges in districts with less than 72,000 general population were labeled as rural; those with more than 72,000 were regarded as urban. The seven types of dropout prevention identified by Lee (1988) are (1) new student support and integration programs, (2) adult learner reintegration programs, (3) peer tutoring programs, (4) peer counseling programs, (5) remedial-developmental programs, (6) comprehensive career planning programs, and (7) a career placement program or office. Data were gathered on the success of the colleges' programs in retaining students and the costs of their operation.

New Student Support and Integration Programs

New student support and integration programs were used predominantly by larger, rural colleges. Still, they were reported to be most effective in smaller urban colleges. The average program required 4.4 FTE staff to operate. Lee (1988) compared the cost of these programs relative to their holding power and found them not to be comparatively cost-effective.

Adult Learner Reintegration Programs

Adult learner reintegration programs were most frequently found in the smaller urban community colleges. They had the strongest holding power among the students of the larger urban community colleges and the weakest performance among the small rural colleges. The average staffing for an adult learner reintegration program was 1.8 FTE, and they were regarded as relatively cost-effective.

Peer Tutoring Programs

Peer tutoring programs were most often established in smaller urban community colleges. Their highest reported holding power was in the larger urban institutions and the smaller rural ones. These programs proved to be relatively cost-effective, requiring approximately 2.4 FTE to staff them.

Peer Counseling Programs

Peer counseling programs were most frequently found in larger urban community colleges, where they evinced good holding power. Only 1 in 10 large rural colleges relied on such peer counseling. Nevertheless, all sizes and types of community colleges that had these programs regarded them as having strong holding power among at-risk students. These programs also proved to be extremely cost-effective in relation to the others examined. The average staffing required for these programs was 2.0 FTE.

Remedial-Developmental Programs

Remedial-developmental programs were the most extensively used interventions for at-risk students in the community colleges studied. All colleges reported strong holding power for these programs, but they were also reported to be the most costly form of dropout prevention studied. These programs were labor intensive, requiring an average of 3.8 FTE to operate.

Comprehensive Career Planning Programs

Comprehensive career planning programs were most often located in large and small urban community colleges. They were described as most effective in the large urban settings. All sizes and types of institutions reported comparatively weaker holding power for these programs. Also, they were not a very cost-effective means to dropout prevention. The average program required 1.9 FTE to operate.

Career Placement Programs and Offices

Career placement programs and offices also were set in the large and small urban institutions. Their holding power was not strong when compared with that of the other six interventions. An analysis of the cost relative to holding power showed that these programs were not a very cost-effective intervention. Their average staffing was 1.5 FTE.

Lee's study (1988) showed that the relative effectiveness of dropout prevention programs varied by the size and type of institution. Urban and rural institutions attracted students who were at risk for different reasons. The study identified several effective intervention strategies for community colleges. The personal and emotional needs of returning adult students can be met in a cost-effective manner through peer counseling. Social integration and support group needs of adult students can be focused through such programs. Also, programs that sought to promote new student integration and support or attempted to provide remedial and developmental assistance were the most widely used and were the least cost-effective ways to retain at-risk students. However, these programs were reported to have the greatest holding power among those at risk. Students at risk have their greatest needs in closing the initial gap between their previous social and academic experience and that demanded of them in college. Closing this gap is costly, yet fundamental to the social and academic integration of at-risk students in community colleges and other higher education environments.

NOT ALL DROPOUTS ARE FAILURES

An important idea to keep in mind when planning a program to arrest attrition and assist at-risk students is that not everybody seeks a college degree. Community colleges, in particular, have been criticized because of the lower number of students who ultimately earn a bachelor's degree (Eaton, 1988). Many students who drop out may have attained their educational goals without completing the educational program of the institution. Although educational programs—be they vocational, general, or liberal arts—are carefully planned to benefit students, they represent the intention of the institution, not the course-taking behavior of students. Both persisters and dropouts report progress in increasing their self-confidence, gaining career skills, understanding and getting along with others, working with others on a team, and developing a meaningful philosophy of life (Hanson, 1988). While college completion may have stronger advantages, college-going also brings benefits. Attitudes and beliefs about learning, study, and college life affect the at-risk students' probability of succeeding. Programs that promote student exploration of postcollege careers help clarify students' goals and self-understanding (Boyd et al., 1988).

Culturally diverse students in predominantly white colleges and universities may benefit from minority student centers. Social networks, informal interaction with other students who are succeeding in college, and support groups are important factors in success for at-risk students. In a predominantly white college environment, minority student centers may foster such relationships, providing places where students may reaffirm their own values, social groups, and informal networks (Terrell & Wright, 1988).

At-risk students are prone to drop out for a variety of reasons. They may be academically or socially underprepared; they may be at a distance, disabled, or simply unclear about their educational and career goals. Research on college students at risk illustrates that dropout prevention is a complex task, not a simple one.

The studies reviewed in this chapter suggest that effective dropout prevention programs are based on and targeted to specific student groups. An effective program for a visually impaired student is different from one to assist an underprepared American Indian. Broad campus retention programs do not work as well as those focused on specific students and their needs.

The importance of family background in retention underscores the need to understand fully the student population to be served. For residential students at small, selective colleges, family background may have only indirect effects on dropout rates. For the student in distance education, family background and environment may be fundamental to the student's academic and social integration into the educational program. For traditionally aged commuter students, family background may be important in the transition from high school to college. As the circumstances of the student vary, the role and importance of factors such as family background vary as well.

The student involvement theory helps explain the role and interrelationship of factors contributing to a student's decision to remain in college or drop out. Similarly stated, the more a student is involved in the academic and social milieu at college, the more likely the student is to persist and succeed. Student success is directly related to the time and energy devoted to postsecondary education.

Fundamental to student involvement are the concepts of social and academic integration. The greater the involvement in coursework, the greater the academic integration and the greater the probability of success. Study skills, previous academic experiences and achievement, and the student's goals affect academic integration.

Social integration results from the friendships, support groups, and networks the students establish to make themselves feel part of college life and the college environment. Social integration is facilitated by recognition and rites of passage into the role of college student. A student's commitment to the postsecondary institution is derived from social integration and influences persistence, progress, performance, and degree completion. Commitment to goals and to institution have direct bearing on persistence. Successful dropout prevention calls for innovative strategies to reaffirm both. Goals may be intrinsic (love of learning) or extrinsic (job preparation). Most students possess both motivations; clearly, however, different students choose postsecondary education for differing degrees of these motivations. Students in vocational programs are more likely to be extrinsically motivated. Students in the humanities may be more inclined toward intrinsic motivation. Students who are unclear about their motivation for being in college are likely to drop out.

Good educational, social, and cultural programs should breed strong institutional commitment. Fundamental to social integration and institutional commitment is a sense of being of the college, not just in the college. Relevant extracurricular activities and informal support groups and social networks foster retention.

Perhaps the easier, least costly way to promote retention is to educate faculty to the powerful and significant influence their informal interactions with at-risk students may have on persistence. The informal interactions decrease an at-risk student's feeling that faculty are there for only the good students in class and that college is more than a process of weeding the academically weak from the able. Equally important are family members who are proactive and supportive. Both faculty and family members can be encouraged to engage the at-risk students in conversations about their education and to take interest in the students' academic lives. Such support persons often become role models and mentors.

Dropout prevention programs that promote student involvement will assist at-risk students. To be effective, they need clearly to understand and appreciate students' varying needs and background, to promote the academic and social integration of students into the college environment, and to reinforce the clarity and strength of students' commitments to their goals and their institution. The research on dropout prevention at the college level is far from complete. The picture that emerges is complex. Nevertheless, there are effective programs and strategies colleges and universities can implement to promote student involvement and to reduce attrition.

REFERENCES

Adelman, C. (1989, November). *The validity of institutional mission.* Paper presented at the annual meeting of the Association for the Study of Higher Education, Atlanta.

Anderson, K. (1984a). The effects of college type and characteristics on educational attainment. Washington, DC: National Institute of Education.

Anderson, K. (1984b). *Institutional differences in college effects: Final report.* Washington, DC: National Institute of Education.

Aschuler, M., & Wallace, W.D. (1983, April). *The effectiveness of a summer prematriculation program for minority medical students.* Paper presented at the annual meeting of the American Educational Research Association, Montreal, Canada.

Astin, A. (1984). A look at pluralism in the contemporary student population. *NASPA Journal, 21*(3), 2–11.

Astin, A. (1985). *Achieving educational excellence.* San Francisco, CA: Jossey-Bass.

Attinasi, L. (1989). Getting in: Mexican Americans' perceptions of university attendance and implications for freshmen year persistence. *Journal of Higher Education, 60*(3), 247–277.

Avakian, A.M., MacKinney, A.C., & Allen, D.R. (1982). Race and sex differences in student retention at an urban university. *College and University, 57*, 160–165.

Bean, J.P., & Metzner, B.S. (1985). A conceptual model of nontraditional undergraduate student attrition. *Review of Educational Research, 55*, 485–540.

Bevilacqua, T., & Osterlink, B.S. (1979). Components of a service program for the mainstreaming of hearing impaired students into regular university programs. *American Annals of the Deaf, 124*, 400–402.

Bieber, T., Kay, C., Kerkstra, P., Ratcliff, J., & Prihoda, J. (1987). *Community colleges and students with disabilities: A directory of services and programs.* Washington, DC: American Council on Education, HEATH Resource Center, and the American Association of Community and Junior Colleges.

Boyd, V., et al. (1988). *Impact of a career exploration component on student persistence* (Research Report No. 9-88). College Park, MD: Counseling Center, University of Maryland.

Braxton, J.M., Brier, E.M., & Hossler, D. (1988). The influence of student problems on student withdrawal decisions: An autopsy on "autopsy" studies. *Research in Higher Education, 28*, 241–253.

Brown, J.V.E., & Robinson, R.D. (1988). The adult male undergraduate: Who stays and who leaves? *College Student Journal, 22*, 95–100.

Bryan, W.A., & Becker, K.M. (1980). Student services for the handicapped student. In H.Z. Sprandel & M.R. Schmidt (Eds.), *New directions for student services: Serving handicapped students.* San Francisco, CA: Jossey-Bass.

Buck, C.B. (1982). *Summer bridge: A residential learning experience for high risk freshmen at the University of California, San Diego.* La Jolla, CA: University of California, San Diego.

Burkhead, E.J. (1980). *Vocational maturity and physically disabled college students.* Unpublished doctoral dissertation, University of Missouri-Columbia.

Calhoun, H., & Brown, T. (1988). A study of former students: Dropouts or stopouts. *Community College Journal for Research and Planning, 6*, 5–14.

Caparosa, C.A. (1985). *Opportunities after high school for persons who are severely handicapped.* Washington, DC: American Council on Education, HEATH Resource Center.

Carroll, J. (1988). Freshmen retention and attrition factors at a predominantly black urban community college. *Journal of College Student Development, 29*, 52–59.

Christoffel, P. (1986). *Minority student access and retention: A review.* New York: College Entrance Examination Board.

College Entrance Examination Board. (1985). *Equality and excellence: The educational status of black Americans.* New York: Author.

Cope, R., & Hannah, W. (1975). *Revolving college doors: The causes and consequences of dropping out, stopping out, and transferring.* New York: Wiley.

Corbie, L. (1983). *SEEK: A study of a compensatory program for educationally and economically disadvantaged students at Herbert H. Lehman College of the City University of New York.* Unpublished doctoral dissertation, Columbia University, New York.

Creamer, D.G. (1982). The management of change as a condition of student retention programs. *Community College Review, 9*(4), 42–50.

Cross, K.P. (1974). *Beyond the open door: New students to higher education.* San Francisco: Jossey-Bass.

Cross, K.P. (1976). *Adults as learners: Improving instruction and reshaping the curriculum.* San Francisco: Jossey-Bass.

Crosson, P.H. (1987, November). *Environmental influences on minority degree attainment.* Paper presented at the annual meeting of the Association for the Study of Higher Education, Baltimore.

Davis, W.E. (1977). *Ethnic minorities at the University of New Mexico: A presidential progress report.* Washington, DC: National Institute of Education. (ERIC Document Reproduction Service No. ED 139 322)

Dellow, D.A., Douzenis, C., & Ross, S.M. (1988). An analysis of course withdrawals at a rural community college in Florida. *Community College Journal for Research and Planning, 6*(1), 3–13.

Donovan, R. (1983). Path analysis of a theoretical model of persistence in higher education among low-income black youth. *Research in Higher Education, 21*(3), 243–259.

Eaton, J.S. (1988). *Colleges of choice: The enabling impact of the community college.* New York: Macmillan.

Epps, E., Gurin, R., Lao, R., & Beattie, M. (1969). Correlates of academic achievement among Northern and Southern urban Negro students. *Journal of Social Issues, 25*, 29–53.

Fleming, J. (1984). *Blacks in college.* San Francisco: Jossey-Bass.

Fox, R.N. (1987). Factors influencing student retention. In F. Kehl (Ed.), *Practical research.* New York: City University of New York.

Gardiner, J.J., & Nazari-Robati, A. (1983). Student attrition research: Implications for retention strategies. *NASPA Journal, 20*, 25–33.

Grossman, E.J., Dandridge, M., Nettles, M., & Theoney, A.R. (1982, May). *Predicting student progression: The influence of race and other student and institutional characteristics on college student performance.* Paper presented at the Annual Forum of the Association for Institutional Research, Denver.

Guon, D.G. (1988, April). Minority access and retention: *An evaluation of a multi-university peer counseling program.* Paper presented at the annual meeting of the Midwestern Psychological Association, Chicago.

Hanson, G.R. (1988, May). *Educational goal attainment: A longitudinal study.* Paper presented at the annual meeting of the Association for Institutional Research, Phoenix, AZ.

Harkins, J.A. (1978). Serving deaf students in postsecondary schools and implications for Section 504. *American Annals of the Deaf, 123*, 47–51.

Hippolitus, P. (1987). *College freshmen with disabilities: Preparing for employment.* Washington, DC: Committee on Youth Development, President's Committee on the Employment and Education of the Handicapped, and the Handicapped Resource Center, American Council on Education.

Jarrow, J.E. (1987). Integration of individuals with disabilities in higher education: A review of literature. *Journal of Postsecondary Education and Disability, 5*(2), 38–57.

Jencks, C., & Riesman, D. (1969). *The academic revolution* (2nd ed.). New York: Doubleday, Anchor Books.

Kay, C.R. (1982). *The relationships between selected student characteristics and measures of satisfaction in community college handicapped populations.* Unpublished doctoral dissertation, University of Missouri-Columbia.

Kember, D. (1989). A longitudinal-process model of drop out from distance education. *Journal of Higher Education, 60*(3), 278–301.

Kember, D., & Harper, G. (1987). Implications for instruction arising from the relationship between approaches to studying and academic outcomes. *Instructional Science, 6*, 35–46.

Kennedy, D., & Powell, R. (1976). Student progress and withdrawal in the open university. *Teaching at a Distance, 7*, 61–75.

Langenbach, M., & Korhonen, L. (1988). Persisters and nonpersisters in a graduate level, nontraditional, liberal education program. *Adult Education Quarterly, 38*, 136–138.

Lee, R.E. (1988). Assessing retention program holding power effectiveness across smaller community colleges. *Journal of College Student Development, 29*, 255–262.

Lewis, J. (1986). The black freshman network. *College and University, 61*(2), 135–140.

McCauley, D.P. (1988). Effects of specific factors on blacks' persistence at a predominantly white university. *Journal of College Student Development, 29*, 48–51.

McElroy, L.J., & Rupp, J. (1979). *Community college services for hearing impaired students in Arizona* (ERIC Document Reproduction Service No. ED 168 618). Unpublished report. Tucson: University of Arizona.

Minnesota University General College. (1982). *The 1980–81 general college retention program: Final report.* Minneapolis: University of Minnesota.

Morrisey, R.J. (1971). Attrition in probationary freshmen. *Journal of College Student Personnel, 12*, 279–285.

Moss, J.R. (1984). *A national directory of four-year colleges, two-year colleges, and post high school training programs for young people with learning disabilities.* Tulsa: Partners in Publishing.

Pascarella, E.R. (1980). Student-faculty informal contact and college outcomes. *Review of Educational Research, 50*(4), 545–595.

Pascarella, E.R. (1983a). Student-faculty relationships and freshman year intellectual and personal growth in a nonresidential setting. *Journal of College Student Personnel, 24*(5), 395–401.

Pascarella, E.R. (1983b). A test and reconceptualization of a theoretical model of college withdrawal in a commuter institutional setting. *Sociology of Education, 56*(2), 88–100.

Pascarella, E.R. (1985a). College environmental influences on learning and cognitive development: A critical review and synthesis. In J. Smart (Ed.), *Higher education: Handbook of theory and research: Vol. I.* New York: Agathon Press.

Pascarella, E.R. (1985b). The influence of on-campus living versus commuting to college on intellectual and interpersonal self-concept. *Journal of College Student Personnel, 26*(4), 292–299.

Pascarella, E.R. (1985c). Student affective development within the college environment. *Journal of Higher Education, 56*(6), 640–663.

Pascarella, E.R. (1986). Orientation to college and freshman year persistence/withdrawal decisions. *Journal of Higher Education, 57*(2), 155–175.

Pfeifer, C., & Sedlacek, W. (1970). *Nonintellectual correlates of black and white student grades at the University of Maryland* (Research Report No. 3-70). College Park, MD: University of Maryland, Cultural Study Center.

Ramist, L. (1981). *College student attrition and retention* (Report No. 81-1). New York: College Entrance Examination Board.

Reed, R.J. (1979). Increasing opportunities for black students in higher education. *Journal of Negro Education, 47*, 143–150.

Rekkedal, T. (1973). *The written assignments in correspondence education: The effects of reducing turn-around time.* Oslo, Norway: NKI-skolen Undervisningssetrum.

Richardson, R.C., Fisk, E.C., & Okun, M.A. (1983). *Literacy in the open-access college.* San Francisco: Jossey-Bass.

Robinson, T. (1988, November). *A cohort analysis of persistence and non-persistence among black students at a historically black private college.* Paper presented at Black Student Retention in Higher Education Conference, New York.

Rotter, N.G. (1988). Student attrition in a technological university: Academic lifestyle. *College Student Journal, 22,* 241–248.

Rudolph, F. (1962). *The American college and university.* New York: Random House.

Seelye, H.N., & Wasilewski, J.H. (1981). Historical development of multicultural education. In M. D. Pusch (Ed.), *Multicultural education: A cross-cultural training approach.* Chicago: Intercultural Network.

Shanley, M. (1987). *An exploratory longitudinal study of retention, persistence, and graduation rates of freshmen seminar course participants at the University of South Carolina during the period 1979–1986.* Unpublished doctoral dissertation, University of South Carolina, Columbia, SC.

Spady, W. (1970). Dropouts from higher education: An interdisciplinary review and synthesis. *Interchange, 1,* 64–85.

Spady, W. (1971). Dropouts from higher education: Toward an empirical model. *Interchange, 2,* 38–62.

Stage, F.K., & Richardson, R.C. (1988, April). *University persistence: Motivational orientations and college withdrawal.* Paper presented at a meeting of the American Educational Research Association, New Orleans.

Steward, R.J., & Jackson, J. (1988). *Academic persistence and black university students' perceived personal competencies.* Paper presented at a meeting of the American Psychological Association, Atlanta.

Suen, H.K. (1983). Alienation and attrition of black college students on a predominantly white campus. *Journal of College Student Personnel, 24*(2), 117–121.

Summerskill, J. (1968). Dropouts from college. In K. Yamamoto (Ed.), *The college student and his culture: An analysis.* Boston: Houghton, Mifflin.

Terenzini, P., & Pascarella, E. (1980). Student/faculty relationships and freshman year educational outcomes: A further investigation. Journal of College Student Personnel, 21(6), 521–528.

Terrell, M.C., & Wright, D.J. (Eds.). (1988, December). From survival to success: Promoting minority student retention. *Monographs of the National Association of Student Personnel Administrators* (Vol. 9).

Thomas, C.H., & Thomas, J.L. (1986). *Directory of college facilities and services for the disabled.* Phoenix, AZ: Oryx Press.

Tinto, V. (1975). Dropouts from higher education: A theoretical synthesis of recent research. *Review of Educational Research, 45,* 89–125.

Tinto, V. (1987). *Leaving college.* Chicago: University of Chicago Press.

Tinto, V. (1988). Stages of student departure: Reflections on the longitudinal character of student leaving. *Journal of Higher Education, 59*(4), 438–455.

Van Gennep, A. (1960). *The rites of passage.* Chicago: University of Chicago Press.

Webb, M.W. (1988). Freshman year retention at three campuses of a large urban community college district: 1983–1986. *Community/Junior College Quarterly of Research and Practice, 12*(3), 213–242.

Welsh, M., Conway, A., & West, K. (1987). *Factors contributing to black student retention at the University of South Carolina.* Columbia, SC: State Commission on Higher Education.

Whitaker, D.G. (1987, November). *Persistence and the two-year college student.* Paper presented at the annual meeting of the Association for the Study of Higher Education, Baltimore.

Williamson, D.R., & Creamer, D.G. (1988). Student attrition in 2- and 4-year colleges: Application of a theoretical model. *Journal of College Student Development, 29,* 210–217.

Wright, B. (1985). Programming services: Special student services and American Indian college students. *Journal of American Indian Education, 24*, 4–7.

Zwerling, L.S. (1974). Experiential education at a community college. In J. Doley (Ed.), *Implementing field expense education: New directions for higher education*, no. 6 (pp. 1–12). San Francisco: Jossey-Bass.

Index